TO PROMOTE, DEFEND, AND REDEEM

Recent Titles in
Contributions to the Study of Religion

TO PROMOTE, DEFEND, AND REDEEM

The Catholic Literary Revival
and the
Cultural Transformation
of American Catholicism,
1920–1960

Arnold Sparr

CONTRIBUTIONS TO THE STUDY OF RELIGION,
NUMBER 25
Henry Warner Bowden, *Series Editor*

GREENWOOD PRESS
New York • Westport, Connecticut • London

Library of Congress Cataloging-in-Publication Data

Sparr, Arnold.
   To promote, defend, and redeem : the Catholic literary revival and
the cultural transformation of American Catholicism, 1920–1960 /
Arnold Sparr.
      p.   cm.—(Contributions to the study of religion, ISSN
0196–7053 ; no. 25)
   Includes bibliographical references.
   ISBN 0–313–26391–4 (lib. bdg. : alk. paper)
   1. American literature—Catholic authors—History and criticism.
2. American literature—20th century—History and criticism.
3. English literature—Catholic authors—History and criticism.
4. Christianity and literature—United States—History—20th
century.   5. Catholics—United States—Intellectual life—
History—20th century.   6. Catholic Church—United States—
History—20th century.   7. Catholic literature—History and
criticism.   8. Catholic Church in literature.   9. Catholics in
literature.   I. Title.   II. Series.
PS153.C3S6   1990
810.9′9222′0904—dc20   89–25853

British Library Cataloguing in Publication Data is available.

Library of Congress Catalog Card Number: 89–25853
ISBN: 0–313–26391–4
ISSN: 0196–7053

First published in 1990

Greenwood Press, Inc.
88 Post Road West, Westport, Connecticut 06881

Printed in the United States of America

∞™

The paper used in this book complies with the
Permanent Paper Standard issued by the National
Information Standards Organization (Z39.48–1984).

10 9 8 7 6 5 4 3 2 1

Copyright Acknowledgment

Extracts from Arnold J. Sparr's "From Self-congratulation to Self-criticism:
Main Currents in American Catholic Fiction, 1900–1960" appear in
chapters 6 and 9 courtesy of *U.S. Catholic Historian* 6 (Spring/Summer
1987): 213–230.

To My Parents, Evelyn and Louis Sparr

Contents

9.   "Yes, We Have No Bernanos." The Search for
        the Great American Catholic Novel, II:
        Catholic Fiction During the Era of
        Transformation   143

PART III DISSOLUTION, THE 1950s AND AFTER

10.   "Ought There to Be a Catholic Criticism?" The
        1950s and the End of the Revival   163

        Endnotes   171

        Bibliography   205

        Index   211

Series Foreword

As early as the national census of 1850, statistics showed that the Roman Catholic Church was the largest single denomination in the United States. Despite that preponderance, or possibly because of it, Protestant groups refused to accept Catholicism as compatible with American religion and culture. Protestant nativists viewed Catholics as unassimilable immigrants, undemocratic residents whose parochial schooling and "loyalty to the pope, a foreign power" precluded participation in republican life. This exclusionist rhetoric lasted into the twentieth century, and most Catholics seem to have accepted it at face value. They flourished in increasing numbers due to more immigration, but they also accepted isolation in cultural ghettos formed jointly by Protestant suspicion and their own acquiescence in secondary citizenship.

In this volume, Arnold Sparr chronicles and analyzes the emergence of Catholic thinkers from their minority status. As they integrated literature, philosophy, and theology in the modern period, they provided educated American Catholics with a unified viewpoint, one that defended the faith and criticized a drifting, fragmented, secular culture. This viewpoint also gave them confidence that they had something valuable to contribute to American culture as a whole.

By 1935 Catholic literary expressions reiterated a simple historical truth, viz., that Americans have always been part of a transatlantic religious community. Up to that time American Catholics had utilized a rigid scholasticism which provided a secure and clear self-definition but at the same time made them appear defensively parochial and moralistic. After 1935 they joined with prominent French and German scholars to see their faith as a cultural force that could transform all of western civilization. This positive attitude began to fade in the 1950s, however, because the dynamics of an anti-ghetto mentality also led American Catholics to accept pluralism. At the end of the period which author Sparr covers, Catholic literature had broken its shackles but had also forfeited a self-conscious identity.

In this latest and most comprehensive survey of the period, Sparr places the study of Catholic literature on a much more sophisticated level. One of his most important contributions is that he shows how the faith content of the Catholic vision, with its utilization of neo-Thomism, fit the historical context in which it emerged and spoke so relevantly. He is both empathetic and critical in explaining how this modern religious perspective changed over the course of decades. From a rigid antimodernism to a blending with many different American voices, Catholic thinkers moved into contemporary times. This volume shows what each step along the way was like and why each one succeeded its predecessor.

Henry Warner Bowden

Introduction

The expression "Catholic literary revival in America" has two dimensions in this study. First, it refers to the impact of the modern resurgence in European Catholic thought and letters upon the American Church between 1920 and 1960. Under the influence of Wilfrid Ward's *William George Ward and the Catholic Revival* (1893) and Abbé Jean Calvet's *Le Renouveau Catholique* (1927),[1] historians traditionally have characterized this intensification of late nineteenth and early twentieth century European Catholic intellectual life as the "Catholic renaissance" or the "Catholic revival."

This work additionally studies American Catholic educational and literary leaders' attempts to induce a similar flowering of Catholic life and culture in their own country—in short, to foster a Catholic "literary revival" in America.[2] The movement thus had both intellectual and organizational aspects. It was the awakening of American Catholics to their modern intellectual and cultural heritage as the achievements of the English, French, and German Catholic revivals were communicated to America. But it was also a movement by a self-conscious American Catholic cultural community to realize its own share of modern Catholic thinkers, writers, and poets. Strongest at the revival's outset in the 1920s, this self-conscious element in Catholic American intellectual life nevertheless continued into the 1950s.

Employing the Catholic literary revival in America as its framework, this study maintains that American Catholic intellectual and cultural life between 1920 and 1960 was driven by three forces: to promote the intellectual standing of American Catholicism, to defend the Catholic faith and its adherents from detractors, and to redeem what was seen as a drifting and fragmented secular culture.[3]

Beginning in the 1920s when low levels of American Catholic intellectual and cultural achievement were criticized by influential voices both within and without the American Catholic community, Catholic cultural leaders led by Francis X. Talbot, S. J., literary editor of the Jesuit weekly *America*, concluded that the time had come for an emergent American immigrant Church to produce writers and thinkers in proportion to her numbers. The strength of Catholic revivals in England and France added urgency to their cause.

Talbot's call for an American Catholic intellectual emergence was seconded by Jesuit youth leader Daniel A. Lord and other Catholic educators who, stung by the anti-Catholic climate of the 1920s, were determined that the Catholic laity must become more articulate in defending the Church against attack. Lord, Talbot, and the American Jesuit educational community played leading roles in the early organizational history of the revival as they looked primarily toward aggressive English apologists like G. K. Chesterton as the prototype for their own movement. Claiming interest in social and cultural renewal, these early Jesuit leaders nevertheless framed their program of reform within a rigid neoscholastic framework.

By the mid–1930s, however, the focus of the revival and of American Catholic intellectual and cultural life began to change. Influenced by the newly translated works of writers and thinkers of the French and German Catholic intellectual revivals as well as by more recent writers of the English revival, many young Catholic American lay intellectuals between 1935 and 1955 began to think of their faith as a social and cultural force capable of transforming western civilization. The Depression brought a new focus to Catholic social thought as modern papal encyclicals addressed the rights of twentieth century industrial labor. There were also new breakthroughs in theology, with thinkers like American Benedictine monk Virgil Michel (*Orate Fratres* magazine) and Europeans Romano Guardini (*The Church and the Catholic and the Spirit of the Liturgy*, 1935) and Jacques Maritain stressing the central importance of the Mystical Body to Christian life and doctrine. There was a concomitant renewal of the laity at this time, as lay Catholics came to realize through the doctrine of the Mystical Body that they *were* the Church, with the consequent duty to witness the Christian message in the modern world.

Intellectual ferment continued on the literary front as educated Catholic Americans during the 1930s and 1940s encountered the Catholic creative writers of Europe—Georges Bernanos, Francois Mauriac, Graham Greene, and others—whose work suggested the outlines of a new Christian realism in modern literature. American Catholics during this second phase (1935–1955) of the revival thus engaged some of the most progressive Catholic minds of the modern era.

William Halsey's *The Survival of American Innocence: American Catholicism in an Era of Disillusionment, 1920–1940* (1980) remains the only comprehensive intellectual history of the twentieth century American Church.[4] Nevertheless, for reasons that will be discussed more fully in chapter 4, I do not believe that a paradigm of "Innocence"—used to characterize the nineteenth century American value system—adequately describes the focus and outlook of a modern religious people. To understand the American Catholic mind, the historian must examine it within its entire structure of faith and belief.

Part of the problem is that Halsey treats Catholic thought and culture ahistorically between the wars. He is correct in maintaining with Philip Gleason that neo-scholastic philosophy was the chief structuring element in the Catholic intellectual synthesis before 1960.[5] The intellectual focus of the Catholic literary revival, especially during its initial stage, supports that interpretation as its early Jesuit leaders sought both self-definition and Catholic intellectual authority by contrasting the "common sense" postulates of a highly conceptualistic neo-scholasticism against the subjective disillusionment of the post–World War I age.

Nevertheless, neither Halsey nor Gleason fully appreciate the intellectual awakening that occurred in the American Church after 1935. Nor do they fully recognize the creative changes within the neo-scholastic synthesis that emerged after that date, as Maritain, fellow Frenchman Etienne Gilson, and others creatively adapted the thought of Thomas Aquinas to modern times. American Catholic intellectual and literary culture thus contained a maturity and scope by 1940 that was absent in 1920. This was due, in large part, to the impact of European Catholic thought upon the American Church after 1935.

I have divided this book into three sections, each corresponding to separate twentieth century phases of the Catholic literary revival in America. Part I, "Origins and Development, 1920–1935," discusses the socio-cultural antecedents of the revival and the self-conscious attempts of the revival's early Jesuit leaders to build a Catholic intellectual presence in America. Part II, "Transformation, 1935–1955," addresses the shift in Catholic revivalist thought from the confrontational literary-philosophical postures of the 1920s and early 1930s to more positive understandings of Catholic faith and practice, as the integral world view of the Europeans penetrated American Catholic intellectual communities and educated Catholic Americans looked toward the essential doctrines of their faith to find solutions to world problems. Part III, "Dissolution, the 1950s and After," chronicles the eclipse of the revival, resulting from a reactivation of the Catholic intellectualism issue, increasing concerns about professionalism within Catholic academia, and liberal Catholic association of the revival with so-called "ghetto culture." Parts I and II conclude with narrative chapters on the American Catholic novel. The search for the Great American Catholic Novel was an important element of the revival and provides a convenient organizing framework through which to summarize and assess major trends in the larger cultural movement.

Religious-cultural movements do not always fall into easily defined decades. Nor do the personalities who lead them. I have designated 1935 as a turning point in American Catholic religious thought, but changes can be seen as early as 1933. That year saw the establishment by Dorothy Day and Peter Maurin of the American Catholic Worker movement, which did so much to inspire the lay Catholic social and intellectual activism of the 1930s and 1940s.[6] In addition, the Catholic publishing firm of Sheed and Ward, which played such a key role in transmitting the literature of the European Catholic awakening to its American audience, opened an American branch in 1933. I have chosen 1935 because it allows time to think of a transition from these events, and because 1935 was the year when the revival began to penetrate most deeply into Catholic American colleges and universities, where it received its greatest impetus and development.

Finally, because a good deal of this study focuses upon midwestern Catholic groups and individuals, one may ask if the Catholic literary revival was chiefly a midwestern event. There are some purely practical reasons for the important midwestern role in the revival. In 1932—the year before St. Louis, Missouri, Jesuits Lord and Calvert Alexander issued their formal summons for an American Catholic revival—St. Louis University was preparing to celebrate its centenary anniversary as the first post-Reformation Catholic University "to be established in the English-speaking world." In anticipation of the event, Alexander wrote that the St. Louis University community, in light of the current European Catholic intellectual resurgence, was justified in thinking that it had been assigned "a special and important role in the Catholic Revival in this country."[7]

Alexander's commentary may explain the intial St. Louis aegis of the revival, but it does not account for the revival's creative midwestern development after 1935 under such figures as Notre Dame University's Frank O'Malley and the midwestern Catholic college teachers associated with the Wisconsin-based Catholic Renascence Society. This study is not prepared to defend Andrew Greeley's thesis that midwestern Catholicism historically has surpassed its East Coast number in originality and vitality because the latter has stood in continued awe of the well-entrenched East Coast "WASP" aristocracy.[8] But it does show an unsophisticated midwestern Catholic confidence not always seen in the Protestant intellectual strongholds of the Northeast. It is further interesting to note that the self-conscious concerns for American Catholic intellectual achievement that both initiated and ended the revival were strongest in the Northeast. But to say that the most progressive phase of the revival belongs to the midwestern Church is to overlook the fact that enthusiasm for the Catholic creative thinkers and writers of Europe reached nearly every level of Catholic American intellectual society after 1935, and that Catholic colleges and universities nationwide initiated courses on their thought. Furthermore, it slights the important role played by New York City-based Sheed and Ward in advancing these thinkers in America, as well as the part played by eastern Catholic publications such as *America* and the *Commonweal* after 1935 in raising the intellectual awareness of educated Catholic Americans.

A concluding word on "Catholic literature" is in order before turning to the main body of this analysis. "Catholic literature" is an ambiguous term. Is it only literature written by Catholics? Or is it literature written primarily from a Catholic-Christian sensibility and point of view? Or is it both?

Moreover, the question arises, "What is literature?" Part of the problem is that proponents of a Catholic literary revival in America took an extremely broad view of "literature" between 1920 and 1960. Father Talbot underscored this formlessness in 1938 when he defined Catholic literature as "the expression of a Catholic's views on every question and problem," extending to "every division of the Dewey [decimal] system" and permeating "every topic treated in books."[9]

Thus, when American Catholic cultural and literary leaders such as Talbot spoke of the Catholic literary revival, they often portrayed the movement as a "glorious renaissance" of modern Catholic thought that was rooting itself in every possible intellectual realm. This revivalist sensibility is crucial in understanding not only the origins and development of the literary revival, but the entire pattern of Catholic American intellectual culture between the wars.

Nevertheless, this study will limit itself as far as possible to those areas of Catholic thought and culture that most concerned educated American Catholics, critics, and cultural leaders between 1920 and 1960: the "renaissance" in Catholic aesthetics, theology, philosophy, and social thought and its application to modern economic, social, and intellectual problems; and the growth and development of the twentieth century Catholic novel. This study, unless otherwise indicated, also employs "Catholic literature" in the same way that Talbot and other Catholic spokespersons used the term during their day—as literature (novels, poems, books of philosophy, history, and theology, magazine articles, and even pamphlets), written by a professed member of the Catholic faith expressing a Catholic-Christian sensibility and outlook toward the subject at hand.

I have run up numerous debts to both individuals and institutions in preparation of this book. The archival staffs at Boston College, College of St. Benedict, College of St. Catherine, Georgetown University, Marquette University, Loyola University of Chicago, St. John's University (Minnesota), Mundelein College, and Notre Dame University were generous in their assistance. I reserve a special word of thanks to Philip Runkle at Marquette and Brother Michael Grace at Loyola who directed me to valuable materials relating to the Chicago Catholic Worker and Chicago Catholic lay movements.

My colleagues at St. Francis College in Brooklyn, New York, also made my task easier. Professor Arthur Hughes carefully read and criticized several chapters and Professors Nino Langiulli and Gerald Galgan offered helpful advice.

A 1981 summer travel grant from the Notre Dame University Cushwa Center for the Study of American Catholicism aided the initial stages of my research. Moreover, it allowed me the opportunity to meet Notre Dame Professor Philip Gleason, who has been a source of never-ending encouragement.

My greatest debt is owed to those special individuals who granted my request for interviews: Margaret Dever, Sr. Mariella Gable, O.S.B., Donald Gallagher, Arleen Hynes, Sr. Kristin Malloy, O.S.B., Ed Marciniak, John Pick, Thomas Stritch, and Leo R. Ward, C.S.C. All gave unselfishly of their time, and, more important, of themselves in bringing life to an important cultural era. Without them this study would not have been possible.

A final word of thanks to Lois Corcoran who typed and retyped the manuscript through all its revisions and to friends and family who patiently saw me through this work.

To all, I am deeply grateful.

Part I

ORIGINS AND DEVELOPMENT,
1920–1935

1

The 1920s: A Time of Troubles

To understand the origins of the Catholic literary revival in the United States, we may usefully contrast the American movement with earlier European Catholic literary movements. Most western European countries experienced late nineteenth century Catholic revivals that produced a great outpouring of Catholic apologetic and creative literature. The most far-reaching actions occurred in France, England, and Germany. Reacting, in large part, to the extremes of late nineteenth century positivistic science and philosophy, these revivals also had similar social antecedents; they occurred at a time when Catholics in these countries were suffering from low intellectual and cultural prestige.

The French Catholic revival occurred against the background of the Third Republic, and, according to Richard Griffiths, coincided with "the first great period of Republican action against the Church."[1] Griffiths writes that the anticlerical policies of the Third Republic, namely the decrees on the congregations and on education (resulting in the laicization of the schools and the suppression of the teaching orders) and other reforms restricting the traditional powers of the French Church, "generated in the average Catholic of the time a spirit of violent opposition."[2]

At the same time, the French Catholic intelligentsia fumed over the antireligious rationalism that had been undermining their status since the days of the eighteenth century *philosophes*. Particularly infuriating to Catholic intellectuals was the smug attitude among Sorbonne positivists who refused to concede a man "could be intelligent *and* Catholic."[3] The disapprobation suffered by the Church during the Dreyfus affair, when many influential French Catholics sided with the anti-Dreyfusards and the anti-Semitic nationalist right, further lowered Catholic prestige among France's intellectuals.

Catholics in England and Germany faced similar problems of standing and influence. Unlike France, "The Eldest Daughter of the Church," the Catholic minority in these countries had been systematically excluded from their nation's intellectual, cultural, and political life since Reformation times. Even after Catholic Emancipation in 1829, English intellectual and literary culture was dominated by Protestants. English Catholics found a major intellectual voice only with the conversion of John Henry Newman in 1845, which commenced the English Catholic revival and the entry of numerous talented writers into the Church.

Germany's nineteenth century Catholic intellectuals also operated under difficult conditions, where, according to Sr. Mary Jane Fiecke, O.S.F., the Protestant hegemony "cast a spell of inferiority over ambitious Catholic writers."[4] The literary revival occurred in Germany, writes Fiecke, because turn-of-the-century Catholic leaders were no longer able "to tolerate the state of inferiority to which Catholicism had ultimately been reduced."[5]

The Catholic literary revival in America had similar social origins. The 1920s was clearly a time of troubles for American Catholics, and particularly her intellectuals. Always a highly self-conscious minority, American Catholic intellectual and cultural leaders during the 1920s and early 1930s felt the eyes of the non-Catholic population upon them perhaps more keenly than ever before.

Several factors were behind this scrutiny, but the major forces that focused attention upon Catholics and Catholicism during this period were: the so-called Catholic Question surrounding Alfred E. Smith's presidential campaigns of 1924 and 1928;[6] the ongoing "revolt against formalism" (in Morton White's phrase) and the challenge to dogmatic belief posed by influential postwar intellectuals;[7] and a number of widely discussed sociological studies impugning American Catholic intellectual ledership and distinction. Catholic American cultural leaders, as a result, were thrown on the intellectual and cultural defensive at the very time, paradoxically, when many believed the postwar American Church stood ready to shed its prewar immigrant image and assume fuller stature in the nation's intellectual and social life.

AL SMITH AND THE CATHOLIC QUESTION

The Catholic Question was actually a series of questions raised by the American liberal community between 1924 and 1928 when Al Smith's qualifications for the presidency were seriously discussed. Voiced mainly by liberal Protestants, the criticism was directed, for the most part,

against nineteenth century papal pronouncements seemingly antagonistic to religious liberty and Church-State separation.

Pius IX's 1864 *Syllabus of Errors*, claiming Vatican sovereignty over the
secular realm, and Leo XIII's 1895 *The Christian Constitution of the States*,
contending a privileged civil position for the Church over other faiths,
were most troublesome to liberals. Even when viewed within their historical context, which nearly every critic ignored, it is understandable
how these declarations provoked fear and speculation when a Catholic
sought the presidency. Many critics wrongly believed these statements
to be backed by claims of papal infallibility, and that it was thus incumbent upon all Catholics to obey.

These fears may have been groundless enough, but they were exac-
erbated, in many cases, by the public actions of the American Church
itself when, during the aggressive postwar years, important sectors of
the hierarchy effectively organized to interject Catholic institutional demands into sensitive areas of the country's civic and moral life. Smith's
candidacy notwithstanding, popular anxiety intensified throughout the
1920s over the direction of twentieth century Catholic growth, power,
and influence. The urban-rural split, the immigration question, prohibition, and new nativist outbursts all stirred interest in Catholicism's
growing social role in America. But a no less important concern was the
aggressive public face of the 1920s Church. One of the most striking
manifestations of postwar Catholic assertiveness was the Church's high
public profile, especially in Catholic strongholds like Boston, Chicago,
and New York City. Moral crusades against birth control, liberal divorce,
and movie sex, and highly publicized attempts to win state and federal
private school aid, were some of the more visible examples of Catholic
group militancy.[8] The election of 1928 thus came at the end rather than
the beginning of an almost decade-long concern about organized Catholic power.

The nation's liberal periodical press—no longer bound by polite prewar restraints—was especially interested in probing the growing social
significance of Catholicism, and many in their number seized upon
Smith's candidacy as an opportunity to review some of these larger
issues. Beginning therefore in the mid–1920s, *Current History*, the *Living
Age*, the *Forum*, the *Atlantic Monthly*, and the *Christian Century* undertook
numerous symposia and editorials on such topics as "The Pope and the
Presidency," "Catholicism and Politics in America," "America and Roman Catholicism," and "The Catholic Church and the Modern Mind."[9]
Some of the questions that Catholics faced in these inquiries were: "Can
a Catholic be loyal to his church, and, as President to his country?";
"Does the Roman Catholic Church officially teach any doctrines which
are contrary to the principles of American government?"; "Does the

Pope still contend for temporal power?"; and finally, "Does the Roman Catholic Church admit of free will in determining the religious predilections of its members?"[10]

Insofar as the Church-State issue was concerned, the attempts of Catholic leaders to answer the Church's detractors met with little success. The Episcopal layman Charles C. Marshall spoke for many critics in 1927 when, in his well-known "Open Letter to the Honorable Alfred E. Smith," he concluded that the dogmatic principles of the Catholic Church were antithetical to American constitutional ideals, and that Smith's election might "precipitate an inevitable conflict between the Roman Catholic Church and the American State irreconcilable with domestic peace."[11] The *Christian Century* likewise editorialized on the eve of the 1928 election that American institutions "would be jeopardized in certain respects by an election of a Roman Catholic to the Presidency."[12]

David J. O'Brien has written that the 1928 political challenge to American Catholicism was the single most important factor in delaying postwar Catholic emergence into the American mainstream.[13] Certainly it intensified Catholic provinciality. Bitter resentment characterized much of American Catholicism's respose to its critics, followed by an equally strong conviction that the Catholic laity must become more articulate in defending and explaining the Church to the non-Catholic majority. Almost unanimously, Catholic spokesmen believed that critics had misunderstood the Vatican's position on Church and State and the American Church's adaptation of that doctrine to religiously pluralistic American society. While some Catholic publications like the *Commonweal* played down the notion of deliberate misrepresentation, the more typical response was that of the Jesuit magazine *America*. Throughout the Smith ordeal, *America*'s editors charged that the American Church was the victim of "misrepresentations, understatements and unwarranted inferences."[14] *America* believed that the liberal community was exploiting the Catholic Question, showing Catholics in the worst possible light, and attributing to them a body of doctrine "which no Catholic ever subscribed to."[15] Even Rev. Peter Guilday, president of the American Catholic Historical Association and one of the nation's most respected Catholic spokesmen, charged in 1929 that during the entire Smith episode the American Church had been victimized "by a studied propaganda of as damnable, obscene and calumnious lies as have ever been broadcast in history."[16]

Were Guilday and *America* correct in their charges? Certainly the anti-Catholic campaign against Smith had its scurrilous side. Ku Klux Klanbacked hate sheets like the *Fellowship Forum* and the *New Menace* were particularly active during the 1928 campaign, evoking images of boozy prelates and Vatican-controlled America. Moreover, even moderate journals like *Current History* and the *Forum*, while disavowing personal bias, nevertheless provided arenas for some notorious anti-Catholics. These included Klan Imperial Wizard Hiram W. Evans and John Jay Chapman. The latter was an old-stock New York Episcopalian who, in 1924, led a personal crusade to block a Catholic's appointment to the Harvard Board of Fellows on grounds that "the outspoken purpose of the Roman Church is to control American education."[17] Chapman again evoked portraits of popery, Romanization, and Jesuitical design in the *Forum* debate, a tactic usually reserved for less literate journals.[18]

Moreover, recent historical studies of the 1928 election also have assigned more importance to the religious issue in relation to traditional interpretations asserting that prohibition, Republican prosperity, and Smith's urban background were more significant factors in his defeat than his Catholicism. Allan J. Lichtman, utilizing quantitative data of 1928 Protestant-Catholic voting alignments, argued that "religious conflict occupied center stage in the competition between Smith and Hoover."[19] Lichtman's data supported Edmund A. Moore's earlier assertion that Smith's religion "played a large, though not wholly calculable part" in his defeat.[20]

There is some accuracy, nevertheless, to James H. Smylie and David Burner's charge that Catholic leaders never really answered Smith's liberal critics—that they never really addressed the full implications of the illiberal postulates of Popes Pius IX and Leo XIII within a modern democratic state.[21] True, Catholics like *Commonweal* editor Michael Williams, Catholic University professor Fr. John A. Ryan, and Smith himself often cited the unequivocal support of the American model of Church-State separation advanced by such liberal "Americanist" prelates as St. Paul, Minnesota archbishop John Ireland and James Cardinal Gibbons; but they overlooked the fact that on the basis of such statements as Leo XIII's *Longinqua Oceani*, the papacy as recently as 1895 merely appeared to tolerate rather than fully endorse modern religious pluralism. Catholic apologists were in an awkward position in 1920s America. They were forced to defend and explain the illiberal prescriptions of a nineteenth century papacy to a liberal twentieth century world.

This section, however, is not intended to show why Smith was defeated in 1928, but, rather, to show how Catholics perceived his defeat. Thus, one must agree with John W. Hattery's assessment that the prevailing mood of Catholics throughout the entire affair "was one of defensiveness."[22] On balance, an us-versus-them attitude dominated, with the majority of Catholic leaders maintaining that religious bigotry was the real issue behind the Catholic Question.

During and after the Smith debacle, Catholics focused their resentment on two key areas. First, many believed that, at least politically, some influential American groups still regarded Catholics as second-class citizens. Many Catholics had interpreted Smith's candidacy as a sign of postwar Catholic social arrival in America. Now much seemed lost.

Claims that Smith's religion disqualified him for the presidency implied that a religious test for office existed, but applied to Catholics only. Any suggestion that Smith withdraw from the race, editorialized *America* in 1927, was equivalent to demanding that "a Catholic cede a Constitutional right."[23]

One of the greatest sources of frustration, however, was directed at the journals that aired the Catholic Question during the campaign. "Our American magazines," wrote *America* in 1928, "are learning a practical lesson already familiar to cheaper journalism: that the Catholic Church is the biggest item of single interest in the market, provided it is attacked."[24] Maintaining that the entire "dispassionate" debate over the Catholic Question was just a sophisticated form of anti-Catholicism, *America* further editorialized that Charles C. Marshall, Chapman, and other liberal Protestants "are not saying anything essentially different from the old rabble-rousers of the Native Americans, the A.P.A., or the Ku Klux Klan. The only difference is that they are now saying it in *The Atlantic Monthly, Current History* and *The World's Work.*"[25]

The negative intellectual image that Catholicism seemed to inspire in the minds of its critics during the Catholic Question debate was particularly troublesome to Catholic spokespersons. Catholics might easily dismiss caricatures of "Rum, Romanism, and Rebellion" as so much anti-Catholic bigotry when it came from Ku Klux Klan nativists, but more wounding were questions raised in the popular press about Catholic intellectual freedom. Protestant critic Chapman indicated how the debate could escalate in a 1925 *Forum* essay when he claimed that the present struggle was "between two opposing forms of thought, one which is related to Authority and the other to the Private Mind."[26]

Chapman, moreover, was not an isolated voice in forcing this issue. Critics, in addressing concepts and doctrines like papal infallibility and ecclesiastical authority, often questioned how free Catholics were in exercising intellectual judgment, not only in the political sphere, but in all realms of thought. One contributor to the *Atlantic Monthly* put it bluntly: "How can an educated man," he asked, in light of the Church's attitudes toward censorship, Church-State separation, divorce, and birth control, "be, become, or remain a Catholic?"[27] The insinuation was that he could not; the Church was no place for someone of independent mind.

With these questions, an essentially political debate about a Catholic's qualification for the presidency was thrust suddenly to the level of intellectual and cultural criticism. This kind of reasoning was especially apparent among those like Chapman who were critical of the assertive public role of the Church in the 1920s. The Church through sheer weight of numbers might interject its demands into the nation's social, moral, and civic affairs; but where, critics asked, was the more positive Catholic influence over culture, the arts, and the sciences? Catholic public and civic power was indeed formidable, admitted Yale University history professor William MacDonald in a 1928 review of Charles C. Marshall's *The Roman Catholic Church and the Modern State*, but its literary and intellectual output, by contrast, was meager. The American Church "on its cultural side," criticized MacDonald, "has been tested and found wanting."[28] Increasingly, Catholic numerical strength in the public sphere was contrasted with lack of Catholic influence in the cultural and intellectual sphere. It was a criticism that would haunt the Church into the 1950s.

CATHOLICS AND THE REVOLT AGAINST FORMALISM

Questions about Catholic intellectual influence and capacity raised during the Smith era were compounded by the ridicule that all believers suffered at the hands of the debunkers and skeptics who also held center stage in the 1920s.

Historians emphasize that antireligious skepticism arrived in America relatively late when compared with the waves of antireligious rationalism that swept Europe as early as the eighteenth century.[29] There was also a difference in tone. In eighteenth and nineteenth century Europe the assault upon credal religion, for the most part, was sharp and overt, as evidenced by the antidogmatic pronouncements of Voltaire and Thomas Huxley. Except for the 1925 Scopes debacle and the modernist-fundamentalist split, there was not the irreconcilable conflict between science and religion in America to duplicate the bitter exchanges between post-Darwinian English materialists and churchmen. Instead, the rationalists' controversy with dogmatic religion in 1920s America was conducted, in the main, under the guise of "broadmindedness," or a "critical attitude." In most cases, also, it was part of an effort by modern thinkers and social scientists to apply the scientific method as far as possible to all realms of human experience, including religion, values, and ethics. Some, like John Dewey, wanted pragmatic experience to replace dogmatic religion in determining values. Others, like Alfred North Whitehead, insisted that religion must evolve to coincide with new developments in science and physics. Still others, like Joseph Wood Krutch, rejected the certitudes of science and religion alike and succumbed to nihilism and hopelessness.

Catholics suffered equally at the hands of Dewey's *Creative Intelligence* and Krutch's *The Modern Temper*. When dogmatic belief is questioned, so is the dogmatic mind. Ever sensitive to their own intellectualism, Catholics during the 1920s were told that traditional religion inhibited self-expression and stifled progress, or that those who believed in the supernatural were living in a world of illusion and superstition. The intellectual implication was unmistakable: Religious belief, somehow, was the mark of an underdeveloped mind.

"Religious orthodoxy," asserted Bertrand Russell in 1929, is "a pursuit inspired by irrational fears."[30] Opening a six-month-long "What I Believe" symposium conducted by the *Forum*, Russell's observations reflected the attitude of many other influential thinkers of his era. Critical of revealed, dogmatic religion, they called for "a wider application of intelligence" toward religion to coincide with the critical attitude that was so much the vogue in postwar American culture.[31]

The editors of the *Forum* thus introduced their "What I Believe" series with the assertion that "the accepted beliefs of the past no longer command respect."[32] Following Russell, H. L. Mencken claimed that religion "has been a curse to mankind . . . by the damage it has done to clear and honest thinking"; Albert Einstein argued that belief in immortality was the refuge of "feeble souls"; and Dewey offered the judgment that all established creeds were "religions of escape" from experience.[33]

Similar pronouncements came from another "What I Believe" symposium in the *Nation* in 1932. Again the suggestion was that belief was the hallmark of an immature mind. "Belief," wrote Cornell University political scientist George E. G. Catlin, "has been a method of adaptation to environment by process of illusion."[34] "I am convinced," insisted literary critic Edmund Wilson, that traditional religions "were made possible only by ignorance, and that all Western churches are obsolescent—in power over the minds that count."[35] Wilson's conclusion, elsewhere, that "few first-rate men" any longer believed in the supernatural[36] seemed to answer a rhetorical question he posed to English Catholic critic Cuthbert Wright in 1929, when he asked: "Who are the great modern Catholic writers and thinkers? There are a few, but, it seems to me, not many."[37] Honesty obligated Wright to remain silent on the issue.

While the antidogmatic bias of these commentators within the popular press was open for every reader to examine, many Catholic spokesmen believed that a more subtle, and ultimately more damaging, prejudice against belief was being perpetrated on the campuses of major secular colleges and universities. Speakers at the 1933 National Catholic Education Association meeting warned of a "materialistic attitude and philosophy" dominating higher education.[38] Other Catholic commentators often analyzed and quoted from textbooks used in secular college psychology, sociology, biology, and philosophy courses to illustrate that many professors were antagonistic to religion.[39]

Thus, during the 1920s and early 1930s, numerous articles and editorials appeared in the Catholic press with titles like: "Is Secular Education Anti-Religious?" and "Atheism in the Colleges."[40] As during the Smith campaign and the controversy over the Catholic Question, the tone of most of these contributions betrayed a deep sensitivity among Catholic intellectuals about their image as believers. They opposed the positivist attack upon belief, but they were equally sensitive to the attack upon those who believe. Thus Catholic editorialists and writers showed a large degree of irritation toward professors "who consider themselves more 'advanced' and 'progressive,' " who "pretend to superiority complexes," and who claim that "religion is a soothing-syrup and church steeples are modern totem poles."[41] It is all so subtle, editorialized *America* in 1931; "There is no prejudice, the professor will say . . . but adopt a critical attitude to determine whether or not it [faith] may be a primitive superstition."[42]

While the antireligious skepticism that marked the thought of so many intellectuals during the 1920s and early 1930s was directed toward all dogmatic religions and not solely toward the Catholic faith, Catholics seemed to feel the sting most keenly. These criticisms came at a time when the Catholic community already felt besieged and misrepresented. The Smith ordeal left many Catholics with the impression that in some circles they were still regarded as second-class citizens. Now it appeared that some moderns regarded Catholics as second-class intellects. Remarked one Catholic layman in 1932, to join the Church was to invite the criticism that one has "stopped thinking."[43]

THE CATHOLIC INTELLECTUALISM ISSUE DURING THE 1920s AND EARLY 1930s

By the early 1930s there was a substantive body of suggestive literature alleging Catholic intellectual insufficiency, if not inferiority. More damaging, however, were a number of empirical studies conducted in the late 1920s and early 1930s correlating church membership with intellectual leadership and distinction. On balance, they appeared to support what the critics were saying. In raw numbers, Catholic America appeared formidable. In 1931 the Church claimed over 20,000,000 members, including 25,000 clergy, 180,000 students enrolled in 552 high schools, and over 60,000 students at 128 Catholic colleges and universities.[44]

But in study after study, researchers presented statistical data confirming that Catholics were not contributing to the nation's intellectual and cultural life in proportion to their numbers. In one leading 1931 study, sociologists Harvey C. Lehman and Paul A. Witty examined the religious affiliation of prominent American scientists listed in the 1927 edition of *American Men of Science*. Only 3 of the 1,189 scientists listed could be identified as Roman Catholic. In addition, the study illustrated that, in proportion to its numbers, the Catholic community was at the absolute bottom in the percentage of scientists produced. Noting that the liberal denominations (Congregational, Episcopal, Unitarian) far surpassed the more dogmatic churches in the ratio of scientists to members, Lehman and Witty speculated that "the conspicuous dearth of scientists among the Catholics suggests that the tenets of that Church are not consonant with scientific endeavor."[45] Catholic spokesmen naturally rejected such a conclusion; nevertheless, the raw data of this and other studies could be ignored less easily, especially in light of similar charges of Catholic cultural insufficiency heard during the 1928 Smith campaign. "Why are so few Catholic educators listed in *Who's Who in America*, *American Men of Science*, or *Leaders in Education*?" asked a correspondent to *America* in 1932.[46] His question expressed a concern that would increasingly preoccupy Catholic cultural leaders throughout the 1920s and 1930s.

While there was a concern for Catholics to contribute to all fields of intellectual endeavor, it seemed to run deepest in creative literature. Again, the root of this concern began with the problem of Catholic self-image. Since Renaissance times, the Church had promoted herself as "The Mother of the Arts." Catholics could point with pride to a long list of writers and artists from Chaucer to Michelangelo who gave substance to that image. Yet the American Church had contributed little to that tradition, and, in fact, seemed to diminish it. She could boast of no American Dante. Nor could she point with pride to an American John Henry Newman or Charles Peguy, or to any Catholic American literary movement comparable to those of England and the Continent.

Whatever image the American Church projected toward literature and the arts was almost wholly negative and obscurantist. Boycotts, censorship, the index of forbidden books, blacklists, and a dismal parade of third- and fourth-rate fictionists was the picture that came to the mind of many critics, both Catholic and non-Catholic alike, when they surveyed the Catholic influence on the American literary scene. Exacerbating this negative image was the fact that a significant number of American writers had actually fled the Church during the 1920s. The apostacy of Theodore Dreiser, James T. Farrell, Eugene O'Neill, and F. Scott Fitzgerald served to underscore all the subtle assumptions of the scoffers and skeptics—that there was a fundamental incompatibility between dogmatic belief and intellectual creativity.

Concern over literary expression thus went to the heart of what was troubling Catholic culture leaders throughout the 1920s and early 1930s. Literary expression was merely another dimension of intellectualism. Moreover, it was a most important dimension, because it raised questions about creativity, independent thought, and intellectual freedom—the same questions that had so disturbed Catholics since the Smith campaign.

"Catholics are so few in the literary world as to create the impression that scholarship and culture are not ours, but belong to others," lamented college literature teacher Sr. Mary Eleanore, C.S.C., at the 1930 meeting of the National Catholic Education Association.[47] Her observation was correct. Literary culture in America belonged to either non-Catholics or to Catholic apostates. It reflected badly upon the Church in either case. With this concern uppermost in their minds, many Catholic critics, teachers, and cultural spokesmen took a hard look at their creative literature during the 1920s and early 1930s, determined to reclaim an area of cultural life they believed rightfully their own.

THE DILEMMA OF CATHOLIC FICTION

"Every one of my literary friends, without exception," complained Wilfred A. Parsons, S.J., editor of *America* in 1930, "has a prejudice against Catholic literature."[48] Parsons was referring mainly to the deplorable state of Catholic American fiction. Throughout the 1920s and 1930s, an army of Catholic literary critics, collegians, and even authors declared that Catholic fiction was "weak, dull, [and] wishy-washy"; that it was like "Peter Pan in the Never Never land"; or that it was "pious and childish."[49] A group of Catholic college students attending the first Catholic Book Club Conference in New York City in 1934 summed up the problem: They were "sick of the pale-faced heroine who rushed into the convent to save her soul," and of books "filled with characters who breathed soft amens at regular intervals."[50] Judging by the reaction of Catholic college students, both at the 1934 conference and in their college quarterlies, Parsons was essentially correct when he complained that most of them "would not be caught [dead] with a Catholic book in their hands."[51]

Parsons's critique notwithstanding, the most searching criticism of Catholic fiction—and of American Catholic intellectual achievement in general—in the postwar era, was delivered by Catholic American layman George N. Shuster. Shuster, a Notre Dame professor of literature who, in 1924, became an assistant editor of the progressive Catholic magazine *Commonweal*, was one of a number of American Catholic lay intellectuals who took seriously questions raised about Catholic intellectual life in the 1920s. His 1925 article, "Have We No Scholars?"—a scathing appraisal of Catholic scholarship and Catholic higher education—represented that concern and set the tone for similar debates over the problem of Catholic literature in the 1920s and 1930s.[52]

Shuster always rejected the criticism that Catholic orthodoxy was a constraint upon thought; but he remained troubled by the fact that the postwar American Church was without positive influence over American culture. Whatever influence it did exercise was narrowly parochial. He was especially concerned as a lay Catholic intellectual about the aggressive public face of the 1920s Church. "Numerical strength," he criticized in 1927, was the weakest and most unwholesome of all forms of power. "It antagonizes groups that are numerically weak," he warned, "just as it annoys those who possess individuality of mind."[53]

Shuster often contrasted the culture-bound provincialism of the American Church with the developed religious outlook and energetic lay Catholic intellectual leadership within the European Churches. A World War I era tour of France—first as a member of the American Expeditionary Force and then as a postwar college student—exposed Shuster to the European Catholic intellectual resurgence and alerted him to similar possibilities in America. European Catholic intellectuals everywhere were stepping to the forefront and positively influencing their nations' art, literature, and culture, he wrote upon his return to the United States in 1920. The young Notre Dame professor urged Catholic Americans to do the same—to become part of a new "World-Force" in modern literature that was reshaping the contours of life and thought.[54]

Shuster criticized Catholic American parochialism in all realms of thought, but he saved his sharpest remarks for American Catholic fiction, especially when compared to mature European varieties. His most devastating appraisal came in *The Catholic Spirit in Modern English Literature* (1922), part of which assessed the American contribution to the international Catholic resurgence. As expected, Shuster found few redeeming names. He did mention the now forgotten Frank Hamilton Spearman and Frances Tiernan (who wrote under the interesting pseudonym, "Christian Reid"), but even in their own day, they were never more than extremely minor figures. Aside from *Robert Kimberly* (1911), a problem novel of marriage and divorce, Spearman's most popular work was *Whispering Smith* (1906), a saga of the American West. Tiernan wrote romantic novels like *Secret Bequest* (1915), the story of a young heiress, who, as a precondition to her inheritance, must persuade her cousin to apostasize from Catholicism, but who is herself converted. Most intelligent readers, Shuster suggested, would likely compare Tiernan's books with "those virtuous but underfed virgins who preside over charity bazaars." On the whole, Shuster concluded, "the great bulk of American Catholic fiction is unintelligent and unreadable."[55]

Shuster's critique of American Catholic fiction and intellectual life constituted some of the most prescient insights of his age. But Shuster was an admittedly isolated figure during these self-consciously troublesome times.[56] Most Catholic cultural leaders—in light of the ordeals of the 1920s—were in no mood to engage in constructive self-criticism. More typical of the era's attitudes were those of Jesuit Daniel A. Lord. Lord, an author, educator, and national director of the Sodality of the Blessed Virgin, a national organization of Catholic high school and college-age youth, was one of a number of influential Jesuit educators and literary spokesmen who would play leading roles in the early organizational phase of the American revival. And in the early 1930s Lord was fighting mad.

Lord, in a series of articles in *America* and the Sodality-published *Queen's Work* between 1929 and 1932, declared that he was tired of the Catholic "inferiority complex" he witnessed in the 1920s. Catholics, Lord decided, must take the offensive. The Jesuit heeded his own advice in 1932, when he declared a "War to the Death" upon the critics of Catholic intellectual and cultural life of the previous decade. Always infuriated by those who sneer at religion, Lord blasted the journals that had aired the Catholic Question and provided platforms for the debunkers and skeptics of the era. "The consistent attitude of these magazines, and dozens of others less cleverly edited," complained Lord, "is that orthodoxy is too stupid for discussion. Only yokels with oats in their hair really are interested in faith or believe in its childish and ridiculous postulates." Civic or social religion is acceptable to them, continued Lord, "but dogmatic religion is too stupid an institution to merit even momentary consideration."[57]

Lord next turned his wrath upon the secular colleges and universities and accused them of systematically undermining the religious beliefs of their students. "They have taken the quiet attitude," he protested, "so much more effective than violent attacks, that religion is superstition [and] men of faith are really men of low mentality."[58]

Lord again underscored his contempt for those who belittled Catholic achievement when he focused upon literature. He was frankly irritated with critics like Shuster and others who objected to "piosity" in Catholic writing. Offering the alternative that would define the earliest stages of the Catholic literary revival, he asserted that "if you can find one line of 'piosity' in any page of [G. K.] Chesterton, [Hilaire] Belloc, Ronald Knox . . . Newman . . . R. H. Benson . . . Sigrid Undset, Bruce Marshall . . . to mention just a handful of Catholic writers, I'll eat this page without butter and mayonnaise."[59]

Lord's colorful but angry challenge gave expression to a decade of Catholic frustration during which a significant part of the American Catholic community felt itself ridiculed, misunderstood, and unrecognized. Now Catholics like Lord were determined to answer their critics—to answer those who belittled dogmatic belief, who doubted Catholic intellectual and cultural sufficiency, and who asked, "Can a Catholic write a novel?"[60] Lord, Wilfred A. Parsons, and the other Jesuits, critics, and educators who directed the initial stages of the revival entered the 1930s compelled by two negative impulses—to defend and to prove. They were determined both to develop an articulate laity capable of defending and explaining the Church to a seemingly hostile world and to prove to themselves and the rest of the American intellectual community that Catholicism was an intellectual and cultural force worthy of respect and recognition. Meanwhile, the mature pluralistic Catholic outlook sought by Shuster in the 1920s would have to wait for less urgent and self-conscious times, as would significant Catholic American discovery of the writers of the French and German Catholic revivals. For now, the Catholic literary revival in America was, by necessity, in other, more pragmatic hands.

2

Francis X. Talbot and the Catholic Literary "Emergence"

Three forces converged during the 1920s and early 1930s to provoke American Catholic attempts to stimulate a Catholic literary revival in the United States. First, a significant number of Catholic publicists, teachers, and literary critics felt compelled to prove both to themselves and to their detractors that Catholic intellectual and cultural life compared favorably with that of the rest of American society. Second, many Catholic leaders, especially those concerned with the education of Catholic youth, were convinced that the Catholic laity must become more knowledgeable about its faith and thereby more articulate in defending the Church against her critics. Third, many of these same cultural leaders believed that in a world menaced by the memories of war, depression, class struggle, and philosophical and spiritual decay, Catholic-Christian orthodoxy offered the only standards, the only fixed body of unchanging "truths" capable of saving the world from chaos.

Thus, the Catholic literary revival was born of a curious mixture of insecurity, protest, and apostolic mission. These forces operated throughout the revival, sometimes simultaneously, often at odds with each other, and frequently within the same individual or organization. Three of the earliest leaders of the revival—Jesuits Francis X. Talbot, literary editor of *America*, Daniel A. Lord, national director of the Sodality of the Blessed Virgin and editor of its organ, the *Queen's Work*, and Calvert Alexander, whose *The Catholic Literary Revival* (1935) stood as the era's most substantive analysis of the international Catholic literary movement—all revealed qualities of intellectual insecurity, opposition, and Christian vision.[1] Yet, each was unique in his approach to the revival, and by studying the thought and activities of each, the various levels in the movement's early stages can be isolated.

Talbot, Lord, and Alexander also illustrate that, for the most part, the initial stages of the revival were Jesuit-led and -inspired. The first lengthy discussion of an actual American Catholic literary "emergence" or revival is encountered in two Jesuit reviews, *America* and the *Queen's Work*, during the late 1920s and early 1930s. In addition, many of the first courses on "The Catholic Literary Revival" were introduced at American Jesuit colleges and universities during the mid–1930s.

The Jesuit role in calling for an American Catholic intellectual emergence was a natural one. First, the Catholic American intellectual and cultural establishment was largely in Jesuit hands during the first third of the twentieth century. In 1932 the Society of Jesus operated thirteen of the fifty-six Catholic liberal arts colleges for men in the United States and fourteen of the nineteen Catholic universities.[2] The latter included such prestigious schools as Georgetown, Marquette, and St. Louis universities. Many of these Jesuit colleges and universities additionally were caught up in a neo-scholastic philosophical revival during the 1920s and 1930s, a movement that both flowed into and gave inspiration and direction to the earliest stages of the literary revival.

The Society of Jesus also loomed large in the Catholic publishing field during this era. Besides *America* and the *Queen's Work*, other Jesuit-edited popular magazines included the *Catholic Mind* and the *Messenger of the Sacred Heart*. Two scholarly journals, *Thought* and the *Modern Schoolman*, were also Jesuit-edited.[3]

Organized by St. Ignatius of Loyola during the sixteenth century to counter the impact of the Protestant Reformation, and historically dedicated to upholding the Catholic position in all matters of faith and morals, the American Jesuit community during the 1920s and early 1930s focused its considerable talents and resources upon the development of a fuller Catholic American intellectual and cultural presence. Encouraging and fostering an American Catholic literary revival was part of that effort.

TALBOT'S VIEW OF CATHOLIC LITERARY ACHIEVEMENT

In 1942 New York area Catholic high school students established a city-wide Catholic book club. They called it the Talbot Club, in honor of Jesuit editor, critic, and writer, Francis X. Talbot. It was the only name that seemed suitable, explained Mary Kiley, the club's first director. At a time when "American Catholic literature was at its lowest, uncreative level," she wrote, Talbot had "lifted the fog, showing Catholic America its own intellectual and literary possibilities, its hope for a new day."[4]

Kiley was correct in at least one respect: Few Americans were more self-consciously concerned about the growth and development of Catholic intellectual and cultural life than Father Talbot.

Talbot was of Irish ancestry, born in Philadelphia, Pennsylvania, in 1889. He entered the Society of Jesus when he was seventeen and took his final vows in 1921. After his ordination, Talbot quickly ascended to prominence within the Jesuit community. In 1923 he was named literary editor of *America*, and he served in that capacity until 1936, when he replaced Wilfred A. Parsons as editor-in-chief. At the same time, he automatically assumed the editorship of *Thought*, a Fordham University-based literary-philosophical quarterly also published by *America*. Talbot edited *America* and *Thought* until 1944. In 1947 he was appointed president of Loyola College in Baltimore, Maryland. He died in 1953.[5]

Talbot's self-conscious concern about the place of Catholicism in American life resulted, in part, from his position as editor of two leading Catholic journals. Because of his honored position in the Catholic community, Talbot was often called upon to act as its spokesman. The 1936 edition of *Encyclopedia Britannica*, for example, contained two Talbot articles on Church affairs. In 1938 Talbot represented the Catholic viewpoint in the Harold E. Sterns-edited *America Now* anthology, where prominent Americans were asked to comment upon contemporary American life. Talbot's position on these and other subjects was forever staunchly and authoritatively "Catholic." The Jesuit throughout his career was ready to take the Catholic side on every issue and to defend the Church against all critics. Talbot's Catholic loyalties were apparent even on the international political front. During the Spanish Civil War he sided with the Catholic Francisco Franco against the Spanish Republic.

Talbot was always proud of the numerical strength of the American Church. In *America Now* he boasted of the nation's 18,428 churches, 21,451,460 Catholics, and 32,668 priests. All served as evidence that Catholicism was becoming a "tremendous national force." The Jesuit assured non-Catholic Americans that the American Church was no longer alien. Three-quarters of her members were now American-born. Catholics had fought in the country's wars, held political office, and served as justices of the Supreme Court. Still smarting from the Smith ordeal, Talbot asserted that America's Catholics might even have gained the presidency, had it not been "withheld from them by undemocratic bigotry."[6]

Talbot found abundant evidence during the 1920s and 1930s to demonstrate that his co-religionists were contributing to the nation's economic and civic life; but he was painfully aware that this did not hold true in the intellectual and cultural realm. Like most Catholic spokesmen at this time, however, he attributed this to social factors, namely, the recent immigrant status of the Church. Thus, George N. Shuster—whose critique of Catholic intellectual life only incidentally acknowledged the immigrant factor while assigning primary responsibility for lack of Catholic influence upon the Church's own parochial outlook—was a major irritant to Talbot throughout this period. Shuster, in Talbot's opinion, was too much of an Americanizer, a "conciliationist" who agreed too quickly with the Church's critics. Both New York City-based editors maintained a polite but frosty relationship until 1937, when their differences exploded over American Catholic support for Franco.[7]

The major difference dividing Talbot and Shuster during the 1920s, however, centered upon the status of Catholic literature and Catholic intellectual life. Shuster's 1922 publication of *The Catholic Spirit in Modern English Literature*—pronouncing the bulk of American Catholic fiction unfit and unreadable—evoked a strong response from Talbot. Reviewing the book in *America*, Talbot departed from his usual two or three paragraph synopsis to devote two full pages to his analysis. Talbot's principal objection centered upon Shuster's "somewhat wide" use of the term *Catholic*. Shuster had purposely avoided sectarian connotations by defining the Catholic spirit as nothing "narrowly controversial," but rather as the "broad, traditionally Christian outlook upon life" that had shaped western culture (*Catholic Spirit*, p. 1). Talbot believed that this approach slighted specific Roman Catholic literary accomplishment. Shuster should have focused upon Catholic writers *per se*.[8]

Talbot conversely maintained that had Shuster been less exclusive in his use of the term *literature*, he easily could have found more abundant American achievements to praise. The Jesuit protested that Shuster had barely touched upon philosophy and theology, and had completely overlooked the economic works of Fr. John A. Ryan (*A Living Wage*, 1906). Talbot also would have listed Catholic American expatriate writers like Francis Marion Crawford and Louise Imogen Guiney under American as opposed to English Catholic letters.[9] Talbot thus alleged that Shuster was overly disparaging of Catholic literary achievement at the very time when American Catholics needed a deeper sense of their intellectual and cultural attainment.

Talbot similarly criticized Catholic colleges and universities during the 1920s and 1930s for failing to expose students to modern Catholic writers. He, like so many other Catholic cultural leaders between 1920 and 1960, looked to the Catholic college as the seedbed of any far-reaching American Catholic cultural movement. It was here that the American Church would develop interested readers and capable writers who would be the literary leaders of tomorrow. "One competent writer produced by each college every five years," reasoned Talbot in 1938, "would bring Catholic literature up to its national quota in the literature of the United States."[10]

But Catholic students, Talbot complained in 1930, had not been told about modern Catholic writers like G. K. Chesterton and Ronald Knox, or novelists and poets like Robert Hugh Benson and Francis Thompson. Instead, Catholic professors focused almost exclusively upon writers like Shakespeare, Alexander Pope, and Charles Dickens in their literature courses. When Catholic professors did mention Catholic books, wrote Talbot, they usually dismissed them as "terribly pious" or silly. The impression given Catholic college students, then, was that "Catholic literature either did not exist or did not matter."[11]

Consequently, Talbot saw red when he heard Shuster and other Catholic critics summarily dismiss all contemporary Catholic fiction—English and American—as overly pious and sentimental. Talbot always insisted that there was more than one tradition in modern Catholic letters. There is the tradition of "masters," he wrote in 1925, and there is the tradition of "scribblers." In that sense, argued Talbot, "the Catholic tradition does not differ from the general literary tradition in its nature." It differed only in its proportions.[12] Talbot was as ready as Shuster to condemn "the puerile efforts that have in the past paraded as Catholic and literary."[13] But the emphasis was upon the past, and throughout the 1920s and early 1930s Talbot maintained that Catholic fiction, like all Catholic literature, was maturing and developing.

As proof, Talbot often pointed to a middle group of contemporary Catholic novelists who, while not of the stature of the Englishman Benson, nevertheless were producing interesting and artistic work. Among these writers, Talbot variously listed Americans Edith O'Shaughnessy, Kathleen Thompson Norris, Lucille Papin Borden, and James B. Connolly. In the English camp, Talbot listed Sheila Kaye-Smith, Isabel C. Clarke, Compton MacKenzie, and Owen Francis Dudley.

While a fuller analysis of these writers is forthcoming, it should be stressed that, aside from Connolly, most of the above wrote either "problem novels" focusing upon some question of faith and morals, or, in the case of the English, followed Benson in dealing with themes of Protestant-Catholic conflict during Elizabethan times. Connolly, although a serious Catholic layman, never introduced specifically religious or moral themes into his stories. His best work, *Gloucestermen* (1930), was a New England sea saga. Talbot's principal interest in Connolly was that he was a Catholic producing literature. Little known and seldom acclaimed outside Catholic circles, all these writers, nevertheless, did represent improvement over the Frances Tiernans and the other pious tractarians rejected by Shuster and Catholic college students during the 1920s. Talbot attempted to focus attention on many of these writers in *Fiction by Its Makers* (1928), which he introduced by asserting: "Never before in English literary history have there been so many brilliant Catholic novelists."[14]

By the late 1920s, Talbot's position on Catholic literature included a number of important assumptions. He believed that Catholic literature, and especially Catholic fiction, was becoming modern and readable. American Catholic letters, no less than in England and continental Europe, were undergoing an awakening. He believed that while it would be wrong to characterize the American movement as a reivival, it was certainly an "emergence." And finally, he believed that the future advance of a Catholic literary movement in the United States was linked directly to the development of an interested and supportive reading public.

Driven by these assumptions, Talbot embarked upon two decades of literary activity designed to lead both the Catholic and the general reading public to a greater respect and awareness of Catholic literary achievement. Most of Talbot's attention was directed toward specific Catholic books and writers—Catholic novelists, poets, essayists, philosophers, and historians who integrated their work with a Catholic orthodox perspective. But he also attempted to create a greater awareness of literary and scholarly achievement by Catholics in general. In this way, Talbot hoped to build an American Catholic literary tradition while, at the same time, silencing the critics of Catholic intellectual and cultural life of previous years.

TALBOT'S LITERARY PLEBISCITES

In 1923 and 1935, Talbot, as literary editor of *America*, sponsored "literary plebiscites" to call attention to Catholic books and writers. In the 1923 contest, *America*'s readers and the nation's Catholic college students were asked to determine "The Best Ten Catholic Books" of the past century. Directed, in part, at Shuster and other 1920s' critics of specific Catholic literary achievement, the contest, asserted Talbot, was intended to "prove to the incredulous that we have a remarkably rich and varied Catholic literature."[15]

The 1935 plebiscite similarly asked readers to nominate an "academy" of contemporary Catholic writers. Modeled after the French Academy, it was to serve as a "Permanent Gallery" of "contemporary immortals" (twenty-five non-Americans and fifteen Americans) at the newly established Gallery of Living Catholic Authors at Webster College in Webster Groves, Missouri.[16] Founded in 1932 with the aid and encouragement of Talbot and his fellow Jesuit Daniel A. Lord, the Gallery's purpose was "to recognize and honor living Catholic authors" and arouse interest in their work.[17] The Gallery's Board of Governors, using the results of the plebiscite as an advisory, were to make the actual selections for the Permanent Gallery.

The board of governors was an impressive group, made up of some of America's leading Catholic editors, critics, and publishers. It included, aside from Jesuits Talbot, Lord, and Calvert Alexander, John Gillard Brunini, president of the Catholic Poetry Society of America and editor of its magazine, *Spirit*; Sr. Mary Madeleva, C.S.C., president of St. Mary's College of Notre Dame and a leading Catholic poet; Notre Dame librarian Paul Byrne; *Catholic World* editor James M. Gillis, C.S.P.; and Catholic publishers Francis J. Sheed (Sheed and Ward) and William Bruce (Bruce Publishing).[18] Thus, the Gallery of Living Catholic Authors—and Talbot's 1935 plebiscite—had the suport of some of America's best-known Catholics.

Similar guidelines were established in each contest. Readers had to confine their nominations to Catholic writers—an obvious swipe at Shuster—and to books written by Catholics. Nominees could not be "near-Catholic," nor could books be written with merely a "Catholic Spirit." All candidates, insisted Talbot in the 1935 plebiscite, must "technically be in communion with the Universal Catholic Church." Willa Cather, a non-Catholic, thus was not eligible for the Gallery, even though her *Death Comes for the Archibishop* (1927) was considered by many to be the best religious novel of the day.[19]

In both plebiscites, Talbot welcomed any book on any subject, as long as it was written by a Catholic, was literature in the generic sense, and was composed with "craftsmanship" and "charm." Neither book nor author need have treated exclusively Catholic topics. The 1935 contest, however, did discourage nominees who had only textbooks or technical treatises to their credit.

Finally, the emphasis was upon contemporary Catholic writers, or in the case of the 1923 Best Books contest, upon writers of the recent past. Talbot's intention here was to encourage his readers to focus upon the books and convert writers of the recent English Catholic revival—Newman, Chesterton, and others.

The results of each vote, as expected, were heavily weighted with English books and writers. The Best Ten Catholic books ranged from Newman's autobiographical *Apologia Pro Vita Sua* (1864) to Hilaire Belloc's *Europe and the Faith* (1920). The only modern fictional work was Irishman Canon Patrick Sheehan's *My New Curate* (1899), a whimsical account of the clash between an old pastor and his brash young assistant. Only three books written by American Catholics were listed, and none of these were novels. The American books were James Cardinal Gibbons's *The Faith of Our Fathers* (1877) (an apologetic work), James J. Walsh's *The Thirteenth, the Greatest of Centuries* (1907, a popularly written history of the medieval Church), and the *Collected Poems* (1918) of Joyce Kilmer.[20]

Similarly, eleven of the twenty non-Americans (reduced from the original twenty-five) eventually selected for membership in the Permanent Gallery of Living Catholic Authors were English.[21] They included such names as novelists Maurice Baring and Sheila Kaye-Smith, historians Christopher Dawson and Christopher Hollis, and controversialists Belloc and Knox.[22] Well-known English Catholic novelist Robert Hugh Benson was neither nominated nor selected because he had died in 1914. Chesterton's death in 1936 likewise excluded his selection. French philosopher Jacques Maritain and Norwegian novelist Sigrid Undset were two of the better-known non-English selections.

The American wing of the Academy was not quite as distinguished, and it was evident that Talbot and the other members of the selection committee were not using the same set of standards here that they had employed with the non-Americans. Talbot found himself enshrined as a "contemporary immortal," along with three other journalists (*Catholic World* editor James M. Gillis, *Commonweal* co-founder Michael Williams, and essayist Agnes Repplier), two historians (Peter Guilday and Carlton J. H. Hayes), one philosopher (Msgr. Fulton J. Sheen), three poets (Theodore Maynard, Leonard Feeney, S.J., and Sister Madeleva) and two novelists (Helen C. White and William Thomas Walsh).

Of the above, only Maynard's reputation was clearly established within the international literary community. But Maynard, in fact, was a naturalized American, having done his best work while in England. White, a University of Wisconsin literature professor, had written two historical novels by 1935, *A Watch in the Night* (1933), based upon the life of thirteenth century Renaissance poet Jacopone da Todi, and *Not Built with Hands* (1935), recounting the clash between Henry IV and Pope Gregory VII at Canossa. Walsh was an English professor at Manhattanville College in New York City. His *Out of the Whirlwind* (1935) was the story of a troubled immigrant worker who flirts with Marxism, but then discovers the nature and destiny of man is best understood in the principles of Catholicism.

Both Walsh and White had received some notice outside of Catholic circles. A 1935 *New York Times* review, for example, placed *Out of the Whirlwind* in the "front rank" of contemporary American social novels, and compared Walsh to the well-known French Catholic writer Francois Mauriac.[23] A reviewer for the liberal Protestant journal *Christian Century* similarly wrote that White's *Watch in the Night* had "no superior" as a historical novel of medieval religion.[24] But Walsh's book was his only novel. In fact, at the time of Talbot's 1935 plebiscite both Walsh and White were probably best known to the non-Catholic world for achievements in other literary fields: White for her scholarly work on nineteenth century English literature (*Matthew Arnold and Goethe*, 1921, and *The Mysticism of William Blake*, 1927), and Walsh for his 1930 biography, *Isabella of Spain*. White would later go on to establish a reputation as a poet.

Talbot's plebiscites nevertheless illustrate several important tendencies in the cultural life of American Catholicism between 1920 and 1935.
First, Catholic cultural leaders like Talbot and Lord during the 1920s and
early 1930s often attempted to demonstrate the vitality of contemporary
American Catholic intellectual and cultural life by identifying with the
accomplishments of European Catholics, especially the English. James
Cardinal Gibbons was not John Henry Newman. Talbot nevertheless
used the results of his first plebiscite as an occasion to praise *American*
Catholic literary life. Reflecting upon the plebiscite in 1924, Talbot wrote
that it was a serious attempt to determine several aspects of "the present
position of Catholics in America." The contest verified, Talbot boasted,
that Catholic Americans possessed "a heritage of unsuspected wealth,"
with books "written with a finish and a literary skill that equals the
greatest achievements of the greatest non-Catholic authors."[25] Talbot
could say this, but only after subsuming the meager American Catholic
literary tradition within the richer English Catholic one. Thus, by jux-
taposing well-known English writers like Newman and Belloc with
lesser-accomplished Americans, Talbot managed to make these diverse
and unequal strains appear to be a single Catholic literary tradition.

This tendency to lay claim to the English was especially strong in the
field of fiction, where the American contribution was embarrassingly
slight. But by pointing to the work of Benson, Baring, Kaye-Smith, and
others, Talbot could claim a Catholic tradition in fiction of at least some
substance. Thus, in a sort of literary imperialism, Talbot annexed the
English Catholic revival to that of the United States, hoping that American Catholic intellectual and cultural life would grow in stature.

Talbot, conjointly, responded to the other frequently heard criticisms
of American Catholic life in the 1920s—that the Church had no scholars,
that only second-rate minds any longer believed in the supernatural,
and that Catholics were not contributing to the nation's intellectual and
cultural life in proportion to their numbers—in similar fashion. He and
other Catholic American cultural leaders during this time singled out
almost any Catholic name that appeared in print, American or otherwise,
as proof of Catholic intellectual achievement. At times, it appeared that
Talbot was willing to celebrate any warm body, so long as it was Catholic,
received the sacraments, and set words to paper.

Talbot's loose definition of Catholic literature helped accomplish this.
During the 1935 plebiscite, for example, it was evident that Talbot was
just as interested in collecting names as in discriminating among them
to determine an academy of "immortals." He admitted as much in 1936
when he stated that one of the primary objectives of the plebiscite was
to produce "a most complete catalogue of the names of practically all of
the Catholics who have published books."[26] Thus Catholic writers like
Fr. Charles E. Coughlin were nominated, along with Maritain, Dawson,
and Undset.[27] Catholic authors of prayer books, spiritual exercises, and

marriage manuals were listed and catalogued within the same literary tradition as Paul Claudel. In this view, Catholic literature appeared to be little more than the sum total of all writing by Catholics.

What may we conclude from Talbot's efforts? On the one hand, his attempts to advertise Catholic writers and Catholic literary achievement, and to call attention to Catholics "because they are Catholics," betray his fundamental insecurity about the place of Catholicism in American life. On the other hand, Talbot's activities represented an authentic attempt to build an American Catholic literary tradition. Talbot's tactic of calling attention to primarily contemporary Catholic literary figures, whether they wrote from a specific Catholic sensibility or not, reinforced the idea that there was a tradition of modern writing and scholarship among Catholics. The New York Jesuit believed that this was a point that had to be made by an emergent immigrant Church. The fact that Catholic creativity and intellectual freedom had been repeatedly questioned by forces both inside and outside the Church during the 1920s intensified his efforts. Long lists of actual Catholic books and writers, moreover, strengthened Talbot's claim that Catholic literature was emerging. Finally, it is true that Talbot often put undue emphasis upon the accomplishments of English Catholic writers, but he, like nearly every other American Catholic literary leader during his time, ultimately hoped that the English would serve as a model for American Catholics to follow, inspiring the American Church to develop writers of her own.

THE CATHOLIC BOOK CLUB, CATHOLIC POETRY SOCIETY, AND CATHOLIC THEATRE CONFERENCE

Talbot's attempt to build an American Catholic literary tradition included manifold projects, aside from his plebiscites. The Jesuit had a hand in the formation of virtually every Catholic American literary association that emerged from the 1920s and 1930s. These organizations included, besides the Gallery of Living Catholic Authors, the Catholic Book Club, the Catholic Poetry Society of America, the Catholic Theatre Conference, the Spiritual Book Associates, and the Catholic Library Association. Most of these groups registered the combination of self-consciousness, protest, and apostolic purpose that characterized American Catholic cultural life during this era.

The Catholic Book Club, founded by Talbot in 1928, was designed to bring "notable Catholic books to the attention of the advanced and intelligent Catholic reader." Offering books "in the modern mode for modern Catholic minds," the club was geared especially toward college-educated Catholic readers, who Talbot feared were reading too many of the "heretical and immoral" books of the period.[28] Talbot thus sought to confront "bad books" with "sane ones."[29] The club's selection committee (whose long-term members included, besides Talbot, historian James J. Walsh, novelist Kathleen Norris, and *Catholic World* editor James M. Gillis) showed a strong preference for European Catholic writers like Maritain, Dawson, and Undset after 1930, as well as such writers as French novelist Francois Mauriac, and German theologian Karl Adam. Many of these writers were published by the London Catholic publishing house of Sheed and Ward, which opened a New York branch in 1933. Talbot and the Catholic Book Club were thus instrumental in stirring the first American Catholic interest in the advanced Catholic writers and thinkers of Europe who would dominate the progressive circles of American Catholic intellectual and cultural life after 1935. Talbot also organized and sponsored an American lecture tour for Undset in 1940.

The Catholic Poetry Society and the Catholic Theatre Conference, formed in 1931 and 1937, respectively, aimed at preserving and advancing a Catholic tradition in these fields. The Catholic Poetry Society grew out of the efforts of Talbot, Francis X. Connolly (a young critic and Fordham University English professor), and Edith Donavan and Frederic Thompson, literary editors at the *Catholic World* and the *Commonweal*. The society's immediate purpose was to recognize and encourage nascent Catholic poets, but Talbot and its founders envisioned the organization eventually as part of a national Catholic cultural movement through which "the Catholic tradition in poetry might be channeled into contemporary modes of thought."[30] Its actual impact, of course, was considerably less, but the society and its magazine *Spirit* did provide a forum for a number of distinguished Catholic poets, including Theodore Maynard, Charles L. O'Donnell, C.S.C., and Helen C. White.

The Catholic Theatre Conference likewise aimed at injecting Catholic principles and values into the nation's cultural life. The organization was the idea of Talbot's friend, Emmett Lavery, a Hollywood screen writer and playwright who was associated with the Federal Theatre Project during the 1930s. Lavery had been impressed by the leftist New Theatre and Yiddish Theatre movements and their success in projecting a definite culture and "way of life to the masses." Lavery envisioned the Catholic theatre in a similar light. In 1936 Lavery wrote in *America*:

I see great audiences as well as fine actors being trained in the Catholic tradition. I see a new market for the works of rising young Catholic dramatists. . . . I see an exchange between the Catholic Theatre and Broadway of sound plays . . . and I see the Catholic way of life opened up to the masses who may never join the Catholic Book Club or identify themselves with the Catholic Poetry Society.[31]

Thus, although the Catholic Theatre movement was aimed primarily at Catholic audiences, Lavery nevertheless entertained the idea that it would eventually impact upon the non-Catholic public. Lavery, in fact, claimed in 1937 that the movement, with its ready-made audiences, equipment, and school auditoriums, had the potential to be "the single greatest force in the 'tributary theatre' of America."[32]

Talbot, an infrequent dramatist himself, actively supported Lavery's efforts, and with his Jesuit confreres Lord and George Dineen (a Loyola University of Chicago drama teacher), helped Lavery launch the first meeting of the National Catholic Theatre Conference in Chicago in June 1937. In its peak years during the mid–1950s, the Catholic Theatre Conference claimed 600 producing groups, mostly affiliated with Catholic high schools and colleges. The Catholic Theatre was less parochial than other projects to which Talbot lent his support. Lavery's list of recommended plays, besides such explicit Catholic productions as Paul Claudel's *The Tidings Brought to Mary*, included George Bernard Shaw's *St. Joan*, Philip Barry's *The Joyous Season*, and Eugene O'Neill's *Days Without End*.[33]

Talbot's goal of establishing a Catholic literary presence in America was thus a multi-dimensional one. There was a genuine apostolic purpose behind many of his efforts: A Catholic literary tradition in America had the potential to change America, and Talbot, like so many other Catholic American leaders between 1920 and 1960, believed that Catholics, given the chance, could do it. But these more positive understandings of the Catholic cultural emergence were often overshadowed—especially during the culturally painful 1920s and early 1930s—by the more immediate concerns of leadership for the sake of leadership, and writers for the sake of writing, by a culturally insecure American Church. Talbot's efforts thus frequently conveyed the sense of Catholics promoting Catholics.

Still, history is not without its insights when we attempt to put Talbot's parochialism into proper perspective. Catholics have not been the only cultural group to struggle to find its national identity. The United States as a nation underwent its own period of "literary nationalism" during the first part of the nineteenth century. English critic Sydney Smith's 1818 sneer, "Who reads an American book?" was not unlike the aspersions cast upon American Catholic intellectual life during the 1920s. The response was surprisingly similar in both cases. Robert E. Spiller writes of nineteenth century Americans: "Indignant protest was one form of their admission of the truth of these criticisms; exhortation to improvement, another."[34]

Or compare Talbot with early nineteenth century American cultural leader Charles Jared Ingersoll. In 1823 Ingersoll delivered his famed "Discourse Concerning the Influence of America on the Mind" before the American Philosophical Society. He sounded much like Talbot one hundred years later. Taking the widest possible view of literature, Ingersoll lauded American literary achievement in all fields of intellectual activity: history, biography, metallurgy, horticulture, ornithology, astronomy, even navigation. In these and other areas, insisted Ingersoll, "there is no reason to be ashamed of our proficiency." Ingersoll's further boast that a single Philadelphia newspaper of the day contained advertisements "by a single bookseller of more than one hundred and fifty publications by American authors from the American Press" are, again, words worthy of Talbot.[35]

In their self-conscious puffery, partisanship, and anxious quest for nationality, the similarities between Talbot and Ingersoll are striking. So, too, were Talbot's concrete activities to build an American Catholic literary tradition similar to the actions of Ingersoll, J. K. Paulding, Noah Webster, and other early nineteenth century Americans. As they had done before, he called for the establishment of "the instruments of literary culture" (colleges, bookshops, libraries, literary societies, and theater groups) which would help realize that quest.

Continuing the analogy, historically, nearly every American minority has gone through a "great names" period in its national cultural development. America's black community underwent such an experience during the 1960s and 1970s, finding a "usable past" in such figures as Crispus Attucks, Phyllis Wheatley, and contemporary black political and cultural leaders of the United States and the Third World. Women, long patronized for their lack of intellectual and cultural achievement, similarly began to find their historical and cultural identities during the 1970s and 1980s. This occurred, in part, because feminist leaders focused popular attention upon the achievements of women who, until recently, were overlooked or ignored in our nation's cultural past.

A self-conscious American Catholic minority had its turn in the 1920s and early 1930s. There was a strain in Talbot and American Catholic cultural life during this time that could not resist fat lists, catalogues, and bibliographies of Catholic names. Talbot's plebiscites, *America* magazine's *One Hundred Best Catholic Books* (1923), the Gallery of Living Catholic Authors, and the numerous literature conferences and book fairs designed to call attention to Catholic books and writers gave expression to that need. After the first annual Catholic Book Fair in New York City in April 1934, Talbot boasted that it contained "the largest assembly of current Catholic books ever gathered in one place."[36] That may be so, responded National Catholic Welfare Conference correspondent Cecelia Mary Young, but she reminded him of a similar fair held in New York City in 1924. Young recalled that the 1924 exhibit had included both displays of Catholic books and autographed photographs and letters from such English Catholic notables as Chesterton and Belloc, and American Catholic poets and writers like Agnes Repplier and Katherine Bregy. "It was a very expensive experiment," admitted Young, "but we had answered the challenge—[that] we have no Catholic writers."[37]

Talbot's single-minded quest for names probably reached a low point when he consented in 1930 to revise, edit, and publish an American edition of Irish Jesuit Stephen J. Brown's bibliography *Novels and Tales by Catholic Writers*. Updated with American writers and publishers, the new addition endeavored "to include all fiction . . . in the English language by Catholic writers, with the exception of some forgotten books of little value."[38] The exception, however, proved the rule. The book was full of such forgettable works as George Williams's *Clubfoot the Avenger* and Rev. Will W. Whelen's *The Ex-Nun* and *The Ex-Seminarian*. For Talbot, however, it was yet another list, and another indication of a Catholic cultural arrival. The same phenomenon of Catholic lists, moreover, was repeated in the non-literary realm during the 1920s and early 1930s, with polls to determine "The Twelve Greatest Catholic Women" in America and the launching of the *American Catholic Who's Who* in 1933.[39] If the contemporary non-Catholic world was ignoring Catholics and Catholic achievement, Catholics would promote themselves.

The 1920s have been called "The Advertising Age," and this was especially true for Catholic literature. "If sauerkraut can be 'put over'— Catholic literature can, too," reasoned one enthusiast in *America* in 1928.[40] Perhaps this best describes the condition of Catholic literature during the 1920s and early 1930s. Catholic literature, like sauerkraut in the wake of World War I anti-German hysteria, was suffering from unwarranted prejudice, primarily at the hands of those who had not tasted its delights. But Catholic literature, and especially Catholic fiction, it was argued, had changed. It was new and improved. Yet many Catholics and the general reading public were unaware of the change. It needed to be advertised. "Let the cause of the contemporary Catholic novel, then, be broadcast," wrote another *America* correspondent in 1925. Pointing to novelists like Benson, Frank Spearman, and Lucille Papin Borden, she urged, "Let the Catholic be reminded that the day of platitudes and tiresome preaching in Catholic fiction has vanished."[41]

"I think we must advertise our Catholic writers," insisted college literature teacher Brother Jogues, C.F.X., at the 1936 meeting of the National Catholic Education Association. "We must become publicity agents. We have been entirely too modest about the growing achievements of our Catholic authors."[42] Catholics during the 1920s and early 1930s appeared to follow his advice. Catholic modesty gave way to Catholic triumphalism. Catholics, as well as their literature, emerged during this period, announcing themselves to a world that had overlooked them for too long.

3

A Revival Is Organized: Daniel A. Lord and the Sodality Literary Campaign

It is always difficult to determine the precise beginnings of literary movements. The origins of the Catholic literary revival in America, however, present few problems. It began, as an *organized* movement, in January 1933 in the Daniel A. Lord-edited *Queen's Work*, the national magazine of the Sodality of the Blessed Virgin. The Sodality, with over one million members, was the nation's largest Catholic youth organization.

Lord, as part of his ongoing effort to stimulate the production of young Catholic readers and writers, commissioned Calvert Alexander, his Jesuit colleague on the English faculty at St. Louis University High School, to write a series of *Queen's Work* articles on John Henry Newman and the major figures of the English Catholic revival. Alexander himself was concurrently preparing a history of English Catholic letters since Newman; it was published in 1935 as *The Catholic Literary Revival*.[1]

Lord used the centenary of the Oxford Movement, a Newman-led effort to renew the supernatural and ecclesiastical authority of the Church of England—ending in Newman's own conversion to Catholicism in 1845—to launch the campaign. He introduced Alexander's articles as follows:

The world is swinging into a great Catholic renaissance. Artists and writers are becoming Catholics in astonishing numbers. Newman's dreams are now being realized. America alone among the nations is slow to take up this new crusade of Catholic truth.[2]

For the next six months, Alexander provided Lord's youthful readers with an impressive overview of the Catholic writers commonly associated with the English movement: Newman, poets Gerard Manley Hopkins, Francis Thompson, and Coventry Patmore, novelists Robert Hugh Benson and Compton McKenzie, controversialists Ronald Knox and G. K. Chesterton, historian Christopher Dawson, and others. Alexander claimed in his characteristically confident style that the worldwide Catholic renaissance was both literary and intellectual, and that while it began with Newman, it continued to the present day. Only in America, Alexander complained, was the Church "without a voice." "Shall we have a Catholic literary revival in America?" rhetorically asked Alexander in his final installment. "We shall," he answered, and the present generation of Catholic high school and college youth "will bring it about." "That is why," he concluded, "we have been studying the authors of the Catholic revival."[3]

Alexander and Lord, like Francis X. Talbot before them, illustrated the outlook common among many Catholic critics, teachers, and cultural leaders during the 1920s and 1930s that a Catholic literary emergence could somehow be deliberately manufactured in America, through inducement, exhortation, and effort. They similarly believed as Talbot— who lent support to the Sodality campaign in *America*—that the American revival, for the most part, could be fashioned through the example of English Catholic literary models. Lord once remarked that "the greatest loss to Catholic authorship in America" was the death of Joyce Kilmer in World War I; as the exemplar of an indigenous American Catholic poetic tradition, Kilmer was the "potential founder" of an American Catholic literary "Resurgence."[5] Lord, doubtless, was exaggerating. The sweet phrases of Kilmer would have made a poor start for the polemical tradition in Catholic letters that Lord and Alexander sought to initiate. Better was combative Chesterton. It was chiefly for this reason that these Jesuits, and many other Catholic educators during the 1920s and early 1930s, looked not toward Kilmer, but toward the outspoken and controversial English for their literary models.

Thus, while Talbot's urgency in establishing a Catholic literary presence in America focused primarily upon self-conscious concerns of influence and prestige, Lord and Alexander added an ideological component to the Catholic literary effort. The Church, in their view, needed not only its quota of modern scholars and writers; it needed Catholics who would counteract the "irreligion" and "immorality" of modern times. For Lord and Alexander, and the wide number of Catholic educators and students whom they influenced during the late 1920s and early 1930s, the Catholic literary revival was no less than "a call to battle." It was a "modern crusade for the welfare of the Catholic Church and of civilization."[6]

LORD, THE SODALITY, AND "INTELLECTUAL" CATHOLIC ACTION

In 1938 Lord indirectly assessed his own role in the Catholic literary revival. His comments came during Fr. John A. O'Brien's symposium on *Catholics and Scholarship* (1938), in which Catholic scientists, litterateurs, economists, and educators assessed contemporary Catholic intellectual life and offered suggestions about how the Church could begin producing scholars in proportion to her numbers. In a paper on "Training Youth for Authorship," Lord explained that when he first began his work with the Sodality in the mid–1920s, he encountered a disturbing "mental habit" among Catholic youth. They seemed to have no Catholic identity, complained Lord, with no pride in themselves or in their religious heritage. On the contrary, Catholic youth seemed timid and inarticulate in the face of the anti-Catholic feeling of the era. Lord continued:

We had to make youngsters talk out, speak their minds, grip their religion in proud hands, face the world knowing that Catholics are the one logical-minded group living; and the one group that holds history in its firm clasp, and can face the future with clear eyes. . . .
. . . More than anything else I was interested in anything that would destroy inarticulateness. That meant an insistence on anything that developed Catholic consciousness and righteous pride in the heritage that is ours.[7]

Lord's observations about Catholic youth came from experience. As national director of the Sodality from 1925 to 1948, he was in close contact with America's young Catholics. The Sodality claimed more than two million members in its peak years during the 1940s, with nearly 13,000 affiliated units in Catholic parishes, colleges, schools of nursing, and high schools throughout the country. From his St. Louis, Missouri, headquarters, Lord directed a staff of seven full-time Jesuits who supplied local units with outlines and suggestions for their regular monthly meetings. Lord, as Sodality director, also edited the *Queen's Work* and oversaw the operation of the Queen's Work Press. The *Queen's Work*, with a circulation of over 100,000 during the late 1930s and 1940s, reached the majority of Catholic high schools and colleges in America.[8]

Lord was a familiar figure on the American Catholic youth scene between 1925 and 1950 as he railroaded across the country giving lectures, delivering retreats, leading Sodality conventions, and conducting Summer Schools of Catholic Action (SSCA). In 1928 alone, Lord presided over twenty Catholic youth conferences attended by over 10,000 high school and college students.

Lord thus held a unique and powerful position in the religious formation of modern Catholic youth. Throughout his life, this uncommon Jesuit, with the ready smile, neatly parted silver hair, and quick, smooth stride, displayed a deep and sensitive insight into the problems and aspirations of modern Catholic youth.

Daniel Aloysius Lord was born in Chicago in 1888, the product of a mixed-religion marriage. His Protestant father traced his English ancestry to William the Conqueror and the first American settlers. His mother was second-generation Irish-American. By his own account, Lord's childhood was idyllic. His autobiography recalls happy days roaming elm-lined, autoless streets on Chicago's suburban west and south sides, family gatherings and picnics, and a devoted mother reading *Robinson Crusoe* and *David Copperfield* at bedtime.[9] Lord credited his mother with his lifelong interest in drama, music, and literature.

After brief attendance at Chicago public schools, Lord finished his education at Jesuit-run St. Ignatius High School and Loyola University, where he excelled in dramatics and edited the college newspaper. He entered the Society of Jesus in 1909, received his M.A. in English from St. Louis University in 1915, and was ordained in 1923. Lord taught English and religion between 1917 and 1920 at St. Louis University and its affiliated high school, and in 1925 was appointed Sodality director and editor of the *Queen's Work*.

Apart from his work with the Sodality, Lord was probably best known for the numerous religious pamphlets he wrote and published through the Queen's Work Press. The bookrack of nearly every American Catholic church between 1930 and 1960 probably contained at least 1 or 2 of the 233 pamphlets Lord wrote during his lifetime. Lord's pamphlets characterize his lifelong attention to the concrete, here-and-now concerns of the average Catholic lay person. They were short, readable, and topical, and primarily addressed some practical question of Catholic faith and practice.[10] At the time of his death in 1955, total sales surpassed twenty-five million, earning him the title of "the greatest religious pamphleteer of his generation."[11] A man of immense energy—a staff member once exclaimed that working for him was "like being tied to the end of a tornado"—Lord also wrote and produced thirty books (including a religion text, a popularly written philosophy, and several novels), fifty plays, twelve musicals, and six pageants. Lord's published work, like his pamphlets, was little known outside of Catholic circles. His month-long "City of Freedom" pageant, honoring Detroit, Michigan, on its 250th anniversary in 1951, did attract over 200,000 people.

When Lord assumed the directorship of the Sodality in the summer of 1925 it was, in the Jesuit's words, "a dying organization."[12] Both the Sodality and the *Queen's Work* were in the midst of an identity crisis. The chief focus of the Sodality, the cultivation of spiritual life through monthly communion, had been abridged by recent reforms of Pius X, who encouraged more frequent reception of the Eucharist. In addition, the *Queen's Work*, established in 1913 as a magazine of general Catholic interest, was finding it increasingly difficult to compete with similarly styled Catholic journals like *America* and the *Commonweal*. Consequently, Sodality membership and *Queen's Work* subscriptions had dropped off dramatically. Upon visiting his scattered Sodality units shortly after assuming the organization's leadership, Lord admitted that they were little more than social clubs or groups for the "piously devout" intent upon their own personal salvation.[13]

Lord revitalized the Sodality both through the force of his own personality and by linking the organization to the newly emergent concept of Catholic Action. Catholic Action was still a relatively undefined area of American Catholic life in the 1920s, with both official and unofficial designations. Pius XI (1922–1939), "The Pope of Catholic Action," gave Catholic Action its official definition in 1922 when, in view of the Vatican's diminishing influence in postwar fascist Italy, he called upon the Catholic laity everywhere to assist the clergy in advancing the Church's corporate interests. Pius XI characterized this lay activity as Catholic Action and, in a subsequent letter to the Italian archbishops, defined it as "the participation of the laity in the apostolate of the hierarchy."[14] Thus envisioned, Catholic Action denoted a tightly integrated laity operating under the direction of the bishops. This version of Catholic Action was institutionalized in the United States in the massively bureaucratic National Catholic Welfare Conference, the official agency of the American bishops, and its affiliated National Councils of Catholic Men (NCCM) and Women (NCCW).

By contrast, a broader, generic designation of Catholic Action, referring to faith-inspired organized Catholic lay activity, emerged almost simultaneously with this official version. This unofficial side of Catholic Action, which possessed little meaningful apostolic focus in the militant 1920s Church, unfolded into the Catholic "lay apostolate" of the 1930s and 1940s and generated some of this century's most progressive Catholic lay activity, including the lay-founded American Catholic Worker movement, established by Peter Maurin and Dorothy Day in 1933.[15]

While Catholic Action, especially under its official designation, often took the form of mobilizing Catholics to protect Catholic group interests, the actual concept of a Catholic lay apostolate had deep theological meaning. In theory, the papacy was calling upon lay Catholics everywhere to make a literal response to Christ's command, "Go, therefore, and make disciples of all nations" (Matt. 28:19). Catholic Action, in this context, always had a compelling, almost intoxicating quality about it. In significant ways, Catholic Action was one of the most powerful forces behind the strong sense of lay Catholic idealism and identity during the interwar years, as Pius XI, again and again, called upon Catholics to organize to extend the "reign of Christ" into every realm of life.

But the Catholic Worker movement was not an option for young American Catholics until the mid–1930s. European-inspired specialized Catholic Action groups (limited to members of a given profession or group, such as workers, students, married couples) likewise were not available in the United States until the early 1940s, when Young Christian Worker (YCW) and Young Christian Student (YCS) groups were formed.[16] Nor were the ideas of Catholic social action theorists like Dom Virgil Michel, an American liturgical scholar who linked the Catholic lay apostolate to the theology of Christ's Mystical Body, well-known before the mid–1930s.

Instead, Lord was correct when he complained that Catholic Action in the 1920s and early 1930s was put forth in the most "nebulous" terms. This was especially true on the parish, high school, and college levels, where lay organizations were not affiliated with the National Catholic Welfare Conference, and where, according to Lord, Catholic Action waited to be "translated from the realm of words into the realm of realities."[17]

It was on this note that Lord determined to give Catholic Action a focus and direction for modern Catholic youth. Starting in 1927 he began to organize the Sodality and the *Queen's Work* around the Catholic Action concept, while developing concrete programs and activities for young Catholics. Moreover, because the Sodality operated under a mandate from the hierarchy, it was designated an official Catholic Action organization.

Lord's idea of the Catholic youth apostolate was chiefly an intellectual one. This was especially true of high school and college students, to whom the *Queen's Work* was directed. Lord always maintained that the chief attacks upon the Church came from intellectual quarters. Thus, he insisted, they must be met by "intellectually educated" men and women.[18] Lord often remarked that there were two types of Catholics: the "hesitant" and the "mentally alert." The first group, according to the Jesuit, lived with a faith only "half-understood." The second, he continued, had "an intellectual grasp of the essentials of the Catholic faith and scholastic philosophy and a ready ability to present these essentials to others." This was Lord's idea of Catholic Action and the lay apostolate: intellectual, vocal, and articulate, dedicted to "the promotion of Catholic truth and the defence of the Church."[19]

The Sodality under Lord became an organization to develop Catholic leaders who "talked, planned, wrote, publicized and acted [their] religion to the full."[20] Beginning in the early 1930s, the St. Louis office endorsed a strong program of Catholic reading, study, and writing for its high school and college affiliates. In 1931 Lord also instituted his Summer Schools of Catholic Action (SSCA) for Sodality members and their moderators. Co-sponsored by the St. Louis University department of sociology, SSCAs were intensive one-week training sessions designed to ground Sodality leaders in the "what, why, and how of Sodality action."[21] By 1933, SSCAs were operating in three separate regions of the United States, averaging 400 students per session. By 1949 cumulative attendance was over 100,000.[22]

SSCA participants received practical training in Catholic Action theory, liturgical renewal, catechetical methods, Catholic play production, and promotion of the reading and writing of Catholic literature. As the Depression unfolded in the 1930s, greater focus was placed upon Catholic social action. Training in how to set up consumers' cooperatives and credit unions was offered at some sessions. St. Louis University sociologist Joseph Husslein, S.J., regularly taught a course on papal social and labor encyclicals at the St. Louis session, while John LaFarge, S.J., conducted a popular class on racial justice at the New York City SSCA. A militant spirit nevertheless permeated many SSCAs, especially during the early 1930s. The theme of the 1932 SSCA, for example, was: "Personal holiness and active Catholicism will conquer the world for Christ." It stressed the need for "apostles . . . who will rise to go forth and openly profess, explain and defend the faith."[23]

THE SODALITY LITERATURE CAMPAIGN

A major component of Lord's Catholic Action program was the development of Catholic readers and writers. Throughout his life, Lord was obsessed with the conviction that books were among the most awesome weapons known to man. "Books," maintained Father Hall, an omniscient, pipe-smoking priest who appeared in a number of Lord's pamphlets, "are one of the really powerful forces that drive ideas into the very soul of mankind." Books "foment revolutions," "start new religions" and "corrupt human hearts." In fact, Lord admitted, as a naive college sophomore he nearly read himself out of the Church.[24]

Like Francis X. Talbot and other American Catholic cultural leaders and educators during the 1920s and 1930s, Lord was especially concerned about the attack upon metaphysics and traditional morality contained in many of the popular works of the period and its effect upon modern youth. Pius XI had voiced a similar concern in his 1929 encyclical, *The Christian Education of Youth*, which warned of "the dangers to morals and religion" that were "cunningly disguised" in the books, theatre, and cinema of the day. The pope again phrased the appropriate response in terms of Catholic Action as he exhorted the laity to increased vigilance in these matters and praised current Catholic groups that were circulating good literature in place of bad.[25]

Lord's objective thus was to expose Catholic youth to Catholic thinkers, novelists, and writers who, in his view, were just as thrilling as the modern amoralists. He wanted Catholic youth to experience modern Catholic writers who were both religious and intellectual and who upheld Catholic dogmatic, philosophical, and moral positions with skill, artistry, and conviction. Such reading, estimated Lord, would both counteract the influence of the crafty moderns over Catholic youth and generate future generations of Catholic writers.

It was against this background that Lord and Alexander launched the 1933 campaign to introduce Sodalists to the achievements of the English Catholic revival. Alexander described the project as "intellectual Catholic Action," and claimed it aimed to achieve two practical results: "The production of Catholic readers and the production of Catholic writers," thus solving two of the Church's greatest needs.[26]

In his first article, Alexander portrayed English Catholic writers "from Newman to Evelyn Waugh" as participants in a "revolt of the arts" against "irreligion" and "unbelief." They were part of a great Catholic cultural awakening, signalling the return of the Church "to the intellectual councils of the world."[27]

Toward that end, Alexander took his readers on an imaginary tour of the English Catholic Poetry Society, where they met Sheila Kaye-Smith ("one of the finest women novelists of Europe"), Maurice Baring (praised by critics "in five languages"), and Alfred Noyes ("whose reputation as a poet is about as secure as any in England"). "There is no group in London," Alexander said, "which includes so many distinguished men and women of letters."[28]

Alexander linked Catholic writing to Catholic Action throughout the campaign, while stressing the aggressive, militant tone of English Catholic letters: Dante's *Divine Comedy* was a "striking example of Catholic lay action" and apostolic zeal. Chesterton's "The Ballad of the White Horse," an epic poem memorializing King Alfred the Great's victory over the Danes at Ethandune, was "sort of a Bible of Catholic Action," because it contained the essential spirit that must animate the current lay apostolate. Alfred's "fight to defend Christian culture against the dark and destructive pagan," claimed Alexander, was "the prototype of our own warfare today."[29]

Finally, Alexander urged his youthful readers to prepare themselves through study, reading, and writing to assume leadership of their own revival. Religion could no longer be a pious, private affair. Catholics in America had "a spiritual and intellectual mission" to perform. It was "no exaggeration," Alexander concluded, "to say that this effort to make the Church articulate . . . is the most important phase of Catholic Action."[30]

By 1933 the broad outlines of the organizational phase of the Catholic literary revival in America were thus in place. Talbot, Lord, and Alexander had set the agenda and established the tone for an American Catholic literary emergence. First, it would be primarily a movement among Catholic youth, linked to Catholic Action, and receiving its most enthusiastic support within Catholic American high schools and colleges. Second, while the movement's practical goals were the development of Catholic readers and writers toward the eventual establishment of a modern American Catholic literary tradition, its early Jesuit leaders just as often framed the revival as part of a larger crusade to save the world from intellectual and cultural chaos. Finally, most of the revival's early leaders took their inspiration from English literary models.

Consequently, the tone of American Catholic literary life, especially in the Catholic colleges during the 1920s and early 1930s, was controversial and combative, imitative of Newman's celebrated exchanges with Protestant Charles Kingsley and "Chesterbelloc's" debates with George Bernard Shaw and H. G. Wells. Chesterton and Hilaire Belloc, wrote Alexander in 1935, "have determined the course Catholic literature has taken in the twentieth century." They have decided that the greater part of modern Catholic literature "should be aggressive [and] polemical . . . one may deplore all this as being detrimental to the interests of pure literature," Alexander conceded, but it was a "necessity of the times," when art and literature were needed to rush to the defense of culture and civilization.[31]

Alexander, Lord, and Talbot played major roles in the organizational history of the American Catholic literary revival. But in broader terms, they were not responsible for the revival. Rather, they were merely giving expression, in literary form, to the revivalist sensibility that rooted itself in the collective Catholic intellectual consciousness following World War I. "The revivalist fervor touched nearly every aspect of Catholic life: intellectual, literary, liturgical, and social," William Halsey writes, as Catholics announced their "return from exile" amidst the intellectual and cultural ruins of a broken and disillusioned world.[32]

Few expressed the revivalist fervor more forcefully than Alexander, both in his life and work. In *The Catholic Literary Revival*, the Jesuit triumphantly noted:

In the midst of the double collapse of Protestantism and the dreams of the Science and Progress cult, the one positive force of importance that remains in the West is the Catholic Church, not dead but more vigorous perhaps than at any time in her career since the Middle Ages.[33]

Alexander, in addition to his literary activities, played a leading role in the American neo-scholastic revival, also at flood stage following the war. Entering the Society of Jesus in 1924 after a brief career as a reporter on the St. Louis *Globe-Democrat*, he was part of a highly self-conscious group of young Jesuit scholars at St. Louis University during the mid–1920s. In 1925 Alexander helped found and edit the St. Louis University–based *Modern Schoolman*, a scholarly journal dedicated to reaching the "American mass mind" with scholastic philosophy.[34] Benjamin L. Masse, another Jesuit leader in the organizational history of the literary revival, was a member of the same graduate seminar that launched the journal. Masse and Alexander both linked the literary revival with the broader neo-scholastic movement. Alexander even described scholasticism as "the official philosophy of . . . the Catholic Revival," and with Masse and other Catholics envisioned a resurgent neo-scholasticism saving the literary world from the same forms of "subjectivism," and "irrationality," that had established themselves in the philosophical realm.[35]

In sum, it was this compound of triumphalism and ebullience, combined with an overriding desire for cultural accomplishment, which fed the revivalist temper among many American Catholic cultural leaders during the 1920s and 1930s. It was what gave the literary revival a sense of urgency, direction, and movement. Inspired by the European example, fired by the idealism of Catholic Action, and viewed as part of a larger intellectual crusade to save the world from cultural chaos, the literary revival had the potential to take on a mind of its own. This, more than any other factor, explains why Catholics could continue to talk so enthusiastically about a literary revival through the 1930s and 1940s while achieving such thin results.

THE REVIVAL SPREADS

The Sodality literature campaign began as a youth movement to generate interest in modern Catholic writers and rapidly gained widespread support across a broad spectrum of the Catholic American educational community. Jesuit schools dominated the early stages of the movement, but the idea of a literary revival quickly established itself at other Catholic institutions as Catholic students and educators, caught up in the revivalist sensibility of the era, picked up the theme. As will be seen, college literary quarterlies played prominent roles in promoting and supporting the idea of an American Catholic literary emergence. Specific courses on "The Catholic Literary Revival," introduced at many Catholic colleges and universities during the 1930s, further accelerated the movement as students were exposed to the actual works of modern (first English, then French) Catholic writers.

Revivalist fervor was at high tide by the mid–1930s. The American Catholic literary and academic landscape was filled with projects, activities, and organizations to foster a real American Catholic literary emergence. The stamp of Lord, Alexander, and Talbot was on many of these projects. Just as often, they were linked to the idea of Catholic Action. Many Catholic colleges during the 1930s had standing literature committees and "Catholic Student Writers' Guilds" specifically established to encourage Catholic reading and writing. A large number of these organizations were Sodality sponsored, with members following guidelines issued by the Sodality office.[36] The national offices of both the Sodality and the Catholic Poetry Society of America during the 1930s provided free literary services to aspiring Catholic poets, essayists, and novelists, encouraging them to submit their work for review, criticism, and possible publication.[37]

Like so many other projects during this era of Catholic mobilization, modest activities often sustained more radical visions. Catholic poets, essayists, novelists, and journalists, it was urged, were really participating in an important intellectual "apostolate." Broadly described as the "Apostolate of the Pen," the goal was "to project Catholic thought" into every intellectual and social field. "Catholic plays," editorialized Talbot's *America* in 1937, "who will write them? For pity sake, when are they going to appear?" *America* identified Catholic play production and the composition of "Catholic popular songs" (with a sense of chivalry and courtship) as two of the most important phases of intellectual Catholic Action.[38] Lucille Papin Borden, a widely read Catholic writer of the 1920s and 1930s, likewise maintained that Catholic fiction writers had an important apostolate to perform and urged her co-religionists to insert "the truths of the Church" into their stories.[39] *Commonweal* editor Michael Williams similarly argued in 1933 that "a great apostolate" awaited "the zeal of Catholic lay writers," while calling for more Catholic dramatists, novelists, and poets.[40] Nor were such summonses confined to the fine arts. In 1929 Alexander challenged Catholic journalists to come to the aid of the Church through an "Apostolate of Publicity," to counteract allegations "that religion is unscientific and a failure."[41]

So pervasive was the idea of a Catholic writing apostolate that it received mention in fictional works produced by Catholics during the 1930s. An example is Hilary Leighton Barth's *Flesh Is Not Life* (1938), a well-written, proletarian-style novel that captures the revivalist temper and awakened social consciousness among young Catholic intellectuals during the Depression. The protagonist, Brendan Grover, a crusading journalist and "Lakeside Catholic Actioneer," argues that the American Church, like communist groups, should develop "a corps of Catholic writers," subsidized, advised, and coordinated by "a centralized Catholic writers' action committee" under the authority of the hierarchy. "I mean a place to live together," insisted Grover, "like the New England communities, with a flaming Catholic Action motivating them where they can study together, get experience and necessary contact with other writers." Appropriately, Grover suggested that Lord, Borden, and Williams coordinate the project.[42]

No less ambitious were the actual plans for training Catholic writers devised by Sr. Mary Joseph, S.L., the director of the Gallery of Living Catholic Authors. The Gallery was established in 1932 at the suggestion of Lord and Talbot to honor contemporary Catholic writers and to create interest in their work. Located at Webster College, a sister college of St. Louis University in surburban St. Louis, the Gallery was launched as a "concrete constructive contribution to Catholic Action." But Sr. Mary Joseph looked forward to the time when the Gallery would evolve into a Catholic university whose sole purpose would be training prospective writers. As "the Catholic Literary Center of the World," she fantasized, the "University of Our Lady of Letters" would offer a strong curriculum in classical literature, and scholastic philosophy and theology, and be staffed with actual Gallery members and other experts in their fields.[43] Faith through the ages no doubt has inspired more ambitious projects. Nevertheless, it was this kind of vision and apostolic fervor which both carried and sustained the literary revival throughout much of its early history.

Of more immediate effect in creating enthusiasm for the newborn Catholic literary movement were the numerous Catholic literature conferences held during the 1930s. Headlines and fragments of news reports in the Catholic press tell part of the story:

Over 200 Hear Catholic Literary Emergence Expounded at Chicago. (Chicago, 1937)

"The Catholic Intellectual Revival" [Speech by Frank Sheed]. (St. John's University, Collegeville, Minnesota, 1939)

Catholic Emergence in Contemporary Literature [Keynote of first annual Catholic Book Conference]. (New York City, 1934)[44]

With a note of enthusiasm and triumph, it was reported that Catholics were gathering in Chicago, Milwaukee, New York, and Denver to study, discuss, and praise the Catholic literary emergence. Accounts of these gatherings were sketchy, but they appeared to follow a similar format: Most would survey the achievements of the English and French revivals, lament the sterility of the American contribution, and end, according to one participant, with an exhortation to "go out and write."[45] Alexander,

Lord, and Talbot were permanent fixtures at many of these conferences, with the latter two Jesuits playing prominent roles in their organization.

No less important were the roles played by English Catholic publisher Francis J. Sheed and his wife, Maisie Sheed Ward, at these gatherings and in the early organizational phase of the revival. Serious and thoughtful Catholics, the Sheeds met through their work as outdoor speakers with the English Catholic Evidence Guild. In 1927, a year after their marriage, they established the London Catholic publishing firm of Sheed and Ward, describing it as a concrete exemplification of Catholic Action and an attempt to give voice to "the growing output of Catholic letters." They opened their American branch in 1933, with the encouragement of Father Talbot.[46]

The Sheeds brought a number of important dimensions to the American Catholic literary effort. Maisie was the granddaughter of theologian William George Ward (1812–1882) and eldest daughter of *Dublin Review* editor Wilfrid Ward (1856–1912). She thus belonged to a family that had been at the very center of English Catholic intellectual and literary life for over seven decades.[47] William George Ward was one of the first Oxford converts, and entered the Church just ahead of Newman in 1845. Wilfrid Ward continued the tradition, as he chronicled the awakening of nineteenth century English Catholic intellectual life in biographies of Newman, Cardinal Wiseman, and the elder Ward. The second volume of this last work, *William George Ward and the Catholic Revival* (1893), would forever affix the term "revival" to what was essentially an unorganized and very limited movement of a small but extremely influential group of English converts and convert writers into the Catholic Church.

The very figure of Maisie Ward thus gave the American movement an air of legitimacy, continuity, and depth. Her own two-volume biography of her father, *The Wilfrid Wards and the Transition* (1934), and *Insurrection Versus Resurrection* (1937), which further chronicled the intensification of English Catholic intellectual and literary life during the first part of the twentieth century, added to her stature as an authority on the Catholic revival and the modern Catholic awakening.

The Sheeds, as the heads of a leading Catholic publishing house, had more than a passing interest in generating interest in a Catholic literary revival and presenting it as a major international event. In 1940 Frank Sheed began editing *Sidelights on the Catholic Revival*, a sampler of selections from books by Catholic writers published by Sheed and Ward over the years. The list was impressive, including most of the modern Catholic thinkers and writers of England and continental Europe. Both Frank and Maisie lectured extensively on "The Catholic Revival," the Oxford Movement, and Newman at American Catholic colleges and universities during the 1930s and 1940s.[48]

Frank Sheed was one of the featured speakers at the Rocky Mountain

Catholic Literature Congress held in Denver, Colorado, in November 1933. It was the largest of the Catholic literature conferences held during the 1930s and the one that left the fullest account of its proceedings. Held at Jesuit-run Regis College, the three-day Congress was attended by over 800 Catholic educators (chiefly nuns and priests) who gathered to discuss "the Catholic revival of letters along the lines made familiar to readers of the *Queen's Work*."[49] The Congress was organized by Benjamin L. Masse, then a professor of literature at Regis. Co-sponsored by the Sodality and the Denver chapter of the National Council of Catholic Women, it was billed as an episcopally-mandated Catholic Action project. *America* magazine, which lent strong editorial support for the gathering, stated that the aim of the congress was "to examine and discuss the European sectors of the present-day Catholic renaissance, particularly the great literary advances recently made in France and England, and to suggest ways and means for a similar advance in the American sector."[50]

The conference overflowed with optimism and self-congratulation. Msgr. J. W. Smith, editor of the *Denver Catholic Register*, characterized the meeting as "the most outstanding Catholic intellectual event in the history of the Rocky Mountains." Msgr. William T. O'Ryan equated the congress with the origins of the Oxford Movement and asked if Americans alone would be without a voice in the current Catholic resurgence. The conference keynote was sounded by Father Lord when he insisted that the Catholic literary revival was not merely the production of books, but a "great binding force" that alone could save the world from discord and chaos.[51]

When the conference turned to the actual achievements of the revival, Sheed lectured on "The Catholic Revival in Europe." Alexander spoke on modern Catholic satire, taking note of the "huge wind of essential and elemental laughter" found in such English writers as Belloc, Chesterton, and Knox. Only Catholics could be true satirists, maintained Alexander, as they alone had the requisite fixed philosophical position necessary to mock modern assumptions. Lord, meanwhile, lectured on the status of Catholic drama, claiming that drama remained the only area where the Catholic renaissance was without realization. It was the "clear duty" of Catholic playwrights everywhere, he maintained, to begin experimenting with their own productions and little theatre projects. Catholic fiction, always considered "the weakest sister" of the revival, was also discussed. Josephine Gratiaa of the St. Louis Public Library described the achievements of Sigrid Undset and noted that Owen Francis Dudley's *The Masterful Monk* was the best circulating Catholic book in over forty American cities. Gratiaa also gave philosophical suggestions about how modern novels might be rewritten so that "the Catholic *Weltanschauung*" would result in happier endings.[52]

In sum, the Denver Congress had all the characteristics of a revival meeting. Fired by apostolic zeal, Catholic Action, and the urgency of the times, the Catholic educators, librarians, priests, and nuns at Denver and at similar conferences held during the 1930s returned to their high schools and colleges inspired to lead a movement that would last into the 1950s.

TWO FRONTS—CATHOLIC AND COMMUNIST: A POSTSCRIPT TO THE SODALITY LITERARY CAMPAIGN

In 1936 James T. Farrell complained of a widespread attitude among American Catholic critics and cultural leaders which demanded that Catholic literature and literary theory serve Catholic dogma, "enforce Catholic moral codes," conform to the Legion of Decency, and "fly the noisy banner of Catholic Action."[53] Farrell drew upon the Catholic example to underscore his own growing disenchantement with left-wing literary efforts during the early years of the Depression.

Catholics and atheistic communists make strange bedfellows, but there were strong similarities between both groups during this period as each sought to organize literature for sectarian purposes. The 1930s has been characterized as the "era of commitment," when it was widely believed that poets, novelists, and playwrights should address the important social issues of their day.[54] Depression-era leftist literary theorists like Granville Hicks and Joseph Freeman thus argued that such concepts as "pure" fiction or art no longer existed. Art and literature, rather, were weapons in the class struggle, and important instruments of social and cultural change. A new theatre, literature, and cinema could redirect values, awaken social consciousness, and transform society. Many young writers within this framework experienced something akin to a religious conversion during the 1930s, as they came together in John Reed clubs, Communist Party-sponsored Writers' Conferences, and leftist theatre companies, persuaded that the committed intellectual could play a vital role in the revolutionary process.[55]

A strikingly similar cultural vision—minus a good deal of its social focus—animated Lord and much of Catholic American literary life during the early Depression era.

Lord always confessed a "sneaking admiration" for the communists. "Communism," he wrote in 1937, understood the "psychology of youth." It recognized youth's idealism, saw the world as a place that could be made better, and enlisted youth as a fighter in a cause.[56] The important ideological struggles of the 1930s dictated that Catholics do the same. The radical left had mobilized to influence culture; the feeling was that Catholics also must assume their role in the fight.

The Catholic literary effort on this important level in the 1930s can be

seen thus as a movement partially designed to counter, or at least cor-
respond to, similar communist and leftist undertakings. Twentieth century Catholic opposition to communism was multi-layered, and to
examine it fully would go beyond the scope of this chapter. But when
Lord and his Catholic contemporaries viewed communism during the
1930s, they saw a philosophical and political system that persecuted
Catholics in the Soviet Union, Mexico, and Spain, promoted atheism,
advocated class hatred, attacked private property (an institution sanc-
tioned by Catholic natural law doctrine), and promulgated a narrowly
materialistic view of man and society.

Materialistic philosophy in other forms—liberalism, positivism, rationalism—had been condemned by the Church throughout the nineteenth century. Opposition to philosophical materialism also explains,
in large part, why Lord, Talbot, and other Catholic critics during the
1920s and 1930s were so opposed to "naturalistic" writers like Theodore
Dreiser who, likewise, enunciated a materialistic, determined outlook
in many of his works. It needs to be stressed that the Catholic literary
effort during the 1930s was directed as much against this element in
American intellectual and literary culture as it was against the radical
left. Philosophically, Catholics could not separate the two.

Self-consciously concerned since the 1920s that Catholics and Ca-
tholicism assume a more prominent place in America's intellectual and
cultural life, and now challenged by the example of the radical left, the
Catholic cultural community during the early 1930s launched its own
"literary front." In 1935 Alexander went so far as to compare Father
Talbot's literary plebiscite—resulting in the selection of Belloc, Dawson,
Maritain, Helen C. White, and others to the Permanent Gallery of Living
Catholic Authors—to the Communist Party-sponsored First American
Writers' Congress, also held that year. Both events, admitted Alexander,
were sectarian. But the Jesuit further insisted that "a revolutionary literature, a literature that draws its creative enthusiasm from ideas antithetical to those currently accepted, must be presented by congresses
and other artificial, private ventures of this nature."[57] Sectarian spon-
sorship was just another indication of the revolutionary temper of modern Catholic writing.

Talbot also took note of the "revolutionary" nature of the Catholic
writers named in his 1935 plebiscite. "They present, to use the same
idea as the communist," wrote Talbot shortly after the plebiscite, "the
united front." "A body of Catholic writers such as we are trying to bind
together," he continued, "is not a limited parochial group engrossed in
parochial boundaries." Rather, he persisted, "it is a pervasive union of
authors held together by a definite system of thought and eager to
indoctrinate all men in that system." These Catholic writers "profess
the Catholic ideology. . . . They offer the Catholic solution to moral prob-

lems, they supply answers to the non-Catholic attack, they create visions founded on the supernatural and they entertain within the limits of the legitimate."[58]

Talbot, Alexander, and Lord were not alone in this viewpoint. Throughout the American Catholic intellectual and cultural community during the 1930s, there was an insistence that Catholics, too, possessed a radical literature and point of view capable of transforming culture— a radicalism rooted in tradition, orthodoxy, sound moral and philosophical principles, and a true understanding of the nature and destiny of man. The 1933 Denver Catholic Literature Congress, the Gallery of Living Catholic Authors, the Catholic Poetry Society, and the Catholic Theatre Conference all institutionalized this spirit, as Catholics came together, solidified ranks, encouraged young hopefuls, and voted "plans of action" to facilitate a new intellectual and cultural order.

Lord attempted to capture this same spirit in the Sodality literature campaign. The Jesuit youth leader, in langue worthy of the 1930s radical left, called throughout the decade for Catholic youth to participate in a literary crusade aimed at fundamental social change: Sodalists were told that they also must become intellectually and culturally committed. Catholic poets, novelists, essayists, journalists, and dramatists were needed to redirect values and influence culture.

Lord's literary campaign, however, was something considerably less in practice. While *New Masses* editor Michael Gold exhibited the figure of activist-intellectual John Reed before leftist aspirants during the early 1930s, Lord's literary role model for Catholic youth during this same period was the combative Chesterton. Upon the Englishman's death in 1936, Lord wrote an "Open Letter" to his Sodalists, inviting them to fill the niche left by Chesterton. "We beg you, beloved young writer," Lord wrote, "step up and take his place, or at least one of his places."[59] Chesterton, in fact, was a rebel, but only in a broad, philosophical sense. Nevertheless, this was the Chesterton that Lord and Alexander were interested in—the Chesterton who, in such early twentieth century works as *Heretics* and *Orthodoxy*, creatively and originally upheld Christian tradition and dogma against the pretensions of *fin de siecle* pessimists, agnostics, and aesthetes.

At the same time, Lord's archetypal Catholic novelist during the early 1930s was Englishman Owen Frances Dudley. Dudley wrote a series of philosophical novels between 1926 and 1948 upholding Catholic dogmatic and moral positions against various materialistic philosophies of the day. His most popular work was *The Masterful Monk* (1929). Set against the background of English high society, Dudley's story pitted the sinister evolutionary biologist Julian Verrers—a thinly disguised composite of Thomas Huxley, James Frazer, and H. G. Wells—against the imposing figure of Anselm Thornton, a humble but knowledgeable monk commissioned by the Church to deflect Verrers's influence. In a series of public debates with all of England watching, Thornton coolly and logically destroyed every one of Verrers's arguments against free will, the supernatural, and Christian orthodoxy.[60]

Dudley was the focus in 1931 of the first feature-length article on a major Catholic fiction writer to appear in the *Queen's Work*. The article surveyed Dudley's life and achievements and praised him for expounding "true Catholic philosophy against the false philosophies of modernism, free-thought, pseudo-science and unbelief."[61] Lord reiterated his preference for Dudley at the 1934 Talbot-sponsored Intercollegiate Catholic Book Conference, where he pointed to the Englishman's work as an example of the "red-blooded" type of Catholic fiction that was needed in today's world.[62]

Many of the other novelists on Lord's Sodality reading list during the 1920s and 1930s reflected Dudley's outlook: Englishman Sir Philip Gibbs, whose *Age of Reason* (1928) rivaled Dudley in attacking behavioristic science and the cult of reason and progress; English satirist Bruce Marshall, whose *Father Malachy's Miracle* (1931) poked fun in more light-hearted fashion at positivistic science and modernist religion; and American Lucille Papin Borden, who wrote novels like *The Candlestick Makers* (1923), upholding orthodox Catholic views on marriage, the family, and birth control.

Thus, while calling for a literary campaign that would produce young Catholic leaders and writers who would work to fundamentally redirect literary and cultural values, Lord's actual focus was primarily protectionist and apologetic (defending and explaining the Church to nonbelievers). This was true of Lord's focus in fiction no less than in other areas of literary life.

The best evidence of Lord's outlook were the articles that appeared in the *Queen's Work* between January and June 1933, the period in which he and Alexander attempted to rally young writers, novelists, poets, playwrights, and journalists to a Catholic literary crusade. *Queen's Work* articles during this six-month period fell, roughly, into four categories: Sodality news and events, Catholic writers, "great Catholics" ("Famous Olympic Athlete [Ralph H. Metcalfe] Becomes Catholic and Sodalist"), and apologetics.[63]

A significant amount of attention was directed toward this last category. An April 1933 article titled "Catholics the Victims not the Authors of Persecution" is representative. Employing the dialogue technique used so effectively in many of Lord's own pamphlets, the article set up an exchange between an articulate Catholic and a curious non-Catholic where the former convincingly demonstrates that while the Church's role as persecutor belonged "to the past," Catholics today were being oppressed in Mexico, Spain, and the Soviet Union, where Church property was confiscated, convents burned, and religious freedom denied.[64] A number of other articles employed the same focus and device. In addition, a regular *Queen's Work* feature at this time was "Joe College vs. Chick Pagan." The feature dramatized scenes in which Joe, a cool, self-assured Catholic youth, regularly debated and defeated his obtuse, agnostic friend, Chick, over such issues as papal infallibility, birth control, and the Church's attitude toward science and research.[65]

On balance, then, Lord's 1933 Sodality literature campaign aimed at developing Catholic writers and leaders much like himself—Catholics who would uphold Catholic philosophical and moral positions, dispell prejudice and error, and defend the Church against attack. Lord expressed this attitude best in his 1935 poem, "The Battle of the Books— Style 1935." Plainly imitative of Chesterton's "The Ballad of the White Horse," the narrative opens on a pagan land overrun by "poisonous books" and "naturalistic" authors who have scornfully rejected God, morality, and religion. Their jeers reverberate throughout the kingdom. But when all seems lost, the sound of "rattling typewriters" is heard over the horizon, as there enter "The Warriors of the Catholic Resurgence." While "pagan publishers" stand in terror, the Catholic warriors chant:

> We'll shoot them with pamphlet
>   and paper and book.
> We'll shoot them with poem
>   and play.
> They crouch in their terror
>   'neath' ramparts of error.
> Who's going with us to the
>   fray?[66]

Such was the apostolic challenge Lord posed to modern Catholic youth. It was a challenge rooted in his vision of a resurgent and confident Catholic youth coming to the aid of Christian morality, orthodoxy, and the institutional Church. This, for the most part, was the meaning that Lord attached to Catholic Action and to the Catholic literary revival.

As it stood in the early 1930s, the American Catholic literary front offered no real alternative to that of the radical left in terms of social thought. In fact, its Jesuit leaders' concerns belonged more properly to the 1920s than to the Depression years of the 1930s. In crucial ways, the movement's chief leaders—Lord, Talbot, and Alexander—were still Catholics turned inward. Their preoccupations were parochial: upholding Catholic group interests, strengthening youth in the faith, supplying answers to the non-Catholic attack, and shoring up morality and decency in a permissive postwar age.

The lay apostolate was consequently seen by Lord and many others of his generation in a very self-centered and provincial way. Indeed, in 1934 the Sodality joined the three other major Catholic Action organizations in America—the National Councils of Catholic Men (NCCM) and Catholic Women (NCCW) and the Knights of Columbus—in supporting a Legion of Decency campaign against permissiveness in the motion pictures. Lord had helped draft the 1930 Motion Picture Production Code that was supposed to serve as a guideline for Hollywood producers, but he soon grew dissatisfied with the code's enforcement and encouraged Catholic youth to boycott films he listed in the *Queen's Work*. The *Queen's Work* staff also sent out regular "white" and "black" lists of motion pictures to diocesan newspapers.[67] The Motion Picture Production Code and the Legion of Decency campaign represented further attempts to exert Catholic influence over the nation's cultural life. Yet like so many other Catholic public activities during this era, they were largely crusading, negative, and moralistic. Catholic Action during the 1920s and early 1930s always seemed to be expressing itself in a rear-guard, protective fashion.

Exacerbating the literary revival's negative focus during this era was the way that the majority of Catholic cultural leaders perceived the changes they sought. Lord, Talbot, Alexander, and most other Catholic cultural leaders of their generation all called for change, but the change they sought was primarily philosophical rather than social. Change, under their terms, meant a return to tradition, standards, and authority, all under the framework of a highly rationalistic and abstract neoscholastic philosophy. Lord, and Catholic educational and cultural leaders like him during the 1930s, thus saw literature as an instrument of propaganda; but unlike the leftists whom they sought to answer, literature was less a social weapon than an intellectual, philosophical, or moral one. Hence their stress upon the polemical Chesterton, Dudley, and Borden.

Whatever the desirability of returning to objective standards of reality, a static and impersonal scholasticism was a poor intellectual base for dealing with the pressing human problems of the Depression. If Catholics were really going to present an alternative to communist ideology, they would have to offer their own positive program of thought and action. Many Catholic intellectuals (Lord included) would eventually find that outlook in the unifying doctrine of the Mystical Body of Christ and the social thought of the Church. This, however, would occur only later in the decade. During the early 1930s, the Catholic literary revival in America was still in its reactionary phase.

4

The Revival as Reaction, I: Catholics against Modernity

Calvert Alexander's *The Catholic Literary Revival* (1935) characterized the revival as a movement in revolt against modern thought. "Catholic literature," the Jesuit wrote, "when we discover it coming into being in the mid-nineteenth century, is a literature of protest against the course being followed by European society."[1] Earlier, Alexander had similarly portrayed the revival as a "protest against the things in modern civilization that deserve to be dynamited."[2] That was a large order, but it illustrates the profound alienation Alexander and many other Catholics of his generation exhibited toward the course of modern intellectual culture.

Alienation from modern thought was a motif that dominated Catholic intellectual, philosophical, and literary expression well into the 1950s. Many popular Catholic novels during the 1920s and early 1930s read like antipositivist tracts.[3] A large number of Catholic philosophical works during the same period record a similar disaffection. Even as late as 1948 Thomas Merton (*The Seven Storey Mountain*) is found reading his way into the Church via the antirationalist expositions of William Blake, D. H. Lawrence, and Jacques Maritain.[4]

Other early twentieth century American groups were equally estranged from modernity. New Humanist critics, Southern Agrarian writers, and fundamentalist Protestants, in many cases, were as vocal as Catholics in their protest against modern cultural relativism and unbelief. But Catholic alienation was broader and, in many ways, more profound. Catholic literary critics during the early 1930s, for example, joined New Humanists Irving Babbitt and Paul Elmer More in sharply attacking naturalistic assumptions in modern philosophy and literature. Yet Catholics ended in rejecting most of the New Humanist program on grounds that it was incomplete—a "half-way house" between modern philosophical materialism and an authentic theological understanding of man.

What precisely did Catholics mean by modern thought? What was the nature of their disaffection? What forms did it take? Was the literary revival wholly reactionary, or did Catholics offer an alternative to modern thought? Answers to these questions point, in large part, to the determining ideas and ideologies behind the earliest stages of the Catholic literary revival in America.

THE INNOCENCE PARIDIGM

The paradigmatic model of "Innocence," since the 1980 publication of William Halsey's *The Survival of American Innocence: American Catholicism in an Era of Disillusionment, 1920–1940*, has become the most popular interpretive framework to explain early twentieth century Catholic disaffection from modern secular thought.[5] Innocence—a construction Halsey borrows from Henry May's representation of late nineteenth century American intellectual and literary culture described in *The End of American Innocence* (1959)—asserts a "common-sense" belief in a rational and predictable cosmos and its inherent moral structure, a belief in progress, and a presumptively "genteel" approach to literature and culture.[6]

Halsey argues that American Catholics purposefully defended these hopeful nineteenth century conventions well into the twentieth century, even as they were being dismantled by materialistic science and relativistic philosophy on the one hand, and irrational war on the other. Latecomers to the promises of American life, Catholics "were unprepared for, and quite naturally opposed to, patterns of thought which appeared to undermine the promise."[7]

Catholics therefore countered the complexities of modernity with the certainties of Innocence. While postwar American secular intellects succumbed to various forms of irrationalism, subjective skepticism, and hopelessness, Catholics during this same period constructed their own cultural world "safe from disillusionment." Moreover, by fusing the nineteenth century credo of Innocence with their own neo-scholastic postulates of an ordered, predictable universe and of man's capacity to master both himself and his environment through the force of human will and reason, Catholics, asserts Halsey, were able to construct a postwar culture that was "at once American and Catholic."[8] Catholics thus would combat pessimism with optimism, while at the same time reaffirming their Americanism by forging a link between their own scholasticism and traditional American idealism.

For all its strength, the Innocence paradigm understates both the nature and the scope of the Catholic position. By confining postwar American Catholic intellectual life to a narrow reaction against disillusionment, the Innocence model makes the nature of Catholicism's controversy with modernity appear much shallower than it actually was. It first offers primarily non-credal, temporal reasons for the Catholic reaction. Then it allows a secular value system to define the parameters of Catholic thought. Innocence, in short, does not meet the Catholic faith on its own philosophical and theological ground. Catholicism is a system of belief and a philosophy of culture that cannot be analyzed adequately within a non-credal framework.

The American Catholic revolt against modernity was much wider in scope than a narrow reaction against postwar disillusionment. When we read what Alexander and other contemporary figures had to say about the origins, nature, and goals of the Catholic literary revival, and when we examine the body of literature and ideas which flowed from that revival, we see that Catholic thinkers worldwide were in revolt against a broad spectrum of modern ideas. We also see that the Catholic reaction began long before the disillusioned 1920s. In fact, Alexander and other Catholic revivalists never seemed to tire of reminding the non-Catholic world that Catholic thinkers as far back as John Henry Newman (1801–1890) had rebelled against the nineteenth century cult of "Reason and Progress," and had predicted the very disorder and disillusionment that this approach to reality would leave behind. Catholics thus liked to congratulate themselves on the fact that they knew all along what the disillusioned critics of the postwar years were just discovering for themselves—that unlimited progress based upon rationalistic science and unaided human reason was an empty promise.

Catholic controversialists like Alexander often employed the phrase "The Modern Mind" epithetically, as a contemptuous expression to designate everything that was wrong with contemporary civilization. But when they became more systematic, they inevitably identified the modern mind with the post-Renaissance, post-Reformation, and post-Darwinian world of secular humanism, religious individualism, and scientific and philosophical materialism. Thus, in Catholic literature and scholarship, the modern mind often found personification in such figures as René Descartes, Martin Luther, Jean Jacques Rousseau, Charles Darwin, Thomas Huxley, and John Dewey. Pre-Vatican II Catholic apologists, neo-scholastics, historians, and cultural critics from Alexander and Fulton J. Sheen to Maritain were nearly unanimous in identifying modern thought with these men and movements as they assigned them varying degrees of responsibility for the modern moral crisis.[9] Because these men and movements loom so large in the twentieth century Catholic critique of modernity, a brief analysis of the main currents of western thought since the Renaissance is in order. Such a retreat will show both how significant areas of modern thought came into conflict with Catholic theological, philosophical, and ecclesiastical positions, and how the Church's early twentieth century response to these events shaped the intellectual outlook of Alexander, Daniel A. Lord, and other early clerical leaders of the Catholic literary revival.

MODERN THOUGHT AND CATHOLIC THOUGHT

One of the most profound movements in the history of modern thought has been the delimitation of supernatural and ecclesiastical authority in the life of western man. With the sixteenth century Renaissance and Reformation came the breakdown of the medieval synthesis through which the Church had dominated western life since the eleventh century.[10] Both the Renaissance and the Reformation constituted a revolt against prescribed, external authority, while fostering a spirit of critical reflection and private judgment.

Following the breakthroughs of the scientific revolution, seventeenth and eighteenth century scientists, philosophers, and even churchmen began to abandon the theocentric medieval *Weltanschauung* and increasingly embraced an empirical framework to comprehend and describe the nature of reality. After Darwin, the scientistic approach was virtually complete, underscoring Carlton B. Hayes's characterization of the last quarter of the nineteenth century as *A Generation of Materialism*.[11]

Philosophical materialism has many dimensions. But most troublesome to the religious mind is its indifference toward ideas about the supernatural origin and destiny of man. Starting with the premise that physical matter is the only knowable reality, the tendency among many nineteenth century philosophical materialists was either to reject or to disregard spiritual assumptions about the nature of God, man, or the universe. Most of the great law-seeking, man-centered "isms" of the nineteenth century—liberalism, rationalism, Marxism, positivism, and agnosticism—were grounded in materialistic postulates. Each came into conflict with a nineteenth century Church that based its authority on truths transcending the realm of subjective human thought, process, or experience. Thus, besides posing a threat to Catholic theology, which begins with the premise that man is a creature under God in need of divine revelation, grace, and redemption, each of these nineteenth century systems posed a threat to the external authority of the Church. The triumph of each meant a subsequent decline in the Church's intellectual, cultural, and political prestige.

Martin E. Marty has described the nineteenth century Church as knowing "almost nothing but hardship, setback, rejection, or neglect."[12] Everywhere throughout the nineteenth century could be heard the heavy hammers of materialistic science and philosophy dealing weighty blows to Catholic authority and belief. All these forces, according to Marty, converged in the last half of the century to produce a "final kind of schism" in which "Christianity and the culture which it had largely informed went separate ways."[13]

Perhaps the greatest challenge to the modern Church came from science. The Darwinian revolution finished what seventeenth and eighteenth century rationalism and empiricism had begun. The eighteenth century vision of a mechanistic universe governed by observable natural laws seemed to achieve confirmation in Darwin's evolutionary theories. Post-Darwinian thought was heavily materialistic and monistic, as social scientists, philosophers, and even novelists enthusiastically embraced naturalistic theories and methods in describing reality. Western man, it seemed, was outgrowing the Judeo-Christian tradition that had formed him, as more and more thinkers substituted naturalistic for theological approaches to human nature and behavior, ethics, law, and literature.[14]

Post-Darwinian analytical philosophy and Freudian psychology radically altered traditional Judeo-Christian and classical conceptions of human reason and human nature. Wilhelm Wundt (1832–1920), "the father of physiological psychology," linked mental life exclusively to biological factors and external stimuli, thus advancing a strictly neurophysiological conception of human thought and behavior. Sigmund Freud (1856–1939), accounted for much of human activity in terms of unconscious drives, frustrations, and repressions. Freud's theories, by revealing the wide area of human behavior that lies outside of conscious control, cast doubt upon the entire concept of rational man. In 1913 John Broadus Watson introduced "behaviorism" into the American psychological lexicon, further eroding non-materialist conceptions of the mind and its processes. Henceforth, the stimulus-response relationship became the basic component of behavioristic psychology, and, as Gerald N. Grob writes, "the distinction between the human and the animal world all but disappeared."[15]

Empiricist-minded post-Darwinians also extended the scientific method into the "life" sciences. Dewey, for example, as part of the postwar philosophical revolt against Hegelian formalism, proposed reducing facts and values to a common naturalistic basis. Dewey maintained in such works as *Experience and Nature* (1925) and *The Quest for Certainty* (1929) that abstract metaphysical idealism isolated values from reality. The ends and the standards of life, insisted Dewey, should be generated from the process of experience, not drawn from some transcendent, otherworldly realm. Dewey's alternative was instrumentalism: the persistent testing of the meaning and worth of ideas, customs, and values in light of their broad social consequences.[16]

The materialist approach to reality also had an impact upon the world of modern literature, although here the impact was decidedly less optimistic. Philosophical materialism resulted in two different points of view.[17] For resolute materialists like Dewey, Huxley ("Darwin's Bulldog"), and Herbert Spencer, the continuity and inevitability of the evolutionary process led to an optimistic view of predictable social progress. Nineteenth century positivists like August Comte (1798–1857) similarly believed that scientific study of man, purely from the standpoint of verifiable material data, would inevitably lead to higher forms of social, political, and religious organization.

But materialism also suggested a mechanistic universe and the idea that man, as a thing of nature, was subject to the indifferent and arbitrary forces operating within that sphere. Theodore Dreiser's reading of Spencer was considerably different from Dewey's. "When I read Spencer I could only sigh," wrote Dreiser in 1922. "All I could think of was that since nature would not or could not do anything for man, he must . . . do something for himself." Of this Dreiser saw little prospect, because man himself was a "product of these self-same, accidental, indifferent, and bitterly cruel forces."[18]

This dark side of materialism accounts for much of the pessimism found in late nineteenth and early twentieth century American fiction, as writers like Dreiser, Frank Norris, Stephen Crane, and Jack London explored the philosophical implications of an indifferent and mechanistic universe. Uncritically mixing vulgarized versions of Darwinian, Spencerian, Nietzschean, and behavioristic theory, they and other "naturalistic" writers of the period focused upon the dilemma of entrapped and determined man. Crushing poverty and bourgeois hypocrisy, for example, drive the innocent heroine of Crane's *Maggie, a Girl of the Streets* (1896), into the arms of the brutish Pete and eventual prostitution and suicide. Similar environmental and physiological factors are, in large part, behind Clyde Griffiths's moral decline in Dreiser's *An American Tragedy* (1926). Again, not man, but vast impersonal forces previl in Crane's "The Open Boat" (1898) and Norris's *The Octopus* (1901). In each instance, frail human beings are helplessly crushed by forces stronger than themselves. Unable to determine their own destiny, they cease to be free moral agents. Rather, they are impotent and powerless in the face of environmental conditions, society, heredity, and nature itself.

Modern philosophical materialism—in either its optimistic or pessimistic form—thus posed challenges to nearly every area of Catholic belief. Its theology of free will and sin was challenged by the naturalistic assumption that man's behavior was determined by psychological, sociological, or biological forces. Its neo-scholastic conception of innate reason and universal ethics was challenged by the pragmatic proposition that there were no antecedent realities rooted either in man's nature or the universe, but that moral norms, social ethics, and law evolve naturally out of contingency and experience. Most important, the Church's theology of salvation and redemption appeared irrelevant in the face of an exclusively material universe governed wholly by mechanistic law. In its indifference to the supernatural in the life of man, modern thought appeared to have forgotten the central images of the Christian faith—the Incarnation, the cross, and the Resurrection. Catholic critics within this context viewed Dreiser and Dewey as of one piece, despite the fact that Dreiser's naturalism ended in disillusionment and Dewey's resulted in liberal optimism. For Dreiser and other literary naturalists, there was no redemption. In the case of the anthropocentric Dewey, man could redeem himself.

THE MODERNIST CRISIS IN THE CATHOLIC CHURCH

All the preceding men and movements constituted external challenges to Catholic intellectual authority. But the century of Georg Wilhelm Friedrich Hegel, Darwin, and Spencer also generated an internal crisis within the Church by the end of the 1890s as subjectivistic and evolutionary theories of religion and religious belief made inroads into important sectors of Catholic philosophy and theology. Pius X condemned these tendencies as "Modernism" in his 1907 encyclical *Pascendi Dominici Gregis* which contained, in the words of John Tracy Ellis, "the harshest and most negative language employed by a papal encyclical in this century."[19]

The shaping influence of Catholicism's early twentieth century struggle against Modernism over the subsequent intellectual life and identity of the early twentieth century American Church has not been sufficiently appreciated by religious historians. True, historians are wont to point out how anti-Modernist sanctions stifled creativity in the theological realm; but a review of the broader intellectual results of the Modernist crisis, illustrating how the anti-Modernist campaign shaped future Catholic (especially clerical) postures toward modern thought systems, has not been explored with much detail.[20]

Modernism as a theological construction is difficult to define.[21] Pius X underscored its formlessness in *Pascendi* when he charged that Modernism was "the synthesis of all heresies."[22] The Modernist movement—which found its principal spokesmen in the French (Alfred Loisy) and English (George Tyrrell) Churches—represented an attempt to bring Catholic teaching up-to-date with the latest developments in modern philosophy and science. Most Modernists expressed dissatisfaction with the narrow intellectualism of Catholicism's own neo-scholastic philosophy. Like the modern thinkers who influenced them—Henri Bergson, Maurice Blondel, and others—Catholic Modernists rejected the idea that faith was entirely an intellectual matter. They maintained, rather, that faith and knowledge were dynamic processes, grounded in intuition, experience, and the drama of life itself. An immanentistic understanding of religious experience, which insisted that God was less known by the intellect than by the affections, was a principal doctrine of Modernism. Another was a nineteenth century historicist attitude toward doctrinal development and the correlative axiom that dogma, too, grew out of experience and thus was linked to the evolutionary process.[23]

The papacy's death blow to Modernism, given the extreme subjectivistic and relativistic theological positions of its leading proponents, was a self-preserving act. Tyrrell's implicit neo-Kantian assumption that the supernatural could not be the object of certain intellectual knowledge was especially deadly to the Church's traditional natural theology and its claim of a rationally known transcendent God. The Vatican subsequently excommunicated Tyrrell and Loisy, silenced others, and reaffirmed scholasticism (already revitalized by Leo XIII in *Aeterni Patris*, 1879) as the preferred philosophical system in Catholic seminaries and colleges.

The Modernist crisis, writes John Tracy Ellis in one of the few studies addressing the intellectual formation of the twentieth century American priesthood, meant very little to the great number of lay Catholics in the United States; but it was a different story for the Church's clergy, particularly those "engaged in education." Modernism and the Modernist crisis continued to overshadow the clergy's intellectual development, Ellis writes, "well beyond W.W.I."[24]

Ellis's study is concerned primarily with the intimidating influence of anti-Modernist attitudes over pre-Vatican II Catholic theological development. But it adds weight to the theme that Modernism as an intellectual crisis generated *antimodern* attitudes that penetrated many other areas of Catholic clerical intellectual life—apart from the theological— well into the twentieth century.

The Modernist crisis and its intellectual aftermath are particularly useful in illuminating the ideological focus of many of the Jesuit clerics who led the early stages of the Catholic literary revival—Lord, Alexander, Francis X. Talbot, and others. Talbot (1907) and Lord (1909) both entered the Society of Jesus in the first decade of the twentieth century. Their intellectual and clerical formation, therefore, coincided with the height of the Modernist crisis. Alexander's 1924 entry came somewhat later, but this younger Jesuit as assistant editor of the *Modern Schoolman* played a leading role in the neo-scholastic resurgence of the 1920s and early 1930s—a movement given new life by the Modernist controversy and, in large part, designed to challenge and deflect modern secular philosophies.

These Jesuits—chronologically, theologically, intellectually—were all touched by the Modernist crisis. They lived through an early twentieth century era when Committees of Vigilance, established to scrutinize books and research and to enforce philosophical and theological conformity, were a regular part of diocesan and seminary life. They likewise were required to take, with all clergy and teachers of philosophy at Catholic colleges and universities at this time, the infamous Oath Against Modernism (*Sacrorum antistitum*), dictated by the Vatican in 1910. The oath required assent to the intellectual, as opposed to the affective, origins of faith and a repudiation of modern subjectivistic epistemologies.[25] More consequentially, those Jesuits absorbed their scholastic philosophy during this era of "post-Modernist repression" from the widely used scholastic manuals of the day.[26] These approved handbooks were frankly apologetic and designed, in large part, to train students to refute non-scholastic "error." The original texts of Thomas Aquinas and the other medieval schoolmen, by contrast, were seldom studied, and the subtleties of Aquinas's metaphysics of existence (which later scholars found to have much in common with modern philosophies of intuition) were largely ignored.

The early published work of Talbot, Alexander, and Lord all give evidence of post-Modernist clerical alienation from the main currents of modern intellectual culture, but that of Lord is most instructive.[27] Nearly all of Father Lord's earliest published works were polemics against modern philosophers and philosophies. Lord's most intensive philosophical thinking came early in his career in a series of articles written for the Jesuit publication *America* in 1917 while he was still a twenty-five-year-old student at St. Louis University. The seventeen-article series, self-consciously patterned after G. K. Chesterton's *Heretics* and *Orthodoxy*, was designed, according to Lord, to explain the riddles of modern "current philosophies" while making the "big high lights" of scholastic philosophy understandable to the "man on the street."[28] The bulk of Lord's ideas, in fact, came from his own classroom notes, taken during his three years of philosophical study at the university. The series thus gives as much insight into post-Modernist Jesuit philosophical training as it does into Lord's own mind.

Most of the ontological, epistemological, and cosmological questions that so engrossed the teaching authority of the Church in its repudiation of Modernism ten years earlier were again probed by Lord. What is the nature of being and existence? Is there a reality outside the thinking subject? What explains thought? How does God communicate himself to man? Does the universe contain an inherent moral structure knowable to all?

Lord's answers were prototypically scholastic: "There is a world of tangible objects outside ourselves." Reality exists. Certainty and consciousness exist. Knowledge "begins with what we learn through the senses," but is completed by the conceptualizing "intellect" (the same for all men at all times) which is able to grasp the "essential nature" of things. Hence, universal and absolute truths exist and are recognizable to all men through human reason. Reason is what separates man from beast while linking him to God. The reasoning intellect, moreover, logically leads man to God, who is understood as "first cause" and "sufficient reason" of all things.[29] Faith, therefore, is an assent of the intellect, and is a completion of an act of reason.

Lord left little doubt that the abstract concepts and stable natures of scholastic philosophy were indispensible antidotes to modern dogmatic relativism, where the Jesuit saw only subjectivism (the deadly Modernist sin), inconsistency, and error. He summarily dismissed all modern philosophical systems—subjective idealism, skepticism, materialism, utilitarianism, pragmatism—for lacking common sense, for promoting doubt and despair, and for sowing the seeds of moral permissiveness and private judgment.[30] Lord, of course, did not really explore these modern systems; rather he presented only caricatures of them. They were—in a style worthy of the best scholastic manuals of the period—straw men to be knocked down by severely formalistic arguments that marched authoritatively and deductively to their conclusions.

Lord's uncompromising early twentieth century enmity toward modern thought underscores Gerald McCool's assertion that following the Modernist crisis, neo-scholasticism assumed a "more aggressive stance against modern philosophy," as it "deliberately" defined itself against positivism, German idealism, Bergsonian intuitionism, and other leading intellectual systems of the day.[31] Lord was not alone. Almost any philosophical, literary, or even fictional work written by Catholic clergy and laity alike during the first third of the twentieth century shows similar intellectual patterns. For example, there was a tendency to see the world in terms of scholastic philosophy and all other philosophies. Also, there was a distrust of non-intellectual epistemologies that, like the Modernists, questioned the limits of the reasoning intellect as the basis of universal understanding and instead laid greater stress upon the knower as the subject, as opposed to the object in the process of knowledge. Further, there was an enmity toward "process philosophies" of any sort which stressed flux, change, and the evolving character of reality, and finally, there was nearly universal disdain for post-Kantian subjectivists—Dewey, Bertrand Russell, and the like—who posited that concepts and conceptual knowledge were mutable and revisable.

Now, in the Modernist aftermath, it appeared these systems and thinkers which had so much to say to modern thought had little to tell Catholics or Catholic philosophers and theologians. Nor did the Church during this post-Modernist era seem to have much use for other post-Darwinians who were just beginning to explore the realm outside human rationality—Freud, Lawrence, James Joyce, Franz Kafka, Friedrich

Nietzsche, and others whose insights into the subconscious and the irrational would be exploited by some of the best minds of the modern era. Scholastic philosophy instead was seen as adequate to explain human existence and reality, a philosophical system rooted in self-sufficient reason and changeless universal truths.

Catholic disaffection from subjectivistic-relativistic modern thought predated the Modernist crisis. But the Modernist crisis—because it brought these intellectual systems into such close proximity to the Church—stiffened Catholic opposition. It sharpened the scholastic critique of modernity and heightened Catholic intellectual identity. Did modern thought lack first principles and an objective view of reality? Was it dominated by mood and prompted by the moment? Did it move chaotically from one intellectual system to another, embracing every new "novelty" about God, man, and the universe? Wasn't Protestantism, too, divided and confused—compromised by its own embrace of modernity? Catholicism, by contrast, represented immutability and cohesion in the face of change, resolute authority amidst the discontinuity of the times. The Modernist crisis—and the Catholic victory over modernism—thus allowed early twentieth century Catholics to represent themselves as guardians at the gate, as one of the few defenders of objective reality in an uncertain and relativistic world. Catholics were knowing veterans. They had fought their battles with modernity and won.

Few would dispute the shaping influence of Vatican II (1962–1965) reforms over subsequent Catholic American intellectual and cultural development in the 1970s and 1980s. Catholicism's early twentieth century crisis with Modernism, from an intellectual standpoint, was equally pivotal. The Modernist crisis, no less than Vatican II, begat an intellectual posture, an attitude and mood that shaped the way early twentieth century Catholics defined themselves and the Church in the world.

In 1933 Lord and his St. Louis University friend and colleague Bakewell Morrison, S.J., head of the university's Religious Studies Department, collaborated on a series of religion textbooks designed to phrase the tenets of the Catholic faith to modern college students in "a vital and impelling manner." The series, which was part of a larger college-wide catechistic reform movement to revitalize Catholic religious instruction, aimed to make Catholic doctrinal positions less abstract and more timely by contrasting them with modern ideas about God, man, and the universe.[32] Lord's contribution *Religion and Leadership* (1933) was designed for use in introductory freshman religion courses.[33] The book reiterated in outline form many of the positions found in his 1917 articles, illustrating how anti-Modernist attitudes, which began with the clergy, filtered down to the laity. Morrison contributed two volumes, *The Catholic Church and the Modern Mind* (1933) and *Revelation and the Modern Mind*

(1936).[34] It is instructive that Morrison began his second volume with an eleven-page detailed analysis of the "not-too-so-far-gone heresy of Modernism" to initiate his contrast of Catholics and moderns.[35] For Morrison, no less than Lord and other Catholics of their generation, the Modernist crisis was a point of departure, an intellectual starting point for looking at themselves and those outside the Church.

Vatican II opened the collective Catholic mind to the pluralistic modern world; the Modernist crisis, by contrast, did a good deal to close it. Following the Modernist crisis, writes Michael Gannon, "the American clerical mind turned in on itself . . . read Chesterton's new book, *Orthodoxy*, with self-congratulatory favor," and compared itself in superior contrast to the wrongheaded "intellectual men" of the century.[36] The Catholic literary revival under the leadership of many of these same clerics followed suit. It was in this spirit that the revival between 1920 and 1935 turned toward the orthodox Chesterton and the authoritative John Henry Newman as the spokesmen and models for the movement.

5

The Revival as Reaction, II: Newman, Chesterton, and Babbitt, Catholic Revivalists

Each age rewrites history to coincide with its own view of reality. Twentieth century Catholic studies of John Henry Newman and Gilbert Keith Chesterton illustrate this point while typifying the keen philosophical and theological differences separating the pre- and post-Vatican II Churches.

Post-Vatican II scholarship has customarily portrayed Newman and Chesterton as religious progressives. Some modern scholars have characterized Vatican II (1962–1965) as "Newman's Council" while proclaiming that Newman's *Grammar of Assent* (1870, a phenomenological analysis of the origins of religious faith) and *Essay on Development* (1845, stressing the unfolding of religious doctrine through time) both anticipated and directed some of the Council's most imaginative reforms. These included the Church's new openness toward ecumenism, theologies of religious experience, and historicist understandings of doctrinal development.[1]

Chesterton likewise has spoken to Catholics in newly different ways since the early 1960s, as scholars have abandoned the journalistic and controversialistic Chesterton in favor of the philosophical and theological one. In *Chesteron, Man and Mask* (1961), for example, Gary Wills—writing during an era when many Catholic thinkers were attempting to reconcile Chesterton's orthodoxy with the insights of post-World War II existential philosophies—argued that Chesterton should be understood as one of the first modern Christian existentialists. As proof, Wills cited Chesterton's deeply humanistic appreciation for the mystery and totality of human experience, in contrast to the narrowly empiricist and idealistic characterizations of mankind's nature and destiny typifying the major secular philosophies of his age.[2]

An existentialist Chesterton or a modernist Newman to most Catholics in the 1920s and 1930s, however, would have seemed a contradiction in terms. Jesuits Daniel A. Lord, Francis X. Talbot, Calvert Alexander, and others of their generation were interested instead in the Newman who defended dogma and revelation to a modern skeptical age, who wrote late in his career that "for thirty, forty, fifty years, I have resisted to the best of my powers the spirit of Liberalism in religion." Newman characterized this spirit as a "false liberty of thought" that subjected human judgment to "those revealed doctrines which are in their nature beyond and independent of it."[3]

Lord, Alexander, and their generation were drawn likewise to the dogmatic Chesterton of *Orthodoxy* and *Heretics* and to the Chesterton who exclaimed through the policeman in *The Man Who Was Thursday*, "The most dangerous criminal now is the entirely lawless modern philosopher."[4] Most American Catholic scholars and teachers during the 1920s and 1930s scrupulously avoided Newman's *Grammar of Assent.* Few fully appreciated Chesterton's sense of paradox.

This chapter assesses Newman and Chesterton's place within the Catholic literary revival and American Catholic thought and literature during the first third of the twentieth century. It also assesses the revival's critical interest in Irving Babbitt and the Babbitt-inspired New Humanist crusade of that same era. Many Catholic critics viewed the New Humanists as potential allies in their mutual campaigns to redirect philosophy and literature away from the naturalistic premises then popular in academic circles toward more objective standards of thought and reality. Younger Jesuit academic critics like Alexander especially perceived in New Humanist classicism a reflection of his own neo-scholastic outlook.

JOHN HENRY NEWMAN

John Henry Newman was born in 1801, the son of a middle-class London banker.[5] Newman's parents were nominally Anglican, but by age fifteen John had embraced a mild evangelicalism. He entered Oxford University in 1817 and in 1822 was elevated to an Oriel Fellowship. At Oriel, Newman initially fell under the influence of Richard Whatley, Thomas Arnold, and a brilliant circle of liberal Fellows known as the "Noetics," so called because they were highly skeptical of any religious knowledge not rationally understood by the intellect. But after encountering the High Church ideas of John Keble, Hurrell Froude, and other Oxfordians, Newman repudiated the Noetics and the positivistic Victorian outlook. Newman's reaction, like similar Romantic and evangelical reactions against Victorian empiricism, soon assumed the outlines of a movement, as he and his Oxford associates attempted to reverse the liberalizing tendencies within the Anglican Church.

The Oxford Movement (*circa* 1833–1845) was essentially an effort to renew the tradition, spirituality, and authority of the Church of England. But in his attempt to uncover the seat of religious authority within his own Church, Newman was drawn deeper into the Catholic tradition. His study of the primitive Church finally convinced Newman that Rome was the Church of Christ's apostles. Newman thus repudiated his own *Via Media* (a theory that the Church of England was a happy mean between the extremes of Roman Catholicism and Protestantism) and "went over" to Rome in 1845. Newman's conversion, as previously noted, precipitated an English Catholic revival of sorts, as many first-rate Anglican minds followed him into the Church.

Newman's works received significant attention in undergraduate English and religious studies programs at many Catholic colleges and universities by the early 1920s. The Englishman's strongest American Jesuit advocate was Daniel M. O'Connell. O'Connell, like Lord, Alexander, Bakewell Morrison, Benjamin L. Masse and other early Jesuit proponents of an American Catholic literary revival, had a St. Louis University background. He entered the Society of Jesus through the Missouri Province in 1903, was educated at St. Louis University, and took his final vows in 1918. In the 1920s O'Connell taught English and composition at Jesuit-run Xavier University in Cincinnati, Ohio, where he gained a reputation as a Newman scholar and edited several college editions of the Englishman's work.[6] He also distributed syllabi and advice to Catholic educators throughout the country, suggesting ways that Newman could be integrated into the college curriculum. Freshman college English, suggested O'Connell in 1923, could usefully employ Newman's *The Present Position of Catholics in England* (1851, a scathing attack upon English anti-Catholic bigotry) to teach undergraduates Newman's techniques as a prose stylist. Newman's more difficult works, *The Idea of a University* (1852, where Newman, among other things, argues for the inclusion of theology in university studies) and *Apologia Pro Vita Sua* (1864, an autobiographical account of Newman's assent to the Catholic faith) could be utilized in upper-division courses.[7]

O'Connell's summons to a "Newmanesque revival" in all American Jesuit colleges and seminaries struck a responsive chord within the Jesuit educational establishment which, as Paul A. Fitzgerald observes, itself was moving toward greater national planning and cooperation at this time.[8] Many Jesuits, including O'Connell (who would assume an increasingly important role in these events when he was appointed national secretary, or Commissarius, of American Jesuit education in 1934), believed that courses on Newman—which combined a cultural approach to Catholicism within a traditional liberal arts framework—would both strengthen the undergraduate curriculum and better prepare students to engage in the "intellectual apostolate" of the day. The fact that courses on Newman and Newman's thought were offered currently at a number of secular colleges and universities—against whom Catholic college administrators constantly measured their school's own academic standing at this time—added weight to the position that his ideas belonged in Catholic schools.

The 1924 and 1928 college bulletins at Loyola University of Chicago and at St. Louis University thus described their newly instituted courses on Newman (offered as an elective through their English departments) in the following identical manner:

Newman: His commanding position in the religious intellectual life of the nineteenth century; life and associations at Oxford; Catholic life; his philosophy of education in *The Idea of a University*; his controversial, apologetic and homiletic works; the great Christian protagonist in the warfare of modern rationalism; the acknowledged perfection of his prose.[9]

Assigned readings, for the most part, were Newman's *Apologia, The Idea of a University,* and *The Present Position of Catholics.*[10] Newman's *Grammar of Assent* and *Essay on Development,* significantly, were seldom encountered. This was true in both Jesuit and non-Jesuit schools, which, in this age, usually followed the lead of the former. Indeed, Fr. Edwin Ryan's 1930 *College Handbook to Newman,* designed as an aid for Catholic college literature teachers, cautioned Catholic educators to guide their students away from these works. Newman's theory on development, warned Ryan, was still under debate and "the extent to which that theory may be used is not yet certain." As for the *Grammar of Assent,* Ryan advised that "one not a theologian had better leave it alone."[11]

Why this narrow view of Newman? In part, it was a consequence of the way Catholics conceived the intellectual apostolate of the day—which was to defend the Church against attack, to refute modern "error," and to uphold religious authority in a relativistic world. The anti-Modernist legacy and the Church's own early twentieth century struggle with modernity, and the presumptive effect this struggle had on subsequent Catholic scholarly development early in the century, moreover, were inseparable from this outlook, and did much to define Newman to this era of the American Church. There is a good deal of irony here because during his lifetime Newman was actually suspected of Modernism when English Jesuit George Tyrrell and other Modernists defended their positions by claiming that Newman's imaginative ideas about religious experience and dogmatic development paralleled their own.[12] But Catholic American religious and literary leaders during the

1920s and early 1930s did not dwell upon this side of Newman or upon the Newman who had serious reservations about unlimited papal infallibility. Instead, they preferred to see Newman as they perceived themselves—as Catholic intellectuals engaged in a relentless war against modern irreligion and infidelity, which in the post-Modernist era was attributed to the rejection of intellect, reason, and objective reality. The Modernist crisis had set the stage; Newman now played the part.

Looking through the many college textbooks, commentaries, and college course descriptions addressed to Newman during the 1920s and 1930s, one is impressed by their tendency to treat Newman's controversy with nineteenth century rationalism—often denoted by Catholic commentators under its broader construction of Liberalism—as the unifying element of his intellectual-religious life. Three college textbooks, all produced and published by St. Louis University Jesuits in the 1930s, illustrate this outlook. The texts are: Raymond Corrigan's *The Church in the Nineteenth Century*, 1938 (a polemical history of the institutional Church and its eventual "triumph" over the forces of modern materialistic thought ending with the anti-Modernist pronouncements of the Vatican in 1907); Morrison's *Think and Live*, 1937 (a popularly written handbook of scholastic philosophy based upon the author's own classroom lecture materials); and Alexander's *The Catholic Literary Revival*, 1935.[13]

Alexander's and Corrigan's books were published under the *Science and Culture Series* of college textbooks edited by St. Louis University Jesuit Joseph Husslein, Dean of the School of Social Service and a close friend of Lord. The series, as Husslein conceived it, was to be a "University in Print," part of an ambitious program by Husslein and other St. Louis Jesuits to bring "Catholic influences to bear on the intellectual problems of the day."[14] Morrison's book was also written in the modern vein, as part of the 1930s Jesuit catechistic reform movement designed to revitalize Catholic religious instruction for modern college youth.

All three of the works, accordingly, depicted Newman as one of the first modern Catholic thinkers to understand the modern mind, to predict its agnostic postures, and to fashion an intellectual response to them. Morrison thus wrote that Newman's prescient critique of modern scientific rationalism, where the latter predicted in his 1851 university lectures that modern empirical science and philosophy would only accept as true what was verifiable by science and reason, had been fulfilled in the twentieth century outlook of modern skeptics like Bertrand Russell. Newman's prediction of the intellectual isolation of religious believers, who in the new age of rationalistic science would no longer be considered "thinking men," was also realized, observed Morrison, by twentieth century events. The remainder of Morrison's volume was dedicated to a "theoretical refutation" of this modern outlook.[15]

Corrigan similarly characterized Newman as a modern prophet who, first through the Oxford Movement and then as a leading Catholic intellectual, struggled with the "mental ills" of his age. Liberalism headed Corrigan's list of nineteenth century disorders, which the Jesuit catalogued with seventy-two other "diseases or symptoms of disease" afflicting the modern mind. Corrigan added that "Newman regarded his fight against this aberration of the century as his life's work."[16]

Newman, in fact, did link the awakening of nineteenth century English Catholic intellectual life to the struggle against the rising tide of rationalistic unbelief. He genuinely feared that the Catholic laity would be unprepared intellectually to address the problems posed to their faith by the growing atmosphere of scientific and philosophical skepticism. Reflecting this lifelong apprehension, Newman wrote in 1877:

I have through all that time thought that a time of wide-spread infidelity was coming, and through all these years the waters in fact have been rising as a deluge. I look for the time, after my life, when only the tops of the mountains will be seen, like islands in the waste of waters. . . . Great actions and successes must be achieved by the Catholic leaders . . . if Holy Church is to [be] kept safe from this awful calamity.[17]

Thus, one of Newman's chief concerns was to strengthen the faithful against the impact of modern infidelity. Newman challenged the Catholic laity to know their religion intellectually and to instruct themselves in all branches of secular knowledge. "I wish the intellect to range with the utmost freedom, and religion to enjoy an equal freedom," wrote Newman in his university lectures, "but what I am stipulating for is that they should be in one and the same place, and exemplified in the same person."[18]

Newman presented this vision most forcefully in *The Idea of a University*, a collection of addresses and essays written and delivered between 1851 and 1858 while he acted as rector of the ill-fated Irish Catholic University. In "A Form of Infidelity of the Day," Newman made a strong plea for the inclusion of theology in the college curriculum while deploring what he predicted would be the coming tactics of unbelief—positivistic science and philosophy, operating under the guise of objectivity, attempting to diminish the importance of undemonstrable theology.[19]

But throughout his lectures Newman was equally adamant in insisting that Catholics become familiar with new developments in the natural and social sciences. Newman wanted a Catholic university where both theology and science would flourish, untrammeled and unimpaired. He likewise insisted that knowledge was its own end, and defended it as a discipline apart from religious and moral development.[20]

Corrigan and Morrison, like most Catholics before 1935, ignored this dimension in Newman's educational thought. It was a literal-minded era of the American Church, and one gets the sense of Catholics during the 1920s and early 1930s scouring the works of Newman for the right quotation to support their own judgments against contemporary religious modernists and philosophical materialists. So eager were some Catholics to appropriate the authority of Newman that they often appeared to be critiquing nineteenth rather than twentieth century thought. The names of Ernest Renan, Hippolyte Taine, Adolf von Harnack, and Fredrich Schleiermacher appear as frequently in Corrigan's and Alexander's critiques of modernity as do Russell, Theodore Dreiser, and John Dewey. Even as late as 1935, Alexander is seen beating the dead horse of "Victorian Progress" long after it had been discredited by events surrounding World War I.

Catholic apologists during the 1920s and early 1930s thus were satisfied to grasp parts of Newman without any real understanding of the whole of his thought. This was especially apparent in Alexander's *Catholic Literary Revival* and its account of Newman's relationship to the Oxford Movement. Newman's own record of the event presented something of a problem for Alexander. In his *Apologia* Newman claimed that the Oxford Movement had really been part of the early nineteenth century Romantic revolt against rationalism. Newman, therefore, acknowledged the debt he and the other Oxford tractarians owed Romantic thinkers like Sir Walter Scott, Samuel Coleridge, and William Wordsworth for awakening the spiritual desires of nineteenth century man.[21]

Alexander's problem was this: As an historian who traced the origins of the Catholic literary revival to the Oxfordians, he had to admit Newman's acknowledged debt to the Romantics. As a neo-scholastic thinker, however, Alexander thought it imperative to disassociate Newman from a movement that posited human sentiment and emotion as the primary guide to truth. The Jesuit wanted no hint of emotionalism or nostalgic medievalism surrounding the rebirth of modern Catholic letters.

Alexander consequently opposed New Humanist critic Paul Elmer More's identification of Newman "with the typical mind of nineteenth century Romanticism."[22] Newman was an antirationalist, conceded Alexander, but "it is equally as obvious that his anti-intellectualism, if we may so call it, was not that of Blake, or Wordsworth, or William Law, or Coleridge." Newman, insisted Alexander, shunned the various substitutes for reason posited by these Romantics—"feeling, intuition, [and] the 'inner light.' "[23]

Newman was antirationalist but he was not anti-intellectual. To the scholastic mind fresh from its battles with Modernism, that was an important distinction. In the scholastic scheme of things there was reason and there was Reason. There was scholastic Reason (*Ratio autem in homine habet locuum dominantis*), which began with the assumption that man, endowed with the higher moral faculties of intellect, reason, and free will, can deductively ascend to truth. Modern reason, or "rationalism," by contrast, dismissed any notion of supernatural or *a priori* truth inherent in man or the universe, and approached reality exclusively through logic, positivistic induction, or empirical fact. The rationalism that Newman opposed, insisted Alexander, was submerged in empirical reason, not the reason that was concerned with "final causes." "Of the two, Rationalism or Romanticism," complained the Jesuit, "it is difficult to say which was the more anti-intellectual."[24]

Alexander therefore maintained that Newman in his controversy with nineteenth century rationalism and Liberalism never abandoned the intellect. Newman denounced positivistic reason, but he embraced *a priori* Reason. A Newman who emphasized emotion over intellect would not only have been a Romantic in the tradition of Coleridge, but would have been uncomfortably close to the religious Modernism of Tyrrell, Henri Bergson, and William James.

Newman was not a scholastic thinker but Alexander tried very hard to imply that he was. In almost syllogisitic fashion, Alexander tried to argue that since Newman was orthodox, and orthodoxy is linked with scholastic philosophy, Newman, *ergo*, was a scholastic. The importance of this maneuver becomes more apparent when it is observed that most American Catholic literary leaders between 1920 and 1960 approached man, reality, and literature from a scholastic perspective. The stock argument heard throughout the literary revival was that while most modern non-Catholic artists, poets, and novelists floundered in a sea of romanticism, "naturalism," or subjectivistic personal systems of thought, making them "prey to despair and frustration," Catholic writers, by contrast, were grounded in the solid, secure foundations of universal truth and Reason.[25]

Modern Catholic writers, Alexander claimed, owed this philosophical certainty to Newman; he was to modern Catholic writers what Aquinas had been to Dante. Newman, maintained Alexander, gave modern Catholic writers the "mind of the Church"—a mind that "recognized the primacy of intelligence without destroying the claims of the heart," and preserved the individual Catholic writer from "wrecking his genius in philosophical blind alleys."[26] Surely, this was the scholastic mind.

Throughout the 1920s and early 1930s, American Catholic writers, critics, and educators projected their own needs onto the complex figure of John Henry Newman. Hence, for neo-scholastic thinkers Morrison, Corrigan, and Alexander, Newman was the most important Catholic thinker of the nineteenth century, upholding scholastic standards and an objective system of reality within a chaotic philosophical and literary world. For literary critic and Catholic cultural leader Francis X. Talbot, on the other hand, Newman was this and more. Newman's reputation as a writer and thinker added stature to the modern Catholic literary tradition that Talbot was so self-consciously attempting to build. He was another source of intellectual standing and prestige. For almost three hundred years before Newman's *Apologia*, observed Talbot in 1922, "a Catholic name seldom appeared on the covers of an English book." But beginning with Newman, Talbot noted, "an army of writers" flowed into the Church.[27] For Talbot, then, Newman was yet another noted and respected Catholic author; another name to add to the Jesuit's long list of modern Catholic writers.

For still other Catholic leaders during the troublesome 1920s, Newman was yet another bulwark against the anti-Catholic feeling of the times. "Find any phase of 1924 prejudice," Daniel M. O'Connell wrote in urging college adoption of Newman's *The Present Position of Catholics in England*, "that has not been skillfully treated in this volume." O'Connell believed that Newman's injunction, "Oblige men to know you; persuade them, importune them, shame them into knowing you," would be sound advice for all"zealous laymen" of the 1920s.[28]

Newman was invoked most frequently during the 1920s and early 1930s, however, to defend religious knowledge in a skeptical secular age. In the view of the Jesuits who led the first stages of the Catholic literary revival, Newman's revolt against Liberalism remained unfinished. Infidelity still stalked the land in the form of philosophical materialism, liberal humanism, and the cult of evolutionary progress. As in the nineteenth century, it was incumbent upon an educated and articulate Catholic laity to turn back the tide.

CHESTERTON AND ORTHODOXY

If Newman was the prophet and inspiration for the initial stages of the Catholic literary revival in America, G. K. Chesterton (1878–1936) was its modern archetype and spokesman. Chesterton as much as Newman dictated the early revival's tone, ideology, and direction. The figure of Chesterton loomed over Alexander's history of the revival. Chesterton's *Orthodoxy* (1908) was ranked with Newman's *Apologia* and *The Idea of a University* as one of "The Best Ten Catholic Books" in Talbot's 1923 plebiscite to draw attention to modern Catholic writers. Chesterton's works appeared sixteen separate times—more than any other writer—in Sr. Mary Louise's *Over the Bent World* (1939), a standard anthology of the literature of the Catholic literary revival used in many Catholic colleges and universities during the 1930s and 1940s.[29]

Catholic critics, moreover, following the anti-Modernist mood of the first part of the century, repeatedly linked Chesterton and Newman in a common ideological battle against modern subjectivist philosophy. "Skepticism is rejected by Newman and Chesterton as vigorously as dogmatism is asserted," stressed Jesuit educator Alfred G. Brickel in a

1919 comparative study of the two apologists.[30] Chesterton's "belliger-
ence," insisted Alexander in *The Catholic Literary Revival*, "was a contin-
uation of Newman's war on Liberalism as something essentially illiberal,
raw, and barbaric."[31] Hence, Chesterton, no less than Newman during
the 1920s and 1930s, was drawn upon to combat twentieth century
skeptics, to defend dogma, and to uphold tradition, standards, and
philosophical and ecclesiastical authority in a relativistic modern age.

American Catholic commentators during the 1920s and early 1930s
have left few extended analyses of Chesterton, and their treatment of
his work is similarly selective and epigrammatic. As with Newman,
however, the historian can get a sense of Chesterton's meaning to the
American Church at this time by looking at the selection process itself—
by looking at the works which Catholic critics and teachers chose to
emphasize.

The works of Chesterton which appeared most frequently in the literature of the American Catholic revival during the 1920s and 1930s (on
the reading lists for courses on the Catholic literary revival, in the anthologies of Catholic authors used in college classrooms, in Alexander's
history of the revival, and in the numerous articles about Chesterton in
the Catholic press) are the following: *Heretics* (1905) and *Orthodoxy* (1908),
two books of essays which pointedly attack the materialist assumptions
of modern science, philosophy, and literature; *The Napoleon of Notting
Hill* (1904) and *The Man Who Was Thursday* (1908), two satirical novels
that contain a good deal of philosophical comment upon modern skeptical systems of thought; and "Lepanto" (1915) and "The Ballad of the
White Horse" (1911), two present-minded epic poems that stirringly
portray historic conflicts between the forces of Christendom and neo-
paganism.

Four general themes emerge from these and most of Chesterton's
other works that deal with the conflict between belief and unbelief. The
remainder of this section will present these themes and examine them
within the context of the works cited.

First Theme: Modern Thought Is in Chaos

The first theme expresses the concept that modern thought has lost
all sense of permanent ideals, tradition, and authority. Modern thinkers,
comments a character in *The Man Who Was Thursday*, have sunk into a
kind of final skepticism "which can find no floor to the universe."[32] In
Heretics and *Orthodoxy*, Chesterton maintains that evolutionary theory,
scientific rationalism, and post-Nietzschean will philosophies have combined to produce a modern skeptical mentality that mocks any attempt
to assert a fixed, objective view of realityy. In *Heretics* Chesterton argues

that moderns like George Bernard Shaw, Henrik Ibsen, and H. G. Wells, in fact, have ended in denying "the possibility of philosophy itself." By "philosophy," Chesterton means a rational system of thought that makes generalizations about first and final causes and objective moral truths and presents ultimate standards by which to judge man, reality, and the universe. Instead, Chesterton writes, "General theories are everywhere contemned. . . . We will have no generalizations."[33] Modern literature, philosophy, and politics will have no talk about ultimate things. "There are no cardinal virtues of Ibsenism," he writes. "There is no ideal man of Ibsen." Shaw's epigram, "The golden rule is that there is no golden rule," perfectly sums up the antimetaphysical spirit of the age.[34]

Shaw's rejection of metaphysics further explained for Chesterton why so many moderns fell victim to every new philosophical fad or yielded to their own subjective thought systems. Shaw adopted a cruelly self-sufficient philosophy of will that worshiped strength and success. Wells, another contemporary, embraced scientific utopianism and the cult of the future. *Fin de siecle* "decadents" took up a determined and passionate aestheticism. Fluctuating between the extremes of hedonistic excess and stoic despair, aesthetes like Walter Pater and Algernon Swinburne rejected all conventions and moral and social values. Chesterton accuses the English philosopher George Moore of having no final philosophy to live by. He was always "walking the world looking for a new one."[35] In Chesterton's view there was something self-indulgent and vain in these excesses. In *Manalive* (1912), Chesterton's hero, Innocent Smith, takes one modern pessimist at his word. Feeling pity for a professor who, in a fit of despair, exclaims that life is not worth living, Smith decides to shoot him—to put him out of his misery![36]

Second Theme: Man Is Restricted by Materialism

A second theme Chesterton espouses is that a material, as opposed to a non-material or metaphysical, approach to reality actually delimits rather than frees modern man. Modern philosophical materialists have merely replaced one set of dogmas (supernatural) with another (material). "The modern world is filled with men who hold dogmas so strongly," insists Chesterton in *Heretics*, "that they do not even know that they are dogmas."[37] One of Chesterton's chief lessons in *Orthodoxy*, *The Man Who Was Thursday*, and *The Napoleon of Notting Hill* is that it is impossible to understand human reality solely through dogmatic materialistic reason. Throughout these works he contrasts the freedom, imagination, and complexity of religious orthodoxy with the cold limits of pure reason. In "The Maniac" (*Orthodoxy*) Chesterton maintains that reason actually leads to insanity: "The madman is not the man who has lost his reason. The madman is the man who has lost everything except his reason."[38] The modern positivist attempts to comprehend paradoxical man exclusively through an empiricist framework. He attempts to explain what human reason and matter alone cannot explain, "and it is his head that splits."[39]

"There is a thought that stops thought," observes Chesterton in commenting upon modern philosophical materialism.[40] Too much rationality ends in destroying what is human in man. That is one of the messages of *Notting Hill*, where James Barker, a Benthamite utilitarian, is totally enclosed in the world of empirical fact. "Of the soul, I cannot pretend to say anything," declares Barker to one of his associates.[41] Completely lacking in imagination, Barker can neither comprehend nor accept the presence of Notting Hill, a medieval-style kingdom set up in the middle of London by the fanatical Adam Wayne, who is as imbalanced toward the romantic side of life as Barker is toward the empirical. Barker thus destroys Wayne and Notting Hill and a dimension of the human experience that his rigid Euclidian mind prevents him from understanding.

Chesterton therefore attempts to illustrate that dogmatic materialism and dogmatic empiricism turn away from human experience. Like Barker and "The Maniac," their universe is soul-limiting and narrow. Life is complex and full of mystery and contradiction. Christian orthodoxy (Chesterton did not convert to Catholicism until 1922), he argues, recognizes this and frees man from the cold prison of rationality.

Third Theme: Christian Orthodoxy Is the Way to Reality

Completing the paradox, Chesterton maintains that Christian orthodoxy is the only philosophy that understands the complex nature of man. It provides the only set of fixed and permanent standards upon which to build a better world. Orthodoxy, rather than stifling progress, is, paradoxically, a prerequisite to progress. Chesterton claims in *Orthodoxy* that most modern philosophies are Christian virtues grown into heresy. "The modern world," he writes, "is full of the old Christian virtues gone mad."[42] Christian principles and dogmas (charity, justice, mercy, humility) cannot exist outside the context of Christian faith and maintain their original meaning and balance. Modern humanitarians like Fabian socialist Robert Blatchford (*Merrie England*, 1894), for example, are so eager to forgive human evil that they end in denying its very possibility. *Notting Hill*'s Adam Wayne is so fanatical about the natural goodness of man that he is blind to the flawed human condition. Wells (*Mankind in the Making*, 1903) similarly speaks of progress without any sense of ultimate moral progress.[43]

But while heresy always passes away, by virtue of extremes, orthodoxy remains, by virtue of its complexity. Only religious orthodoxy, Chesterton maintains, understands the paradox that is man. It satisfies both the head and the heart and prevents the intellect from consuming itself. As the "Higher Dialectic," orthodoxy provides the equilibrium and balance to life that is missing from other systems of modern thought.

Chesterton thus argues that dogma is a pre-condition to progress. "If we want reform," writes Chesterton in *Orthodoxy*, "we must adhere to orthodoxy."[44] "No body [sic] has any business to use the word 'progress,' " persists Chesterton in *Heretics*, "unless he has a definite creed and a cast-iron code of morals. No body [sic] can be progressive without being doctrinal."[45] Progress has no meaning without definite and ultimate standards toward which to advance. Chesterton, like Newman, then, argues that development can occur only when there is something fixed enough to develop.

Fourth Theme: Attack the Forces of Unbelief

The final Chestertonian theme emphasized by American Catholics during the 1920s and 1930s is the Englishman's call to Christians to take action against the forces of modern unbelief. This theme appears most dramatically in "Lepanto" and "The Ballad of the White Horse."[46] Both are poems of conflict and crisis, past and present. "Lepanto" memorializes the 1570 battle in which Don John of Austria, Philip of Spain, and other Catholic knights of Europe rallied to the call of Pius V to throw back the Ottoman Turks and the forces of Islam. In "The Ballad of the White Horse" Chesterton similarly describes how Christian King Alfred the Great roused the Anglo-Saxon chiefs of England to hold off the Danes at the battle of Ethandune (878).

Each poem, however, plants the message that victory is far from complete. Surveying his triumph, Alfred predicts the future return of the heathen in new and modern dress, armed with "scroll and pen."

> They shall not come with warships,
>   They shall not waste with brands,
> But books be all their eating,
>   And ink be on their hands.[47]

In this eighth and final book of the poem, Chesterton appears to be speaking directly to the twentieth century, predicting most of the modern theories that will threaten Christian belief anew: fatalism, skepticism, materialism, a "detail of sinning/And denial of the sin," and deterministic tales "of curse in bone and kin."[48] The struggle thus is an eternal one because it is a struggle between two different attitudes of mind.

The survey of Chesterton's ideas yields a sense of his meaning to the American Catholic literary revival, which in large part began as a movement to resist the materialistic premises of modern thought, to defend the Church against all critics, and to reestablish objective standards of truth in a confused and chaotic world. Chesterton attempted all of this. He both challenged and satirized the most cherished assumptions of modern unbelief. He took the entire argument against dogmatic Christianity, and, with some success, stood it upon its head. He turned all the traditional arguments against orthodoxy back upon themselves: It is religious orthodoxy that is liberal, and modern thought that is illiberal. Orthodoxy frees, deterministic materialism and narrow rationalism restrict. Unbelief stands in the way of progress, orthodoxy leads to true progress.

Chesterton, moreover, managed to do all of this with a sense of detachment and whimsy. This was best symbolized by Chesterton's lifelong friendships with his "arch-enemies," Wells and Shaw. Chesterton's was an urbane apologetic, a combination previously unknown to a defensive American Church.

Enhancing Chesterton's appeal, especially among the Jesuit clerics who led this first stage of the revival, was the fact that he was an outspoken anti-Modernist. Chesterton throughout his career regularly crossed swords with liberal religionists who would accommodate dogma to the spirit of the age. "It is always easy to be a modernist," Chesterton writes in *Orthodoxy*, and to embrace "fashion after fashion."[49] Chesterton also wrote the introduction to Fulton J. Sheen's *God and Intelligence in the Modern World*. Sheen's 1925 book delivered one of the sharpest attacks upon religious modernism ever written by an American cleric.[50]

American Catholic critics, controversialists, and educational leaders thus turned to Chesterton no less than to Newman during the first three decades of the century for inspiration, argument, and conviction. In the words of a eulogy by Daniel A. Lord upon Chesterton's death in 1936, the Englishman had put "the proud aesthetes" in their place, and pointed out the "absurdities" of modern pessimists "who taught a philosophy that life was too horrible to bear or thought they were humanitarians when they stripped man of his Father in Heaven."[51] Even as late as 1940, a spokesman before the annual meeting of the Franciscan Educational Conference urged his colleagues "to develop not pious, sentimental scribblers, but strong, virile writers in the true artistic and philosophical tradition as G. K. Chesterton."[52]

Indeed, Chesterton's iconoclastic apologetic was especially appealing to many American Catholic undergraduates grown weary of syllogistic scholastic apologetics. In 1935 St. Louis University student Harold Wilson even credited Chesterton with saving his soul. Wilson had rejected scholastic apologetics as too dry and formalistic, and was wavering on the brink of agnosticism. Chesterton, wrote Wilson, was "what I needed." He represented a "militant aggressiveness and less formal apologetics." Wilson continued to describe—in language worthy of a college sophomore—his happy encounter with Chesterton and "The Ballad of the White Horse":

The subterranean fires of wrath which the crust of doubt and stratified rock of indecision had for a long time repressed in the onetime agnostic, Chesterton broke out with such violence when finally let loose that they seared like some great blow-torch all the godless, faithless, senseless heterodoxies of the day leaving them gray, burnt, crisps strewn in futility at the foot of the Church.[53]

The University of Notre Dame underscored less dramatically how much Catholic colleges and universities valued Chesterton as an apologist when in 1937 it established an award for excellence in the field of "practical apologetics" in honor of Chesterton.[54]

That same year Alexander gave his own opinion of Chesterton's importance to Catholic letters and the Catholic literary revival:

G. K. Chesterton gave to modern Catholic writers the one characteristic by which they are termed modern—the characteristic of fighters as well as writers. From the moment of his awakening to the realization of the indivisible conflict between barbarism and Christianity, he enlisted as a fighter in this great, modern war.[55]

Alexander was paying tribute to Chesterton's tone and style, but the imagery and sense of conflict contained in his statement also carried a deeper meaning. His words expressed the widespread sense of crisis that was almost universal among Catholic thinkers and writers during the 1920s and 1930s. Catholic thinkers, worldwide, were convinced that western civilization had reached a critical juncture in its history. It was at a crossroads, and its intellectual and cultural choices would determine its very survival. Western civilization, it was argued, could continue along the post-Renaissance, post-Reformation, post-Darwinian road of unrestrained individualism, religious subjectivism, national particularism, and philosophical materialism, and slip further into disorder and chaos, or it could return to its Christian humanistic roots: the Judeo-Christian heritage, a unifying philosophy and culture, and first principles about man's spiritual dignity and destiny.

These were the positive theological and cultural alternatives that European Catholic thinkers like Christopher Dawson and Jacques Maritain emphasized in such works as *The Modern Dilemma* (1932) and *Religion and Culture* (1931). But while the Jesuit leaders of the American Catholic revival before 1935 were familiar with the works of Dawson and Maritain, they nevertheless seemed more eager to embrace classical, as opposed to Christian, humanism as a solution to modern problems. They still preferred scholastic formalism. They would save a troubled twentieth century civilization, but it would be through "intelligence," "Reason," and "will." For these reasons, Catholic cultural leaders like Alexander were always more at home with the Aristotelian metaphysics of Irving Babbitt than the integral humanism of Maritain. Moreover, Babbitt's own "Battle of the Books" during the 1920s and early 1930s better coincided with the belligerent state of mind in which Alexander and many other American Catholic literary and philosophical leaders then found themselves. In Babbitt and like-minded critics, Catholics could claim strong ideological allies in their warfare with modern thought. It was against this background that the American Catholic literary revival embraced Babbitt and the New Humanist movement.

TWO REVIVALS, CATHOLIC AND HUMANIST

The New Humanist and Catholic revivals originated at approximately the same time.[56] True, Babbitt had sketched the major outlines of the New Humanism as early as 1908 in *Literature and the American College* and more fully in *Rousseau and Romanticism* (1919); but it was not until the late 1920s that he and other New Humanist thinkers—Paul Elmer More, Norman Foerster, George Roy Elliott, and Stuart Pratt Sherman—gained widespread attention, when Seward Collins opened the pages of the prestigious *Bookman* (superseded in 1932 by the *American Review*) to New Humanist criticism.[57]

By 1930 the major American Catholic philosophical and literary journals—*America, Commonweal, Thought,* the *Modern Schoolman*—were also expressing keen and sympathetic interest in the movement. Between April and September 1930, *America,* under the literary editorship of Talbot, published eight major articles analyzing the New Humanist movement and assessing its meaning for American Catholic literary and philosophical opinion. The Jesuit-published *Modern Schoolman,* a journal dedicated to the revival of neo-scholastic philosophy in the United States, similarly ran seventeen articles on the New Humanism and New Humanists between 1930 and 1935.

What was the meaning of the New Humanism to the Catholic literary and neo-scholastic revivals? American Catholic literary and philosophical leaders during the 1920s and early 1930s viewed the New Humanists on several different levels. First, many regarded the New Humanists as comrades-in-arms against modernity, kindred voices asserting universal standards of intelligence against the scientific reductionism and debilitating relativism of their age. Second, many welcomed the New Humanist program and its emphasis upon the higher faculties of the intellect, reason, and free will, as preparing the ground for a similar revival of scholastic principles. Closely following this last view, many Catholic cultural leaders hoped that the New Humanism would break down modern philosophical prejudice toward scholastic philosophy, and thereby win a fresh hearing for Catholic thought in the American intellectual-literary community. Thus, like so many other episodes in the Catholic literary revival, the Catholic encounter with the New Humanism was inextricably linked to the early twentieth century quest for intellectual status and respectability.

Writing in 1930, Talbot observed that New Humanists and Catholics had much in common. In an article titled "Humanism Is Against," Talbot sought to compare the Catholic and New Humanist literary movements and to enumerate "some few aspects of the contemporary chaos" that the New Humanists opposed as "savagely" as he did.[58] Talbot noted that both movements shared common enemies: "The little Olympians of the past decade or two"—debunkers like Edmund Wilson and H. L. Mencken, the *New Republic* and the *Nation*, and critical realists such as Theodore Dreiser and James Branch Cabell. Talbot believed that their relativistic and irreligious attitudes were symptomatic of the modern moral crisis. The Jesuit found Catholics and New Humanists similarly opposed to the naturalistic presumptions of modern thought: positivistic science and deterministic psychology that reduced human behavior to "uncontrolled impulses" and "primitve desires," and a modern philosophical pragmatism that assumed "truth is a relative, a mutuable, and a fickle thing."[59]

Talbot's analysis was unsystematic and personal, but more advanced Catholic philosophical minds during the 1920s and early 1930s spoke of similar affinities between Catholic and New Humanist thought. Alexander, for one, claimed in 1930 that the New Humanists "have admitted that they are linked in essentials with those spiritual upholders of orthodoxy in England, G. K. Chesterton, and Hilaire Belloc."[60] Benjamin L. Masse, who likewise played a leading role in both the Catholic literary and neo-scholastic revivals, also saw a coincidence between the New Humanism and the current Catholic literary movement. "By placing himself in direct opposition to naturalism," Masse wrote of Babbitt in 1934, the latter was "joining hands" with European Catholic thinkers like Chesterton, Belloc, Maritain, Dawson, and Arnold Lunn.[61]

Much of the New Humanist critique of modern intellectual culture did mirror Catholicism's own critique of modernity since Renaissance times. Babbitt and other New Humanist critics, not unlike Alexander, Masse and many Catholic thinkers in the 1920s and early 1930s, blamed naturalism and romanticism for the subjectivity, drift, and confusion of modern thought. In *Rousseau and Romanticism* Babbitt maintained that Rousseau's idealization of natural and uncorrupted man had led to an erosion of objective norms of behavior, discipline, and restraint. "Faith in one's natural goodness," complained Babbitt, "is a constant encouragement to evade individual moral responsibility." Romantic literature, he charged, extoled primitive man and blamed society for corrupting his spirit.[62]

New Humanist thinkers, no less than Catholics at this time, likewise asserted that modern thought had overstated man's ties to nature and the environment. They charged that naturalistic science and philosophy had submerged man's being too completely in matter and had thereby deprived him of his dual nature and classical conceptions of both mind and matter, body and spirit. Now all was matter, and mind, which had previously transcended matter, was tied to the sensory perceptions of the particular organism. Modern naturalistic philosophy and literature, criticized Babbitt, had left man mindless, a mere product of natural impulse and environmental conditioning.

Babbitt's New Humanism thus defended human freedom, the integrity of the intellect, and the natural capacity of mankind to understand fundamental reality—the same axioms that were so central to scholastic thought through the ages. But unlike scholasticism, it did so without appeal to dogma, revelation, or ecclesiastical authority. Instead, Babbitt and the New Humanism were determined to meet the twentieth century non-religious mind on its own intellectual ground, finding necessary intellectual support for their theories not in orthodox-Christian but in classical Far Eastern conceptions of human duality and universal consciousness.

Against current monistic postulates of naturalistic human nature, New Humanists thus maintained that man possessed—in Buddhist-classical fashion—a dual nature and identity: a "lower self," driven by natural impulse, emotion, and desire; and a "higher self," that was the seat of reason, intelligence, and restraint. Babbitt called this higher instrument of control the *"frein vital"* (vital control) or, with Paul Elmer More, the "inner check." Norman Foerster called it the "inner authority." But while all of these thinkers maintained that this higher ethical self stood apart from nature and matter, none, in keeping with their modern empiricist focus, was willing to concede that it had supernatural origins.[63]

The New Humanism, even with its deficiencies, enjoyed great popularity within the American Catholic literary and collegiate community well into the 1940s. It filled a void in the absence of a fully developed Catholic academic criticism. Babbitt's defense of traditional humanistic studies was welcomed also by many 1930s Catholic educational leaders who, like the New Humanists, were troubled by the increasing "electivization" of modern American higher education. St. Louis, Marquette, and Notre Dame Universities all offered upper-division courses in New Humanist criticism beginning in the 1930s. Marquette's offering, "Modern Humanism," was taught by Victor H. Hamm, a Catholic layman who wrote his Harvard dissertation under Babbitt in the early 1930s.

Alexander and Masse (who was at Regis College in the mid–1930s) were examples of teachers who integrated New Humanist theory into their regular English courses.

Alexander and Masse especially were eager to point out similarities between their own neo-scholastic and New Humanist principles. As young Catholic intellectuals they were self-conscious about the cultural isolation of American Catholicism and the low regard that scholastic philosophy suffered outside the Catholic intellectual community. It heartened them to see Catholic doctrines and principles embraced and articulated by a group of non-Catholic scholars. "Babbitt was raising questions that concerned the fundamentals of civilization," Masse wrote upon Babbitt's death in 1933, "and he was answering them as we would have answered them."[64] Father Alexander agreed. In the presence of a New Humanist, Alexander wrote, "You can give full rein to your anti-romanticism and suggest Blake and Shelley should be studied by psychiatrists. . . . You can even," the Jesuit continued, "quote St. Thomas as an authority."[65]

The New Humanism thus reinforced Alexander and Masse's conviction that Catholicism, amidst the confusion of the times, was destined to become an intellectual force in modern America. Babbitt, through Aristotle, was making Aquinas respectable to the modern intellect. Perhaps the New Humanism presaged the advent of the "intellectual Catholicism" sought so earnestly by these Jesuits and other proponents of the Catholic literary revival. Moreover, the New Humanism, despite its cranky demeanor, did claim a positive aesthetic and program of reform. Catholics wanted their literary revival seen in the same light.

Alexander was therefore almost self-congratulatory when, in a series of 1930 articles in the *Modern Schoolman* addressed to the New Humanism, he pointed out that the movement was using "as its principal weapons the arguments that have been current as commonplaces in Catholic circles since the beginning of neo-scholastism."[66] New Humanists insisted that western civilization was in need of a philosophical system that "gives proper place to the importance of the intellect and free will," noted the Jesuit. These were principles that a despised Catholic scholasticism had been saying all along. Alexander conceded that Babbitt and the New Humanism had not explicitly called for the return of scholastic principles to modern philosophy. But "the fact remains," he said, that in calling for the return of "freedom and intelligence" the New Humanism was advocating a program that scholasticism "may be pardoned for thinking her own."[67]

Yet, not all was agreement between Catholic and New Humanist critics. As early as 1928 Babbitt's most accomplished pupil, Anglo-Catholic critic T. S. Eliot, while sympathetic to the New Humanism, had exposed the fatal philosophical flaw that underlay the entire movement. Eliot observed that the New Humanism, by refusing to admit any transcendent or supernatural origins of its "higher self," in effect was relying upon the natural to check the natural. Eliot thus reminded its leaders that the New Humanism was tied to the very naturalism it so violently opposed. "Either everything in man can be traced as a development from below," Eliot noted, "or something must come from above." There was no middle way. "You must either be a naturalist or a supernaturalist."[68]

By 1932 the editors of the *Modern Schoolman* were noting similar problems. The New Humanists, they argued, were proposing an unworkable "Via Media." They were operating on a "mythical humanist plane between naturalism and supernaturalism."[69] Catholic critics thus increasingly insisted throughout the early 1930s that the New Humanism was in need of dogmatic religion, and particularly its philosophical cousin, Catholicism, if it hoped to make a lasting impact upon American intellectual and literary culture.

Perceptive Catholic scholars, however, soon recognized that this sort of criticism cut two ways. They recognized that in their very criticism of the New Humanism's intellectual shortcomings, they were raising questions about Catholicism's own failure to exercise intellectual leadership in the United States. In short, where were the Catholic Babbitts? Where were the Catholic leaders who could seize control of the New Humanism and direct it into Catholic channels? During the early 1930s then, there was an increasing call for serious Catholic critics and scholars to step forward and "complete" the New Humanism. True, one motivation was certainly to correct New Humanist "error," but there was also the conviction that here, finally, was an opportunity for American Catholics to assert intellectual and cultural leadership.

It was thus with some uneasiness that Notre Dame professor and literary critic Camile McCole discussed "Humanism's Challenge to Catholicism" in a 1930 article in *America*. McCole admitted that the New Humanist movement posed new and serious questions for American Catholic intellectual and cultural life. The New Humanists, observed McCole, had reminded Catholics of their "heritage as Catholics" and their own intellectual and philosophical tradition. "What are we going to do about it?" asked McCole. "Just how prepared are we to use these weapons? We must admit we have been inarticulate too long."[70]

Alexander was especially distressed that so few Catholic scholars could be found to take command of a movement that, in his view, was their intellectual and philosophical birthright. Unhappily, it again illustrated to the Jesuit that America's intellectual and cultural leadership was in non-Catholic rather than Catholic hands. The time was ripe for a workable philosophy that could reap the windfall of America's apparent desire to return to tradition and authority, wrote Alexander in 1930 in paraphrasing the concerns of minor New Humanist critic Sherlock Gass. It was unfortunate, added Alexander, that it was not Catholicism, but some "watered-down edition of it," that was "doing the reaping." "What we badly need in America," he insisted, "is a crop of men who know their scholastic philosophy, and know their literature and art, and what is more important, know them both together." Thus, Alexander urged his co-religionists to step out of the shadow of the New Humanists, to become more articulate, and thereby restore the Church to her rightful position as "Mother of the Arts."[71]

Alexander's call for a new generation of American Catholic scholar-critics was thus strikingly similar to Talbot's anxious appeal for American Catholic writers during this same era of the American Church. In both instances, that curious mixture of self-promotion and apostolic mission that dominated the early stages of the Catholic literary revival was evident. America's Catholics would redeem western civilization while at the same time bringing long-sought-after intellectual and cultural stature to a self-conscious, emergent immigrant Church.

6

The Search for the Great American Catholic Novel, I: Catholic Fiction to 1935

The novel "has a very definite and important role to play in the Catholic Literary Revival," wrote Georgetown University student James Albano early in 1936, but thus far, he continued, "its status is one of anticipation rather than achievement."[1] Albano, himself an aspiring young writer, identified a problem that was to trouble the American Catholic literary movement from beginning to end. Catholics believed they possessed the message, but they were sadly aware that they lacked persuasive and talented messengers, especially in the area of popular culture where the Catholic voice could receive its largest audience. The search for The Great American Catholic Novel is thus an important episode in twentieth century American Catholic life because it confirms on the popular level trends and attitudes that were occurring at other levels of Catholic society. To wit, the search for The Great American Catholic Novel, like the literary revival of which it was a part, reveals the three central themes that shaped American Catholic intellectual and cultural life between 1920 and 1960: the need to promote, to defend, and to redeem.[2]

THE NOVELS OF FRANK H. SPEARMAN, KATHLEEN THOMPSON NORRIS, AND LUCILLE PAPIN BORDEN

Given the American Church's minority status during the first third of the twentieth century, it comes as little surprise that the Catholic novel before 1935 exhibited the same defensiveness described by Paul R. Messbarger in his detailed study of nineteenth century American Catholic writers. In fact, the basic definition of Catholic fiction during this later era differed little from that of the previous century. In the opinion of writer and critic alike, a Catholic novel was a novel (1) written by a Catholic; (2) set against a specific Catholic background; (3) addressing an important matter of Christian faith or morality; and (4) professing a definite Catholic point of view.[3] The issues might change over the years, but the novel's polemical-didactic purpose remained the same.

With few exceptions, two concerns dominated the thematic structure of the American Catholic novel during the first third of the twentieth century. Of primary importance was the sanctity of Christian marriage and the family and the threat presented to these traditional institutions by liberal sexual attitudes, interfaith marriage, divorce, and birth control. The other important concern was the danger to religious belief and objective standards of right and wrong posed by the profusion of modern materialist philosophies. This second theme was often intertwined with the first, as Catholic writers frequently linked the modern breakdown in moral conduct with the subjectivity and chaos of twentieth century thought. Thus, the predominant themes in pre–1935 Catholic fiction roughly paralleled the well-documented concerns of the Catholic hierarchy during this time, as they mobilized the faithful against Margaret Sanger and the National Birth Control League on the one hand, while delivering ultimatums against Modernist theologians on the other.

One could focus upon a number of early twentieth century Catholic writers whose work reflected these themes, but three stand out: Frank H. Spearman, Kathleen Thompson Norris, and Lucille Papin Borden. All thought of themselves as Catholic writers and received the approbation of most Catholic reviewers. They also contributed extensively to the Catholic press in articles devoted to parochial issues of the day.

Reared and educated during the late nineteenth century, Spearman (1859–1937), Borden (1873–1948), and Norris (1880–1960) belonged in temperament and outlook to the pre-World War I era. Spearman was of early American heritage. Raised in the Congregational church, he converted to Catholicism when he was twenty-five.[4] Like many twentieth century American Catholic writers, Spearman did not devote full attention to stories dealing with religious themes. In fact, he was probably best known for his epics of the nineteenth century American West. His most popular novel, *Whispering Smith* (1906), later adapted to the screen, was a western railroad saga. Spearman's religious novels were *Robert Kimberly* (1911) and *The Marriage Verdict* (1923).[5] Both address the problem of interfaith marriage and divorce.

Norris grew up in a large middle-class family in San Francisco, California. Deeply religious (as a youngster, she dedicated herself to the Virgin and "wore blue for years"), Norris found her security shattered by the almost simultaneous death of both parents.[6] As the eldest daughter, nineteen-year-old Kathleen was left with the responsibility of keeping home and family together. Her experiences as a young working woman on her own in the city became the source of many of her stories. Norris began writing seriously after her marriage to Charles Gilman Norris, brother of Frank Norris (*The Octopus*), and their subsequent relocation to New York City, where Mr. Norris also published novels while working for *American Magazine*.

Norris's girlhood ambition to be a "distinctively Catholic writer" soon yielded to the harsh realities of New York City publishing. As Norris later wrote, she was told constantly by secular publishers (most of her novels were published by Doubleday) to "soften the Catholic atmosphere" in her stories. Thus, early on Norris turned to the more generic theme of "the problem of the decent girl of today" out in the modern world.[7]

The decision opened more doors to non-Catholic publishers but, at the same time, permitted Norris to direct her readers' attention toward the moral themes of family, marriage, and divorce which so preoccupied Church authorities at this time. Moreover, Norris became adept over the years at slipping subtle references to Catholic faith and practice (prayers at bedtime, a prize won at a "Catholic fair") into her work, leaving little question that most of her heroines came from Catholic backgrounds. Thus, while Norris's only truly Catholic novel was *Little Ships* (1925)[8]—a very readable semi-autobiographical account of an extended Irish-American family living in San Francisco—she nevertheless received wide Catholic support. Her novels (seventy in all) enjoyed particular favor among Catholic schoolgirls, even into the 1950s. Norris also enjoyed the special friendship of literary critic and *America* editor Francis X. Talbot and served on the selection committee of Talbot's Catholic Book Club during the late 1920s and early 1930s.

Unlike Norris and Spearman, Lucille Papin Borden's identity as a Catholic writer was unequivocal. A lay Catholic aristocrat by birth and inclination, Borden grew up in an old St. Louis Catholic family that traced its lineage to British and French royalty. Her 1898 marriage to wealthy New York milk heir Gerald Borden further enhanced her status. Serious Catholics, the Bordens divided their time between their New York City residence and the cultural centers of Europe, where they listed as their friends English Catholic writer Robert Hugh Benson, numerous Vatican prelates, and three twentieth century popes. Borden boasted in 1945 that Pius XI had once told her that all her books were in the Vatican library.[9]

Borden's major Catholic novels included *The Candlestick Makers* (1923), *Gentleman Riches* (1925), *From Out Magdala* (1927), and *Silver Trumpets Calling* (1931).[10] Published by The Macmillan Company, which maintained a special religious division for writers of Borden's ilk, they were unblushingly Catholic in theme, characterization, and tone.

If one were to synthesize a common plot line from the many stories that make up the body of Spearman's, Borden's, and Norris's work, it might read as follows: unmarried man falls in love with unhappily married Christian woman, thus confronting woman with the moral dilemma of divorce. Or: weak-willed heroine falls in with permissive (usually non-Catholic) crowd who affect quotations from Bertrand Russell and seduce her with talk of divorce, birth control, and realtivistic-hedonistic lifestyle. Each plot and subplot sets up dramatic situations that force the protagonist to choose between the attractive but more ephemeral path of divorce, immorality, and subjectivity, or the harder option of virtue, family responsibility and adherence to Christian dogma.

Thus, in Norris's *Mother* (1911), Margaret Paget, a decent but restless young woman who seeks freedom and independence in the big city, is placed in the position of choosing between the subjective attitudes and lifestyle of her free-living, mostly childless and divorced city friends, or the more mundane but meaningful joys of homemaking and childrearing represented by her mother. The love of a traditional young man who admires the mother she dismissed as old-fashioned opens Margaret's eyes to the fact that she and her beloved brothers and sisters might never have been born had her mother practiced her own selfish philosophy of life.[11]

Norris's *Margaret Yorke* (1930) is also a story of choices.[12] Margaret, a pretty young woman who flees with her child from an unhappy first marriage with an unprincipled older man, is confronted with the problem of divorce when she falls in love with another. Despite well-meaning appeals from the latter, Margaret remains true to her "vows." As happens in many of Norris's stories, the disagreeable spouse dies, clearing the way for Margaret's new union.

Sometimes, however, death does not intervene. Such a case becomes the occasion for Spearman's *Marriage Verdict*, where the author skillfully builds drama around the ancient canon law concept of Pauline Privilege (the assumption that Christians may "legally" break bonds with unbaptized partners if the latter refuse to permit the free and untrammeled practice of the faith) and annulment, as the hero and heroine rush to the altar before the rejected spouse can pretend to change his misguided ways. Annulment is also the solution to the heroine's dilemma in Borden's *Gentleman Riches*.

The other theme that dominated American Catholic fiction during this period—the chaos of modern thought and the breakdown of objective moral order—was less pronounced than the first theme of Christian marriage and morality. Nevertheless, while the primary focus of most Catholic American writers during this period was upon narrower questions of personal morality, the underlying assumption in most of their stories was that divorce, birth control, and permissiveness were a consequence of the subjectivism and relativism that, in their view, permeated the leading philosophies of the day. "I think everything was better before the war," intones a wise priest in Borden's *Silver Trumpets Calling*, commenting on the alarming rise in the American divorce rate. "Most modern ethics," he adds, "or rather, want of them, came out of the war."[13] It was principally through asides like these that Borden, Spearman, and Norris made their case against modern thought.

These writers' choice of villains and the books they read is also revealing. Invariably, villains in these stories are philosophical relativists. Skeptical of religion, they adhere to subjective standards of morality and reality. "[George Bernard] Shaw is right, and don't you think for a second that he isn't," chirps callow Van Murchison to innocent but naive Gail Lawrence in Norris's *The Lucky Lawrences* (1930).[14] Van's hedonistic-relativistic attitude would later get Gail's younger sister, Ariel, "in trouble."

Borden was particularly adept at linking her villains to modern materialist philosophies. In *Silver Trumpets Calling*, the story of a heroic Russian princess and her efforts to rescue Russian children from communist rule, the chief villain, for example, is the Soviet social system itself, with its policies of "eugenic breeding" and "registry marriages," and its "godless" view of humanity. In *Gentleman Riches*, Borden's chief antagonist is the sinister Ewen Hayle, who almost succeeds in extinguishing the spiritual life of the weak-willed Ginestra Dane. Hayle, the reader learns, had been led down the "path of indifferentism" through reading volumes of natural science, socialist theory, Darwinism, and primitive philosophy. Happily, Hayle mends his ways and finishes life as a Franciscan brother.

The novels of Spearman, Norris, and Borden, inasmuch as they lack the complexity and social realism found in the major works of the period, give popular expression to the paradigm of Catholic Innocence popularized by William Halsey and other scholars of twentieth century American Catholic thought. As Halsey insightfully notes, while major postwar American writers like John Dos Passos and Ernest Hemingway were exploring the increasing change, impenetrability, and ambiguity of modern life, Catholic writers during these same years barely touched upon these themes. True, a subplot of Spearman's *Marriage Verdict* focuses upon a management-labor dispute, but that was not the point of the story. It is also true that Norris did not blink at the fact that working women on their own, passion, divorce, and premarital sex were inevitable consequences of the changing status of women in the post-World War I era. But in *Mother* and many of her other stories, Norris looked back to a simpler, more wholesome world. Indeed, many of Norris's stories have a nineteenth century Horatio Alger-like quality about them, with virtuous heroines frequently rewarded by material security and success, usually in the form of marriage to a promising young man.

Idealism, not realism, was the primary message of Norris and other Catholic writers of this era. Their intention was to show that right existed and that virtue counted; that there was an objective moral structure inherent in the universe, and to follow its laws promised certainty, happiness, and salvation.

Given the partisan nature of the Catholic novel at this time, Catholic characters seem to see this moral structure more clearly than others. Subjectivism, relativism, and the like, simply do not work for most Catholic heroes and heroines in these stories. For example, in Norris's *The Lucky Lawrences*, the Catholic heroine, Gail Lawrence, soon discovers she does not really belong to the "smart crowd" she once found so attractive. Feeling miserable and alone, Gail admits that her "training was not right, her background was not right" and she would be a fool to pretend differently.[15] Similarly, Alice MacBirney's divorce from her profligate husband in Spearman's *Robert Kimberly* nevertheless leaves her feeling depressed and empty, with something in her subconscious telling her that while her divorce may be perfectly legal in the eyes of the State, she still had disturbed some higher moral law. Alice's non-Catholic fiance, Robert Kimberly, by contrast, finds her ennui incomprehensible.

An overriding message in Catholic fiction during this period was thus that Catholics were different somehow, and it was the demands of their faith that made them so. "The world will always think us wrong, a peculiar people and with principles beyond its comprehension," comments the stern archbishop to Kimberly after refusing the divorced Alice remarriage in the Church. "We cannot help it."[16] This was the price one paid for maintaining principles and standards in a subjective world.

CATHOLIC CHARACTERIZATION AND CATHOLIC IDENTITY

Separation is often a necessary corollary to innocence. This deeply felt sense of Catholic differentness overshadows the characterizations not only of Spearman, Norris, and Borden, but also of most other Catholic writers of the period. In nearly all cases, Catholics are described as a people apart. "I am a Catholic. Divorce has no meaning for us," haughtily proclaims Yolande to her unprincipled husband Gifford in Isabel C. Clarke's *Fine Clay* (1914) when Gifford (a non-Catholic) reveals that he had previously married and divorced. Thus, wrote Clarke, Yolande chose "the path which alone was open to her as a Catholic." She leaves Gifford because under Catholic moral theology, she has "never been" his wife.[17] While most non-Catholics in pre–1935 Catholic novels are uncertain about first principles and are without a theology of birth, death, and marriage, Catholics, by contrast, are ruled by fixed standards of right and wrong. Armed with a firm philosophy of life, Catholic characters almost always see more deeply into reality and thus are able to deal more meaningfully with life's joys and tragedies. Paul Jarrette, an agnostic university professor and fallen-away Catholic in Ethel Cook Eliot's *Her Soul to Keep* (1935), finds that he is without fundamental resources to fall back upon when faced with the impending death of his critically ill wife. Even his familiarity with voguish modernistic conceptions of the soul and "spiritism," gained from reading the likes of William James and Sir Oliver Lodge, is not enough to reassure Paul of his wife's eternal survival. Lucia Rue, a Catholic friend who had lost her own husband in an automobile accident a few years before, sadly reflects that had Jarrette believed in the Resurrection, he might have spared himself this terrible agony.[18]

Lucia Rue illustrates an additional dimension of Catholic characterization during this period. Even though Lucia has received less formal education than many of her university friends, she is, nevertheless, considerably more enlightened than they. While their educated and "advanced" friends fall under the sway of every new philosophical, psychological, and sociological theory, are led by fashion or popular opinion, and believe that to reject religion is a sign of progressive thinking, Catholic heroes and heroines, by contrast, hold steadfastly to the timeless, common-sense principles and traditions of their faith. The modern sophisticate may be more clever than the dogmatic believer, but he is never wiser. This usually becomes apparent in a debate, with the Catholic coolly and quietly presenting the Church's answer to an important moral or philosophical question while exposing the modern solution as shallow and ephemeral.

Because they belong to a demanding faith, Catholics, furthermore, almost always possess greater strength of character than non-Catholics. In Borden's *The Candlestick Makers* (1923), which describes the evils of eugenics, family planning, and birth control, a group of non-Catholic women (against their better "instincts") are pressed into attending an offensive lecture on abortion by the freethinking Hildegarde, a strong advocate of such practices. They fear that to decline would make them appear less modern. Catholic woman Faith Desmond alone refuses to participate, despite condescending asides that she is "medieval" and "priest-ridden."[19]

Catholic characters subsequently are more efficient and self-possessed, and act as a stabilizing influence upon those around them. During times of crisis, they know what to do. They have the power of prayer and the certainty of their faith behind them. When her foster daughter Jane's life is threatened by a difficult delivery, Lucia Rue in *Her Soul to Keep* quickly organizes the remaining members of the family to pray for her. Calling home, she orders her two younger daughters to recite the *Memorare* for Jane. "Light the votive candles and the vigil light in my room," adds Lucia. "Go now."[20]

In many cases this special reservoir of strength is manifested physically. Catholic characters usually stand taller and walk straighter than non-Catholics. Faith Desmond (*The Candlestick Makers*) has "clear eyes," suggesting her inner virtue and keen insight into life.[21] Kate Walsh of Kathleen Norris's *Little Ships* is similarly spirited and pretty. She is "the happiest of creatures," despite her humble surroundings and heavy responsibilities as eldest daughter in caring for her poor, down-on-their-luck, Irish family.[22]

Recognizable by their high moral tone, quiet dignity, inner strength, steady values, and realistic attitude toward life, Catholic characters are usually secretly respected by their non-Catholic friends. Non-Catholics soon realize that Catholics have something they lack, "something definite and tangible to grasp."[23] A conversion usually follows. Diana Travers, the weak-willed heroine of *The Candlestick Makers*, is led into the Church through the example of Faith Desmond. Hildegarde also finds salvation. Mortally wounded by an inexplicable attack from her pet parrot, she is baptized by her Catholic husband, Michael, and dies kissing the crucifix. In *Her Soul to Keep* Paul Jarrette (who, it turns out, is really the father of Jane's illegitimate child) is likewise drawn back into the Church through the efforts of Lucia Rue. Paul confesses his sin and shortly marries Lucia.

A number of specific historical factors, apart from the rather diffuse explanatory paradigm of Innocence, can account for the cultivated sense of differentness found in the Catholic novels under discussion. First, one cannot discount the disproportionate influence of English Catholic letters upon American Catholic literary culture during the first three decades of this century. English Catholic writers like Isabel C. Clarke, Owen Francis Dudley, and Robert Hugh Benson were turning out sectarian novels of Catholic life long before Borden, Norris, and other Americans. In Dudley's *Masterful Monk* trilogy (1929–1948) the Catholic philosophical novel reached the state of the art, where the Catholic position (stated through the imposing figure of Brother Anselm Thornton) on important philosophical and moral issues of the day was constantly contrasted with, and shown superior to, that of an assortment of sinister amoralists, materialists, and "pseudo-philosophers."[24]

Benson (1871–1914) was the most respected Catholic novelist of his day. During a brief but prolific literary career, this convert son of the Archbishop of Canterbury wrote nearly a dozen historical novels. *Come Rack! Come Rope!* (1912) portrayed the harrowing adventures of recusant Catholics during Elizabethan times. Benson's Catholics in nearly all these works are a people literally set apart, physically and religiously. Mainly of aristocratic blood, they live in enclaves (usually in old Catholic houses) and are looked upon with suspicion and hostility by their Protestant neighbors. Most show unusual conviction, devotion, and courage in remaining steadfast to the faith, despite penal laws, charges of political treason and "popery," and, in some cases, the gibbet.[25]

Both Benson and Dudley had a large American Catholic audience. Benson's *By What Authority*, 1904 (based upon the life of English Jesuit martyr Edmund Campion) ranked second only to Canon Patrick Sheehan's *My New Curate* (1899) as the most popular Catholic novel in Father Talbot's 1923 plebiscite to determine "The Best Ten Catholic Books." Dudley's novels frequently were assigned as supplementary reading in Catholic college philosophy courses during the 1930s.[26]

American Catholic writers, critics, and readers thus found in English Catholic writers Benson and Dudley, no less than in Newman and Chesterton, a modern Catholic literary tradition and another Catholic subculture with which to identify.[27] The consequences of this Anglo-American Catholic cultural union were not always fortunate. By identifying so closely with the English Catholic tradition, American Catholic fiction during the 1920s and early 1930s remained, for the most part, both imitative and didactic. More important, the example of English Catholic clannishness only reinforced already strong Catholic American tendencies in that direction during this same period.

The English influence notwithstanding, historians and sociologists have long known that sectarianism itself can be an important source of group identity for people outside the social and cultural mainstream. R. Laurence Moore's *Religious Outsiders and the Making of Americans* (1986) throws important light upon this theme.[28] Moore illustrates that nonmainstream American religious groups—Mormons, nineteenth century Catholics, twentieth century Protestant Fundamentalists, Jews, Afro-American churches, and Christian Scientists—purposefully employed the rhetoric of outsiderhood as a strategy to establish their own self-definition and identity during their American historical development. Moore argues that outsiderhood, once embraced, communicated a sense of "chosenness" that was both culturally binding and redemptive, allowing these groups to stand in critical opposition to many aspects of American society while simultaneously laying claim to their share of it.

Moore's insights are similarly relevant to the study of early twentieth century American Catholicism and the Catholic American Church. For one, the paradigm of Catholic Innocence—which is merely another manifestation of outsiderhood—takes on a wider, more pragmatic context under Moore's construction. The history of American religious outsiderhood demonstrates that, in crucial respects, the social record of twentieth century American Catholicism did not differ significantly from that of other non-mainstream religious groups. All, in some way, were forced to "invent" themselves out of a sense of opposition to the mainstream.

Apart from Moore's study, moreover, history reminds us that sectarian self-enclosure is not necessarily confined to self-conscious religious groups. Here again the experience of twentieth century Catholics invites comparison to that of early nineteenth century Americans, when this nation's first cultural leaders, stung by sneering accounts of American character and culture in the European press, found vindication by constructing an elaborate mythology that belligerently contrasted Old World decadence, idleness, and despotism with New World "republicanism," practicality, and "innocence."[29] We see that pre–1935 Catholic American writers such as Spearman, Norris, and Borden (and the characters through whom they spoke) responded in much the same fashion, as they defined the Catholic American subculture in polar opposites from the culture that had dismissed it. Liabilities thus were transformed into assets under American Catholic writers and cultural leaders during Catholicism's time of troubles in early twentieth century America. Like Spearman's inflexible archbishop, Catholics admitted they were orthodox, and were proud of it. Catholics were indeed different, and better because they were different!

"The Church," boasted Talbot in 1938, "remains traditional." Echoing the plot line of many of the pre–1935 Catholic novels he reviewed with acclaim, Talbot continued: "It flits not with the upstart reformer or philosopher of the century, it wavers not with the fads of the time, it wriggles not with the pressure of the extremes."[30]

Early twentieth century American Catholic fiction writers, not unlike Father Talbot and the anti-Modernist clergy of his generation, thus posed Catholic tradition and orthodoxy in virtuous contrast to a rootless and flabby secular culture. Others might accommodate paganism, but Catholics would not. The most despicable character in Catholic novels of this period was the apostate, the Catholic who would trade his or her faith for admission to the secular world.

A self-conscious American Catholic subculture thus discovered in its own fiction of the first third of the twentieth century that it possessed "exquisite qualities as a race" (to borrow a phrase from Henry James). In their very Catholicism, Catholic Americans found their own unique cultural identity and the key to their American cultural role. "American civilization," Talbot said, "needs [Catholic] ideas, dreadfully, and . . . this civilization can be saved only by the infiltration of the Catholic theory of human and divine relations."[31]

It may have been a tremendous religious burden to remain the last believers in America, but it was also an occasion for pride. Like "Lucia Rue," "Faith Desmond," and "Brother Anselm," Catholics could hold their heads high during the 1920s and early 1930s secure in the knowledge of the superiority of their values. Living apart from the world, they would act as a light to the world, a special people with a special destiny.

Whatever framework one uses to understand their intention, the novels of Norris, Spearman, Eliot, and Borden properly belong to the separatist Catholic "ghetto." Denominative, antisecular, and aggressively apologetic, they reflect the intellectual and cultural isolation of the American Catholic cultural community during one of the most difficult periods in its national history.

By the mid–1930s, however, a new mood permeated the American Church. Open, interactive, socially conscious, and, in many ways, self-critical, it would prove fertile ground for the next generation of American Catholic writers.

Part II

TRANSFORMATION, 1935–1955

7

The Transformation of the Catholic Literary Revival in the American Catholic College During the 1930s and 1940s

The mid–1930s represented a transition period in the Catholic literary revival and in the development of American Catholic religious thought. As in all transition periods, a number of contradictory emphases stood side-by-side. The promotional-apologetic theme in the Catholic literary revival remained a strong and constant factor. Lucille Papin Borden persisted in writing Catholic novels upholding Catholic moral and philosophical positions well into the 1940s, and indiscriminating Catholic critics like Francis X. Talbot continued to review them with predictable acclaim. Neo-scholastic philosophy still held the status of ideology in most American Catholic intellectual circles.[1] And there were still mid–1930s summonses by Daniel A. Lord and others for American Chestertons.

The history of American Catholicism in the 1930s, however, will be remembered not for how much it resembled the 1920s, but for how much it represented reversals in the mentality of the previous decade. The events of the 1930s had much to do with these changes. The Depression called forth new developments in Catholic social thought and, more than any other twentieth century event, forced Catholic Americans out of the parochial group-interest mentality that marked the 1920s Church.

New theological emphases—the Incarnation, the liturgy, and developments in Christology and the theology of the Mystical Body—also reshaped the intellectual outlook of many Catholic Americans. These theological breakthroughs were also linked to 1930s events as the challenge of Protestant neo-orthodoxy, the spiritual crisis between the wars, the rise of dehumanizing totalitarian ideologies, and finally war itself, forced Catholic thinkers, first in Europe and then in America, to give new content to the fundamental mysteries of their faith. These new theological emphases did not overturn the neo-scholastic philosophical hegemony, but they did result in more meaningful categories through which Catholics could address the spiritual crises of the age.

The neo-scholastic synthesis itself was revitalized during the 1930s as European Catholic thinkers like Etienne Gilson and Jacques Maritain repudiated the hyper-rationalism of the scholastic manuals in favor of a return to the "real" Thomas Aquinas—the Aquinas found in the original texts.[2] Scholasticism after 1935 was less essentialist and abstract and more willing to deal with the contingencies of individual existence and the concrete questions of the day.

There was thus a positive tone and dynamism to post–1935 American Catholic intellectual life that was absent from the negative postures of the previous era. This was due in large part to the impact of Europeans and European developments in Catholic thought upon the American Church. Moreover, many of the leading Catholic lay intellectuals behind the European resurgence actually lived in America after 1935. The most notable were Gilson and Maritain, who by the late 1930s were permanent refugees from fascism. Their physical presence added to the air of freshness and movement besides providing models for American lay Catholic intellectual achievement.

All of these factors resulted in an extraordinarily fertile period in American Catholic intellectual development after 1935: Maritain, Gilson, Christopher Dawson; Popes Leo XIII and Pius XI; Georges Bernanos, Francois Mauriac, and Graham Greene; social Catholicism, Catholic culture, and the liturgical movement. These were the thinkers, concepts, and ideas that dominated the most progressive circles of American Catholic intellectual and cultural life after 1935. When scores of idealistic young Catholics spoke of creating a new synthesis of religion and culture between 1935 and 1955, it was upon these men and ideas that they chiefly drew. It was principally the American Catholic college student who benefited from this post–1935 reorientation of Catholic thought and the creative American Catholic encounter with the Europeans. Courses on "The Catholic Literary Revival" introduced into the American Catholic college curriculum beginning in the mid–1930s often served as the first contact point between American Catholic undergraduates and the avante-garde Catholic thinkers of Europe. Courses on Catholic social doctrine were also introduced at this time. Many Catholic students left those courses with a deepened understanding of their faith as an intellectual and cultural force in the modern world.

The following two chapters discuss these courses addressing the Catholic literary revival and Catholic social thought, and how the Catholic intellectual and literary revival actually penetrated a representative number of midwestern Catholic college and university communities between

1935 and 1955, the period that coincided with the greatest intellectual ferment. The discussion includes both Jesuit and non-Jesuit institutions. The Jesuit schools treated include Loyola University of Chicago, Marquette University, and St. Louis University. The non-Jesuit schools include St. John's University (Collegeville, Minnesota), the College of St. Benedict (St. Joseph, Minnesota), Mundelein College (Chicago), the College of St. Catherine (St. Paul, Minnesota), and the University of Notre Dame at South Bend, Indiana.

COURSES ON "THE CATHOLIC LITERARY REVIVAL"

By 1940 American Catholic colleges and universities offered a wide variety of courses in modern Catholic literature. In that year the Franciscan Educational Conference (a national organization of Franciscan secondary and college teachers) surveyed Catholic colleges and universities, asking them to list all courses in "Modern Catholic Literatures" offered at their institutions. Of the 120 schools that responded, 75 (62 percent) indicated that they offered at least one course matching that broad description. Most revealing was the number of courses specifically examining the Catholic literary revival. Specific courses on "The Catholic Literary Revival" were listed by 25 (33 percent) of the 75 schools offering courses in modern Catholic literature.[3]

The closest rival to explicit courses on the Catholic literary revival was a course on "Newman" offered by 14 of the respondent schools.[4] The likelihood exists, though, that Newman was also studied in relationship to the revival since he was linked to its origins.

A closer look at our sample of midwestern Catholic colleges and universities adds specificity to the Franciscan study. By 1945 all eight of the midwestern schools sampled offered either fixed courses on "The Catholic Literary Revival" or courses treating aspects of the revival.[5] Loyola University, for example, listed a course on "Modern Catholic Writers" as early as 1924, describing it as "a review of the Catholic revival in English letters."[6] Marquette University offered a course in "The Catholic Spirit in English Literature" as early as 1931 but changed the title to "The Catholic Literary Revival" in 1935, underscoring the tendency during the mid–1930s to isolate and treat the revival as historical event.[7]

The revival received as much attention in midwestern non-Jesuit as Jesuit schools. St. John's University was offering a course on "The Catholic Literary Revival" by 1935, two years before Jesuit-run St. Louis University introduced such a course.[8]

The majority of the courses treating the Catholic literary revival were introduced into these midwestern schools between 1931 and 1945 and coincided with a set of concerns seen as early as the mid–1920s when many Catholic college leaders called for the introduction of Newman into the curriculum. These concerns included increasing distress over the progressive vocationalization of Catholic college and university studies as Catholic insitutions responded to the demands of post-World War I urban-industrial culture, anxieties over the departmentalization of knowledge and the attendant demise of humanistic studies, and, finally, the apprehension shared by many Catholic college administrators and teachers that Catholic higher education was losing its old vision of unity and function.[9] The deepening socio-cultural crises of the 1930s further added to these concerns.

American Catholic higher education experienced tremendous institutional growth between 1930 and 1950. In 1930 there were 102,000 students enrolled in Catholic colleges, seminaries, and universities in the United States. By 1948 the total enrollment was 293,000, an increase of 153 percent.[10] But many Catholic American educational and cultural leaders expressed real dismay that graduates of Catholic colleges and universities were being sent into the world as businessmen, teachers, and technicians, but not as Catholics. Even within the shrinking liberal arts curriculum there was a concern by many Catholic educators that there were too few courses that specifically addressed the Catholic-Christian heritage. Franciscan educator Victor Hermann thus complained before the literature section of the 1940 Francisan Educational Conference that contemporary Catholic students were regularly exposed to "the glories of Emerson's transcendentalism" but seldom encountered a Catholic structure of ideas in their Catholic college literature courses. The conference ended with a resolution encouraging all friars engaged in teaching literature "to be ever mindful of our Catholic literary heritage, both in their criticism and in the selection of content for study."[11]

Increasingly, then, Catholic educational and cultural leaders called upon Catholic colleges and universities during the 1930s and 1940s to revitalize their curriculum. Catholic college leaders believed that amidst the growing confusion, disintegration, and disorder of the age, the Catholic college, aware of its overriding purpose, had something positive to give to the world. A resolution at the 1933 meeting of the National Catholic Education Association therefore declared:

Because a materialistic attitude and philosophy have dominated secular education, giving it a divided and distorted view of life . . . the Catholic colleges emphatically assert that their function is to give a totality of view regarding life, in which God and the things of God have their proper place.[12]

It was this intellectual and academic environment that was most responsible for the introduction of courses on the Catholic literary revival into the Catholic college curriculum during the 1930s and 1940s. Inspired by a drive toward intellectual and cultural synthesis both within their own educational establishment and the larger Catholic community, American Catholic college leaders sought to give modern students a structure of ideas and a vision of life that was thoroughly Christian. Preparation for salvation was one goal, training for Christian leadership, another.

The formats for the courses on the Catholic literary revival introduced at midwestern Catholic colleges and universities beginning in the mid–1930s naturally reflected the strengths and preferences of the individual instructor, but some patterns do emerge. In general, these courses had three main objectives: (1) to expose Catholic undergraduates to their Catholic literary heritage; (2) to study the revival as a historical event; and (3) to discuss the social and cultural implications of Catholicism within the modern world.

Thus, in 1935 Marquette University described its course on "The Catholic Literary Revival" in the following manner:

English 145: This course concerns itself with the Catholic contribution to English letters from 1800 to the present. Selections from such representative Catholic authors as Newman, [Francis] Thompson, [Conventry] Patmore, [Alice] Meynell, Belloc, Chesterton, Dawson, [Maurice] Baring, Sheila Kaye-Smith are studied. . . . The course further stresses the phenomenon of the Catholic revival and its manifestations in modern English literature. Such topics as the cultural and artistic implications of Catholicism . . . are discussed.[13]

The College of St. Benedict described its 1936 course on the "Literature of the Catholic Revival" somewhat more tersely:

English 49s: Newman, Thompson, Meynell, Patmore, Chesterton, Belloc, Maritain, Dawson, Christopher Hollis, and others.[14]

Finally, the College of St. Catherine, which initiated its course on the revival in 1942, described its focus as "a study of the development of the Catholic point of view in fiction, poetry, essays, biography, and drama since Newman."[15]

We thus see that while these courses were primarily literary in focus, they also turned their attention to Catholic social and cultural thought (Dawson, Maritain, Hollis, Belloc), just as Calvert Alexander (*The Catholic Literary Revival*) had done in his history of the revival in 1935.[16] Catholics, as previously noted, always took a broad view of their literary revival, seeing it as a component of the larger Catholic intellectual revival manifesting itself in all realms of modern thought.

The gradual introduction of French, German, and other European Catholic thinkers and writers into the body of these courses was another developing pattern in the 1930s and 1940s. Initially, there was a strong

English flavor to these courses. This was due, in part, to the continued influence of Alexander's Anglocentric *Catholic Literary Revival*, which was often used as the primary textbook. By the late 1930s, however, English Catholic apologists like Chesterton, Belloc, and Ronald Knox were sharing the stage with newly translated French writers like Maritain, Bernanos, Mauriac, Paul Claudel, Leon Bloy, and Charles Peguy. The thoughts of important twentieth century Catholic theologians such as German Karl Adam and German-Italian Romano Guardini also began to be addressed.

Two major anthologies, specifically designed for use in courses on the Catholic literary revival—Sr. Mary Louise's *Over the Bent World* (1939) and Jesuit Francis B. Thornton's *Return to Tradition* (1947)—signaled this change. Both anthologies contained extensive selections from French and German Catholic writers, although Sr. Louise's book, compiled with the assistance of Jesuits Alexander and Lord, was still heavily weighted in favor of the English.[17] Thornton's anthology, however, represented the most dramatic change. It contained an entire section on recently translated modern French Catholic writers including selections from Bloy's *The Woman Who was Poor* (trans. 1939), Bernanos's *The Diary of a Country Priest* (trans. 1938), Maritain's *Art and Poetry* (trans. 1943), and many others. Another section on "The Liturgical Revival" that included selections from Virgil Michel's *The Liturgy of the Church* (1937), Adam's *The Spirit of Catholicism* (trans. 1935), and Guardini's *The Spirit of the Liturgy* (trans. 1935) illustrates the increasing influence of the liturgical movement upon American Catholic intellectual life and culture after 1935.[18]

THREE MODERN CATHOLIC THINKERS: MARITAIN, DAWSON, AND MICHEL

"Cultural Catholicism" and its corollary, "Catholic culture," were much-used terms within the American Catholic educational and intellectual community between 1935 and 1955. These terms, along with such phrases as "organic unity," "synthetic vision," and "integral Catholicism," writes Philip Gleason, became almost buzz words of American Catholic discussion beginning in the mid–1930s.[19] The concept of Catholic culture nevertheless did derive from a larger intellectual framework. For the most part, when Catholics employed the term, they were drawing upon the ideas of the necessary relationship between religion and culture articulated by three modern Catholic thinkers often studied within the context of the Catholic literary revival: Maritain, Dawson, and the American Benedictine monk Virgil Michel. It was through these thinkers that many Catholic undergraduates first awakened to the intellectual dimensions of their faith and its cultural and social implications for modern times. A discussion of these men's ideas and their impact upon the intellectual and religious development of American Catholics during the 1930s and 1940s follows.[20]

Dawson and Maritain, like so many figures in both the English and French Catholic revivals, were converts to Catholicism. Instrumental in the conversion of each were patterns of ideas they encountered in their university training. Dawson's (1889–1970) road to Rome reflects in certain respects that of earlier Oxford convert John Henry Newman. As a Trinity College student in the pre–World War I era, Dawson saw in the authority of Rome an attractive alternative to the seeming discontinuity of his own Anglican congregation. The encouragement of Oxford classmate and recent Catholic convert E. I. Watkin and future wife Valery Mills persuaded Dawson to enter the Church in 1914. Dawson's Oxford encounter with the thought of German sociologist Ernst Troeltsch and the latter's analysis of the necessary relationship between religion and culture also played a key role in Dawson's intellectual development.[21]

Maritain (1890–1968), who was of liberal Protestant background, came to Catholicism by way of French vitalist philosopher Henri Bergson. As a biology student at the Sorbonne during the early 1900s, Maritain became disillusioned with the narrow scientism promulgated by his teachers. His friend Charles Peguy encouraged Maritain to attend the lectures of Bergson at the College de France, where, in Bergson's non-positivistic affirmation of spirit, intuition, and free will, Maritain found the "sense of the Absolute" for which he had been searching. Encouraged by Leon Bloy, Maritain converted to Catholicism in 1906, as did his wife Räissa.[22]

Michel (1890–1938), unlike Maritain and Dawson, was a born Catholic and raised by a strong religious St. Paul, Minnesota, German Catholic family. But Michel, too, underwent a sort of conversion. While studying scholastic philosophy at Belgium's Louvain Unversity during the mid–1920s, the young Benedictine became absorbed in the ideas of the liturgical movement then underway in the elite Catholic circles of Europe. He was especially impressed with Belgian liturgist Dom Lambert Beauduin's efforts to restore the neglected doctrine of the Mystical Body of Christ to a central place in the theology of the Church. The socially minded Michel saw in the concept of the Mystical Body a totally new way of looking at a unified humanity and a dynamically vital force for social and cultural change.[23]

When Michel returned to the United States in 1925 he made the Benedictine Abbey at St. John's University a center of liturgical studies. In 1926 Michel, with the help of St. Louis University Jesuit Gerald Ellard, founded the liturgical review *Orate Fratres* to diffuse the liturgical movement throughout America. Ellard (1894–1963) played a key role in promoting the liturgical movement within the American Jesuit community during the 1930s. His *Christian Life and Worship* (1933), stressing the importance of the Mystical Body in Christian life, was a standard text-book used in Jesuit college sophomore religion classes during the 1930s and 1940s and served as the first introduction of many college-age Catholics to the social implications of the liturgy. The book proved so popular that its Catholic publisher (Bruce Publishing Company of Milwaukee, Wisconsin) issued a separate edition for the general public. The college edition ran through nineteen printings and sold over 63,000 copies between 1933 and 1963.[24]

Catholic undergraduates during the early 1930s encountered Dawson and Maritain through the *Essays in Order* series, begun in 1931 by the English Catholic publishing house Sheed and Ward. Dawson served as the series' general editor and contributed two essays. The series represented a remarkable intellectual event. It was, in effect, an extended symposium on Catholic thought addressed to the problems of the day. Its list of contributors was impressive. They included, apart from Dawson and Maritain, German philosopher Peter Wust (*Crisis in the West*, 1931), English critic E. I. Watkin (*The Bow in the Clouds*, 1931), Russian emigre-philosopher Nicholas Berdyaev (*The Russian Revolution*, 1931), and others. The series captured the sense of cultural crisis and ferment that characterized much of Catholic social and cultural thought during the 1930s. Dawson set the tone for the series in his "General Introduction" in 1931:

Western civilization to-day is passing through one of the most critical moments of its history. In every department of life traditional principles have been shaken and discredited, and we do not yet know what is going to take their place.[25]

This apocalyptic tone and the sense that the West was passing from one order to another also dominated the writing of Maritain and Michel. Maritain was convinced that western man between the wars was living in a midnight hour of civilization.[26] Michel, too, believed that the world was in an age of transition that was questioning all its old beliefs and habits.[27] The constant theme of these writers was that the old order—liberalism, bourgeois individualism, and the doctrine of necessary progress—had run its course. They believed that if the West was to survive, it must move toward new patterns of corporate life and spiritual unity.

This sense of crisis enhanced the perception among Catholics, and particularly Catholic intellectuals, that they had a special role to play at this critical point in history. We are witnessing today, wrote Wust in 1931, "the return of Catholicism from exile."[28] Alexander attempted to convey this same sense of urgency and crisis in his 1935 *Catholic Literary Revival* which, in large part, was inspired by the *Essays in Order* series.

Dawson, Maritain, and Michel all blamed the breakdown of European unity on secularization and the divorce of religion from life. Dawson's analysis of this historical problem was particularly provocative. The central thesis that dominated nearly all of Dawson's writing during the 1930s and 1940s was that religion was the integrating principle in every culture and that a society that had lost its religious roots was a dying culture.

Dawson allowed that all cultural development was affected by material factors, but he insisted that a civilization received its form from its religious tradition. Thus, Dawson was critical of modern historians and sociologists for minimizing the formative impact of religion upon culture. In *Enquiries into Religion and Culture* (1934), one of his first major works treating the relationship of religion and culture, Dawson wrote:

We are only just beginning to understand how intimately and profoundly the vitality of a society is bound up with its religion. It is the religious impulse which supplies the cohesive force which unifies a society and a culture. The great civilisations of the world do not produce the great religions as a kind of cultural by-product; in a very real sense the great religions are the foundations on which the great civilisations rest.[29]

The religious dynamic, Dawson contended, was the great unifier in society because it, more than any other cultural element, informed society with an inner bond, animating society toward a common set of aspirations and ideals.

Dawson utilized this same interpretive framework to argue that the medieval Church provided the spiritual energy that shaped the intellectual and cultural institutions of modern Europe. "Before the coming of Christianity," wrote Dawson in *The Modern Dilemma* (1932), "there was no Europe."[30] Part of Dawson's analysis of the Church's importance to European cultural development is a familiar one: the critical role of churchmen like Thomas Aquinas in transmitting classical culture to the medieval West, the importance of the monastic orders in keeping learning alive during the early Middle Ages, and the significance of the papacy, especially during Carolingian times, in cementing European unity.[31] Dawson broke new ground, however, when he attempted to demonstrate that Christianity continued to inspire the intellectual and cultural development of Europe long after the breakup of the medieval synthesis.

Dawson argued in convincing historic terms that the major secular intellectual and cultural movements that shaped and unified the West since the Renaissance—liberalism, humanism, and the idea of progress—received their inspiration from Christian ideals. They were the substitute faiths, the quasi-creeds of a secularized West, providing the spiritual dynamic that ordered and animated western man with the common vision and spirit necessary to the survival of every culture. Maritain also turned to this theme in *Religion and Culture* (the first *Essay in Order*, 1931) and *True Humanism* (1938).[32] To cite just one example, Maritain and Dawson both argued that the idea of progress was a secularized version of a Judeo-Christian teleology that posited a divine purpose and overall design to the universe. Judeo-Christianity, unlike the great eastern faiths, observed Dawson, did not aim at deliverance of the body from the sensible world. Rather, it aimed at the complete transformation of humanity to a higher level of being. This ideal of restored humanity received its greatest confirmation in the Christian doctrine of Christ's Incarnation, which in Christian dogma continued through space and time.[33]

Dawson and Maritain, much as G. K. Chesterton before them, insisted that Christian ideals could not long endure when severed from their historical or theological roots. Both thinkers reminded a secularized West during the 1930s that it was reaping the consequences of that separation. Bourgeois humanism, divorced from its Judeo-Christian foundations, had degenerated into an anthropocentric worship of man by man. The "Religion of Progress" had ended in bourgeois culture, economic and social atomization, exploitation, depression, and war. Western societies were embracing the new quasi-creeds of the 1930s—fascism, communism, and nationalism—as twentieth century spiritual substitutes for a spent and discredited nineteenth century liberalism.

In the great age of system-building between the wars when left and right extremes were both emphasizing collective solutions for economic and social problems of the day, Dawson, Maritain, and Michel insisted that the West could achieve unity only by a new integration of religion and culture. Religion had animated, unified, and transformed the cultures of the past, and it could do so again. "I believe," wrote Dawson in concluding *The Modern Dilemma*, "the Church that made Europe may yet save Europe."[34]

Dawson and Maritain sometimes seemed possessed by the historical ideal of medieval Christendom, but both employed the concept analogically. What they had in mind was a temporal civilization taking its inspiration from religious values.[35] This would be accomplished not through legislation, party movements, or amendment, but through the individual Christian living out the social and cultural implications of his or her faith.

Dawson, Maritain, and Michel all stressed the importance of the Christian citizen in realizing a new synthesis of religion and culture, but Michel, by placing the concept of the Mystical Body of Christ at the very center of Christian living, did so with the most concreteness and sophistication. The Mystical Body, according to Catholic theology, is the community of Christians united to Christ through baptism. Christ is the vine and the members of his Church are the branches. Together with Christ, the faithful form a single, living, supernatural organism, permeated and vitalized by divine life. So formed, the Mystical Body is Christ's way of continuing the Incarnation through time. Christ accomplishes through the faithful what he once accomplished through his physical presence on earth—the redemption of mankind. By entering into the Mystical Body, Christians not only enter into a brotherhood and sisterhood with Christ, they also become another Christ. St. Paul summed up this mystical union with Christ when he wrote, "It is no longer I that live, it is Christ that liveth in me" (Gal. 2:20). Through the liturgy (the common public worship of the faithful united in Christ giving praise and sacrifice to the Father), Christians give concrete expression to this concorporal union with Christ and one another.

The concept of the Mystical Body and its expression in the prayer of the liturgy thus had radical personal and social implications. This was especially apparent to Michel, Gerald Ellard, and social activists within the orbit of *Orate Fratres* and the Catholic Worker. Michel saw in the Mystical Body an integrating principle of Christian living, with the spirit of the liturgy permeating "all human contacts and activities with the spirit of Christ."[36] Christians could not ignore the "profound social character" of the doctrine of the Mystical Body, wrote Ellard in *Christian Life and Worship*.[37] Christians should first restore themselves and then restore society. In the words of Michel's biographer Paul Marx, Michel and those associated with the American liturgical movement truly believed that "liturgical life could regenerate all of Christian society and, through it, eventually all of human society."[38] Again, the Mystical Body was used analogically. It was a way to present the broad outlines of a new social and cultural order. Like Maritain's "New Christendom" based upon the "Humanism of the Incarnation," the Mystical Body was a model for a more integrated human community and a counterforce to the self-centered individualism of modern times. But its realization was dependent upon the efforts of individual Christians. Hence Maritain and Dawson, no less than Michel, called upon the laity to penetrate culture with Christian principles.

Dawson urged the laity to become "agents" of Christian culture, reminding them that the era of passive Catholicism was over.[39] Maritain demanded no less than a rededicated "Christian heroism" directed toward the "socio-temporal realisation" of the gospels.[40] Michel challenged Catholics to penetrate every dimension of culture, from architecture to literature, "imbuing," "leavening," and "vivifying" it with the liturgical spirit.[41] In this way Catholic culture would transform secular culture, infusing it with a new philosophy and outlook on life.

Dawson, Maritain, and Michel, not unlike most Catholic thinkers before 1960, were scholars, but they were scholars of a particular type. While post-Modernist era neo-scholastic commentators earlier in the century like Fulton J. Sheen, Alexander, and Lord approached the re-

construction of western civilization from a rigidly ahistorical and epistemological perspective, the focus of Dawson, Maritain, and Michel was
historical, liturgical, and cultural. Their view of humanity, the Church,
and history was concrete and theological, rather than conceptual and
abstract. James Hitchcock observes that Dawson, in fact, was treated
with condescension by many academic neo-scholastic philosophers in
the 1930s and 1940s because his historical generalizations were perceived
as a "lower order of significance than those supplied by metaphysics."[42]

Maritain also preferred metaphysics to history, but his concrete approach to the problems of human personality and human community
matched that of Dawson and Michel. The titles of Maritain's works
during the 1930s and 1940s—*Freedom in the Modern World* (1935), *Natural
Law and Human Rights* (1942), and *Christianity and Democracy* (1944)—
suggest this concreteness. Indeed, apart from his practical application
of neo-scholastic principles to human affairs, Maritain's chief contribution to the neo-scholastic revival of the 1930s and 1940s was his recovery,
with Etienne Gilson, of the existential components within Aquinas's
metaphysics, thus encouraging neo-scholasticism to move from an essentialist outlook and terminology to explore more fundamental questions of individual being and existence.[43] Aquinas therefore assumed a
theological breadth and scope in Maritain not fully disclosed by traditional scholastic thinkers.

The influence of Dawson, Michel, and Maritain can be seen on almost
every major lay Catholic movement in the American Church between
1930 and 1955. Catholic Action, the Young Christian Student, Young
Christian Worker, and Christian Family movements all attached themselves to the liturgical movement. The Catholic Worker (established in
1933) had ties with all three thinkers. Maritain, who was a visiting lecturer at the University of Chicago during the late 1930s and lived and
lectured in the New York City area during the World War II era, became
a friend of both Peter Maurin and Dorothy Day. In 1936 Maritain made
two separate visits to New York City's St. Joseph's House and partici-
pated in one of Maurin's celebrated Friday evening "Round-Table Discussions." Maritain's topic was "A New Christendom," where he urged
American Catholics not to withdraw from the problems of the modern
world, but to unite with others "toward making a new social order."[44]

Dawson was "must reading" among Catholic Workers during the
1930s and 1940s. The movement's penny tabloid, the *Catholic Worker*,
often posted Dawson on its reading list and reviewed all of his books.
Maurin even condensed Dawson's *Catholicism and the Bourgeois Mind* into
one of his *Easy Essays* in 1936.[45]

Michel, among the three, had the strongest personal ties to the Catholic Worker. Catholic Worker historian Mel Piehl writes that Michel and
Day "immediately recognized one another as allies," because of their

strong mutual emphases upon lay Catholic social action based upon the social justice implications of the liturgy.[46] Day constantly connected the liturgical movement with the Catholic social justice movement and corresponded regularly with Michel and Gerald Ellard. Michel, for his part, wrote a number of articles for the *Catholic Worker* and spoke at various Catholic Worker houses during the mid–1930s.

It was at Maurin's suggestion that Michel established an undergraduate seminar on "Catholic Backgrounds and Current Social Theory" at St. John's University in 1936. The course was designed "to form active Catholic laymen by having them inquire into the nature and function of living Catholic culture *vis-à-vis* modern secularism." Under the direction of selected faculty, St. John's students addressed such topics as "The Catholic Literary Revival," "The Liturgical Movement," "The Principles and Achievements of Neo-Scholasticism," and the "Theological Basis of Christian Social Theory."[47]

All topics were studied with reference to their role in social and cultural reconstruction. Dawson, Maritain, and Michel were assigned reading. Catholic sociologist Paul Hanley Furfey, a Sulpician priest who taught at Catholic University, was also studied. In *Fire on the Earth* (1936), Furfey promulgated a "Supernatural Sociology," a radical Christian social ethic based upon "personalist action" and the theology of the Mystical Body.[48] According to Piehl, Day and other Catholic Workers grounded their own movement in Furfey's thought. "For several decades," Piehl wrote, Furfey's ideas offered "the clearest theoretical rationale for an American Catholic radicalism."[49]

The St. John's University undergraduate seminar and Furfey's own course on advanced Catholic social thought introduced at Catholic University in 1935 illustrate the profusion of such courses throughout the American Catholic college community at this time. All of the midwestern schools cited earlier had introduced courses on Catholic social thought by the end of the decade—spurred on by both the drive toward a more integrated Catholic curriculum and Depression-time attempts to present Christian solutions to modern social and economic problems. Marquette University introduced separate courses on "Christian Social Policy," "Corporate Worship and Christian Solidarity," and "Catholic Social Justice" between 1934 and 1937. Loyola University began a course on "Catholic Economic Thought" in 1935. A course on Catholic social doctrine was introduced at Mundelein College in 1934.

Most of these courses had a similar focus, as they attempted to expose Catholic undergraduates to the best Christian social thought of the day. Marquette's course on "Corporate Worship and Christian Solidarity," taught in 1936 by Father Ellard, for example, focused upon the social implications of the doctrine of the Mystical Body, the dynamics of Furfey's "Supernatural Sociology," and the relationship between the liturgical movement and Catholic social action.[50] At Marquette and other schools, special emphasis was placed upon the social encyclicals of popes Leo XIII (*Rerum Novarum*, 1891) and Pius XI (*Quadragesimo Anno*, 1931) as starting points for a Catholic program of social and economic reform.

Both encyclicals employed scholastic natural law ethics to clarify the rights and duties of labor and management in the modern industrial age. The natural right of property was upheld, but both documents recognized the need for state intervention to regulate the conditions of labor and further maintained that employers had the moral obligation to pay a living wage to their workers, apart from the pressure of so-called "economic laws." The right of workers to form trade unions and to strike, if necessary, was also asserted.[51]

The central importance of the social encyclicals to the American Catholic program of social reconstruction was underscored in 1935 when the National Catholic Education Association Committee on Social Studies issued a suggested program of study on *Rerum Novarum, Quadragesimo Anno,* and other twentieth century social encyclicals for use at all American Catholic colleges. Written by Joseph Reiner, S. J., Dean of the College of Arts and Letters at Loyola of Chicago and a leading social activist, the outline was titled *A Syllabus on Social Problems in Light of Christian Principles, with Special Reference to the Encyclicals of Popes Pius XI, Benedict XV, Pius X, and Leo XIII.* Following the committee's mandate, Reiner recommended that such a course "be given to every [Catholic] college student . . . and that it should be required of every candidate for a degree."[52] Not all Catholic colleges carried through on Reiner's ambitious plan. Nevertheless, such a course was required at Loyola and Mundelein during the late 1930s and early 1940s.

The ideas of Maritain and Dawson, the liturgical and Catholic Worker movements, and the development of Catholic social doctrine under the social encyclicals all represented significant developments in the religious thought of Catholics after 1935. Catholic social thought before 1930—apart from such progressive thinkers as American sociologist Fr. John A. Ryan—had been primarily conservative. Now in the Church's own social encyclicals Catholics could find a systematic body of religious thought that sharply attacked laissez-faire attitudes and institutions, showed a willingness to put limits on the right of private property in accordance to its social function, promoted trade unionism, and recognized the need for government intervention to provide for the common good.

Dawson, Maritain, and Michel could sound no less radical in their own critique of the social and moral consequences of unrestrained individualism. Sidney Hook recognized this when he wrote of Maritain in 1940 that the Frenchman's critique of "bourgeois man" and modern economic liberalism "would not be out of place in a socialist tract."[53]

Nor would Michel's call for a new economic order based upon the brotherhood of man. This kind of economic and social critique—and positive program for reform that followed—was especially appealing to Depression-era Catholics who remained opposed to Marxism, but nevertheless were searching for meaningful economic and social change.

Catholicism in the 1930s was thus beginning to take on an intellectual and social dimension that was exciting to college-age Catholics and intellectuals of the era. Its theological voice—vivified by the radical personalism of the Catholic Worker and the Mystical Body theology of the liturgical movement—also began to assume more meaningful dimensions within the Catholic cultural synthesis. Neo-scholastic philosophy still dominated the Catholic world view, and in some academic circles, as James Hennesey writes, still served to "shore up" those Catholics who thought of themselves as a people "certain and set apart";[54] but the theological emphases of the 1930s encouraging Catholics to incarnate their faith in the world served as a counterforce to this attitude. There was no room for Innocence and detachment from the world in Catholic religious and social thought of the mid–1930s and 1940s. That period was over. Catholics now were encouraged to cooperate with the world and its institutions—economic, social, cultural, and political—and work for their improvement.

CATHOLIC COLLEGIANS REACT TO THE REVIVAL

In 1942 St. Louis University professor and Catholic educational theorist William J. McGucken, S. J. offered an overview of American Catholic higher education. Commenting upon the "renascence" of Catholic thought in Catholic American colleges during the past decade, McGucken noted that something "has happened" to the average Catholic undergraduate. He "is more Catholic, more apostolic," observed McGucken. "His faith means more to him, he has a more intelligent grasp of it." "Something of the vivifying breath of the Catholic Renascence has swept through our Catholic colleges here in America," McGucken continued. "The voices of Belloc and Chesterton and Maritain and Fulton Sheen—to mention but a few—have proclaimed to the world the greatness of our Catholic heritage."[55]

The Jesuit further noted that Catholic undergraduates during the past decade had encountered "the great pivotal dogmas of the Faith," including the Incarnation, the Mystical Body, and the liturgical movement. "What undergraduate today," asked McGucken, "does not know the great encyclicals intelligently, does not set a right appreciation upon their worth?" "In a word," McGucken concluded, "that about which we have talked so long is beginning to take form and substance; Catholic lay leadership has become a reality on the college campus and in the college classroom."[56]

Many within the American Catholic educational and cultural community during the 1940s would challenge McGucken's roseate view of the Catholic undergraduate. Indeed, one of the major criticisms of American Catholic higher education heard during the 1940s was that Catholic colleges and universities had failed to achieve the integration called for in the previous decade. Thus, in 1947 Chicago auxiliary archbishop Bernard J. Sheil, one of the most progressive Catholic American social thinkers of his time, complained, "It is an experienced fact that the graduates of Catholic schools are notoriously deficient in a practical and competent knowledge of Catholic social thinking." According to Sheil, Catholic college graduates were "just as individualistic and reactionary" as those coming out of secular colleges and universities. Most Catholics, criticized Sheil, "have not even read the papal encyclicals."[57]

Sheil's observations doubtless were correct. Nevertheless, his statement obscures the real intellectual ferment that had been taking place among a significant number of college-age Catholics and their teachers since the mid–1930s. True, not all Catholic undergraduates were interested in Maritain, Dawson, or Michel. Nor were they all interested in the social encyclicals, the literary and liturgical revivals, and the Catholic Worker movement. But a large number of articulate and highly motivated educated Catholics were. In total, their activities and interests after 1935 constituted something of a movement. In the long run, they played an important role in the maturation of American Catholic intellectual and cultural life prior to Vatican II.

Cyril Echele, Richard Finnegan, Donald Gallagher, and Arthur Kuhl were students at St. Louis University during the mid–1930s. Echele and Gallagher were philosophy majors. Finnegan and Kuhl were preparing for careers in journalism. All four men were regular contributors to the university's literary quarterly, the *Fleur de Lis*. Gallagher, a transfer student from New York City's Fordham University, succeeded Finnegan as the magazine's editor in 1935.

It was a heady era, recalled Gallagher in a personal account of those years: Chesterton, Belloc, Dawson, and Maritain were all being recommended by their teachers. "They simply seemed to be very exciting. We did look upon them as a movement going on." Gallagher encountered Chesteron, Belloc, and the encyclicals of Leo XIII in Fr. Raymond Corrigan's popular course on the nineteenth century Church. Fr. Louis Forrey's course on "The Catholic Literary Revival" focused on some of the same thinkers, as well as the creative writers of the European Catholic emergence. "It was a delight and unexpected find," Gallagher recalled, to discover the modern Catholic intellectual tradition: "Catholicism was part of the western tradition, it wasn't just on the periphery of things."[58] Campus lectures by Catholic publishers Frank Sheed and Maisie Ward and English Catholic writer Arnold Lunn reinforced this awareness.

The *Fleur de Lis*, as the literary organ of St. Louis University students and faculty, recorded much of the intellectual ferment of the times. In 1933 editor Finnegan announced that in light of the "stirrings" of new Catholic life "in every sphere of thought and action," the quarterly henceforth would be conducted as "a magazine of the Catholic Revival."[59] What followed was a steady stream of articles and editorials that acquainted students with the various figures of the European Catholic movement, presented the Catholic literary revival as a modern intellectual and cultural force, and critically discussed the prospects of a similar emergence in the United States.

The influence of Dawson, Maritain, and the *Essays in Order* group was prominent in many of these articles. This was especially true of those addressed to the breakdown of liberal culture and the necessity of establishing a new integration of religion and life. Dawson, Maritain, and Russian philosopher Nicholas Berdyaev, editorialized Finnegan in December 1933, had pointed out the "disintegrating tendencies" of modern times, and had "raised their voices against the cant of progress and the ridiculous pride of the age." "Man," Finnegan said, "has proven to be a poor god."[60] In a March 1934 essay titled "The Bourgeois Spirit in America," Cyril Echele likewise drew upon the ideas of Dawson, Maritain, and Berdyaev to denounce the materialistic values underlying modern

middle-class culture. Paraphrasing Berdyaev, Echele identified "bourgeoisism" as a false faith whose self-centered spirit had enfeebled Catholics and non-Catholics alike. Now with the loss of confidence in this "quasi-faith," continued Echele, "our mighty middle class kingdom has been shaken to its foundations." Echele insisted, as Dawson had, that "the creative element in human culture is spiritual," and when that is lost, culture and life distintegrate.[61]

Other Depression era *Fleur de Lis* essays focused upon many of these same themes. The idea that true economic, social, and cultural renewal must begin with Christian-Catholic principles was a strongly reiterated student theme, as was the conviction that any new synthesis of religion and life in the United States depended upon the leadership of Catholic intellectuals like themselves and the Catholic colleges and universities that they attended. In his 1934 article "The Catholic Literary Revival, its Need in the United States" Finnegan thus wrote, "An American Dawson is badly needed, but which of our American Catholic universities could produce him?" Finnegan maintained that "accomplished [Catholic] writers" would not appear in America until its Catholic colleges and universities were "renewed in their spirit." What was needed was the deepening of American Catholic intellectual life along the lines suggested by the Europeans.[62]

As a philosophy major, Donald Gallagher naturally looked toward scholastic philosophy as a solution to modern problems. "Go to Thomas," enjoined Gallagher in a 1936 article. Aquinas, Gallagher insisted, was "the Apostle of our time," and Thomism was at the very center of the "intellectual Catholicism" so urgently needed in the modern world. Gallagher nevertheless was sharply critical of the "cribbed and cabined" scholastic philosophy taught in many Catholic schools at the time. Gallagher's solution was to return to the "real Aquinas." This was the Aquinas not of the manuals and textbooks, but the one being uncovered by Frenchmen Maritain, Gilson, and other European Thomists of the era.[63] It was exciting for Gallagher to see these thinkers actively applying Thomistic principles to the actual problems of the day.

The desire of Gallagher and his St. Louis University friends to do something concrete about Depression-era problems took practical form in July 1935 when Echele, Arthur Kuhl, and other St. Louis University students established a Catholic Worker group in the city. Their first meeting, recalled Echele, "had been prepared by years of academic training."

All those present . . . were steeped in the literature of what was called the Catholic intellectual and literary revival in Europe, represented by such figures as Chesterton, Belloc, Christopher Dawson, [and] Jacques Maritain. . . . We were well acquainted with the liturgical movement in Europe and America. . . .

. . . We had developed the germ of Catholic consciousness and the Catholic attitude toward life. . . . We longed for the day when people who think would once more devote their talents to the service of the Church.[64]

After an abortive attempt at running a Catholic Worker farm in nearby Fredericktown, Missouri, the group opened a St. Louis House of Hospitality in October 1936. Gallagher, who had joined the group earlier that year, lived with Echele in a back room of their Franklin Street headquarters while completing his senior year at the university.

The St. Louis Catholic Worker sponsored a full program of activities: weekly meetings and speakers, study groups on the social and personal consequences of the liturgy, a Catholic bookshop, and outreach to the city's poor and unemployed. On the social and intellectual front, Echele and Gallagher were selected to maintain contact with labor groups in the city, to support C.I.O. unionization, and "if possible, to infiltrate the ideas of the papal encyclicals into their ranks." The same tactics were directed at the city's youthful Marxists who were headquartered a few doors down from the Catholic Worker.[65]

"We learned and planned our technique chiefly from our study of the life and work of Jacques Maritain," wrote Echele, "especially his practical philosophy."[66] Maritain's formula for a "New Christendom"—where the latter had carefully distinguished between the laity acting as Chruch members as such and the laity acting as citizens under the influence of Christian values as the starting point for the reconstruction of a new social order—was an especially important intellectual concept for the St. Louis group.[67] It represented a Christian theory of politics—unlike previous nineteenth century "thesis-hypothesis" Church-State formulas— that respected the autonomy of the temporal sphere. Religion and life were to be united in the believer and the citizen, not in the "consecrational state." The "New Christendom" thus would be at once sacred and plural, with individual Christians creating with other citizens the outlines of a more just society.[68] This was particularly pleasing to American Catholics who had long defended pluralistic conceptions of politics and society. Echele, Gallagher, and other St. Louis Catholic workers framed their own approach to social and cultural reconstruction around this formula, seeing in the "New Christendom" a charter for lay Catholic social action.[69]

The theology of the Mystical Body also figured prominently in the intellectual and social outlook of the St. Louis group, as it had for other Catholic Workers throughout the country. The doctrine, recalls Gallagher, "was very much a part of our thinking and living."[70] This was especially true in the group's approach to social justice and race relations. The attitude was stated most forcefully in *Royal Road*, a 1941 novel by Arthur Kuhl, based, in part, upon his Catholic Worker experience. Kuhl's story draws parallels between the life and sufferings of a gentle black man, Jesse Stewart, and the passion and death of Jesus Christ. Born in Bethlehem, Pennsylvania, and raised in Nazareth, Kentucky, Jesse lives in poverty in a Chicago ghetto. Jesse is wrongly accused of rape and murder, thrown into an indifferent and racist criminal justice system, and dies abandoned and broken in the electric chair.[71]

Kuhl's story is sentimental and overdrawn and owes too much to Richard Wright's earlier *Native Son* (1940), but it nevertheless constituted a dramatic portrayal of the Christian belief that "we are all one in Christ" and that violence done to one member of His Body is violence done to Him. The work, moreover, coincided with a number of other Catholic novels during the 1930s and 1940s that also used the doctrine of the Mystical Body to attack Catholic bigotry toward blacks, communists, and Jews.

Coincident with the formation of the Catholic Worker, clusters of committed young lay Catholic intellectuals emerged elsewhere in the country. In Chicago during the late 1930s the movement centered around Edward (Ed) Marciniak, John Cogley, and James O'Gara. Marciniak and Cogley were students at Loyola Univeristy, and O'Gara was at the University of Chicago. Marciniak recalls the sense of awakening he and his

Catholic friends experienced when they first discovered Maritain, Dawson, the Catholic Worker movement, and the social teachings of the Church:

All of a sudden there was this new world for me, a world of great intellectual vitality. There were many of us, and we read avidly, every learned Catholic magazine we could locate. . . . Sometimes our sessions would go from Sunday afternoon right through to early Monday morning—one week Maritain; the next, perhaps, the [1938 Republic] steel strike.[72]

In Maritain, Dawson, Virgil Michel, and other modern Catholic thinkers, Marciniak and his Loyola University friends found an intellectual approach to the faith not previously encountered on the parish or home level. A faith previously presented in private-personal terms was now seen to have social, even radical, implications. It was an exhilarating experience for Marciniak, the son of an immigrant Polish grocer and steelworker, to see Catholic intellectuals addressing the most pressing social and cultural problems of the day.

No less moving was Marciniak's discovery of the Mystical Body. Like young Catholics elsewhere, it was exciting for Marciniak to find the dynamic "inner aspects" of the Church taking precedence over the devotional, juridical, and institutional. Marciniak now was awake to the fact that "the Church was *we* [sic]," the laity *"were"* the Church. For young Marciniak, the doctrine of the Mystical Body was "the most important theological concept" of his generation and a compelling command for lay Catholic social and cultural action.[73]

The Chicago Church during the 1930s and 1940s afforded a number of concrete opportunities for Marciniak and other young lay Catholics to put their faith into practice. The greatest was offered by the Chicago Inter-Student Catholic Action organization (CISCA). CISCA was a city-wide federation of Catholic high school and college Sodalities and other student groups. The organization was formed by Loyola University Jesuit Joseph Reiner in 1927, with the approval of national Sodality director Daniel A. Lord.[74] Reiner was one of a number of highly influential Chicago area clerics in the 1930s and 1940s who dedicated their careers to the formation of lay Catholic leaders.

CISCA membership by 1935 numbered over 20,000, with nearly all of Chicago's fifty Catholic high schools and eight Catholic colleges and universities represented. Each Saturday morning up to 600 Sodality representatives would meet at Loyola's Loop Campus to discuss and develop plans of action to bring back to their local units for the coming week. The CISCA program focused upon four key areas of lay Catholic life: the liturgy, mission support, literature, and social action. The last area filled a serious gap in Father Lord's Sodality program. According to a colleague who knew both men, "Fr. Reiner taught Fr. Lord whatever the latter knew about Catholic social thought and action."[75] Under Reiner and his charismatic successor Martin Carrabine, S. J., CISCA leaders went into Chicago area high schools and colleges to talk on Catholic social thought, distributed copies of the *Catholic Worker* to Chicago workers, and volunteered in the city's hospitals and community centers. In the early 1940s, CISCA led a successful struggle to integrate Chicago's rollerskating rinks.[76]

Marciniak, Cogley, and James O'Gara were all active in CISCA. Marciniak served as CISCA president in 1938, during his senior year at Loyola. That same year, Marciniak and Alex Reser, "an intellectually inclined German Catholic railroad worker," opened a Chicago Catholic Worker house on Blue Island Avenue.[77] Cogley and O'Gara soon enlisted in the movement. Within four months the group was publishing the *Chicago Catholic Worker*, with Marciniak and Cogley as editors.

The *Chicago Catholic Worker* closely followed its New York City counterpart in its personalist theology and outlook; but a distinguishing feature of the Chicago group was its accent upon literature and the arts in a program of Christian social and cultural renewal. This resulted mainly from the influence of Cogley and O'Gara, who both had a deep respect for the social power of creative writing. The *Chicago Catholic Worker* thus actively supported the Chicago Catholic Labor Theatre, begun by Catholic Worker Philip Seaman in 1939, as a "medium for spreading Catholic concepts of social problems."[78]

One production put on by the Chicago group was Lord's *Storm-Tossed*.[79] Written in 1936 as a means of dramatizing the social justice implications of the Mystical Body and the papal social encyclicals, the play represents Lord's own growth in the social teachings of the Church. By 1935 Lord had also written a book on the Mystical Body that stressed the doctrine's importance as a motivating force in lay Catholic action and its revolutionary implications for social justice and world solidarity.[80]

Storm-Tossed focused upon these same ideas. Set in the midst of a bitter labor dispute, the story contrasts a group of "Catholic Workmen" with a second group of young communist radicals in their efforts to win the hearts and minds of striking workers. While the communists preach class hatred and proletarian revolution, the Catholic activists make speeches about the stewardship of wealth and social solidarity based upon the radical fellowship of the Mystical Body. The moral of the play is that in terms of social thought, Catholics "have all the Communists have and so much more."[81]

The Chicago Catholic Labor Theatre emerged only toward the end of the Depression and probably had only limited influence over Chicago's working class; but it nevertheless added an important dimension to the Catholic literary front begun earlier in the decade. Presenting "only plays of social significance based on Catholic philosophy and theology," the Chicago movement represented the socially relevant drama absent from the Francis X. Talbot-supported Catholic Theatre movement of the 1930s, which had been interested more in presenting plays upholding Catholic moral standards than in using the theatre as an instrument of social change.[82]

The Chicago Catholic theatre group, moreover, epitomized what the *Chicago Catholic Worker* was attempting to do throughout the city during the late 1930s and early 1940s. In editorial after editorial directed at Chicago's large Catholic working class, Cogley and Marciniak urged workers to "get out and read a copy of the Popes' encyclicals." "The Popes tell us," wrote Cogley in 1938, "that we have a moral duty to join unions and to protect ourselves and our fellow workers from being exploited." "If Christ were living today," he claimed, "he would be a union man."[83]

The *Chicago Catholic Worker* ceased publication in June 1941 as many Catholic Workers throughout the country split with Day over the pacifist issue or, like Cogley and O'Gara, were themselves drafted into the armed services. After the war, however, both Cogley and O'Gara returned to Chicago eager to establish a new Catholic journal that would address the concerns of young Catholic intellectuals who had grown to maturity during the Depression and the war. They found a strong supporter in Father Carrabine, who was looking for a forum for promising CISCA journalists and writers. With the backing of Carrabine and under CISCA auspices, Cogley and O'Gara founded *Today* magazine in 1946, "a publication written by students for students."[84]

Today adopted a wide focus, with youth-oriented but well-written essays on current movies, articles on dating hints for teen-agers, and feature stories on figures as diverse as Peter Maurin and DePaul University basketball coach Ray Meyer. The magazine nevertheless remained a very Catholic publication—not in the sectarian sense, which Cogley and O'Gara abhorred, but in the sense that the Catholic faith was seen as a premise for lay Catholic thought and action. In a steady stream of comment during the late 1940s, Cogley stressed the need for Catholic students "to fulfill their vocation to the world." What was needed, Cogley emphasized, were Catholic leaders—"Christians in the World" who would "incarnate" their faith into "the social, cultural, political and economic life of our times."[85]

Today's orientation, like the *Chicago Catholic Worker* before it, was thus social and cultural, although as the Depression ended and post-World War II Catholics moved into the middle class, the emphasis on social action shifted from economic-labor problems to broader concerns of fair housing, civil rights, world peace, and parochialism in the Church. *Today* also maintained a strong literary emphasis, which was sustained by the large number of students from midwestern Catholic women's colleges who contributed to the magazine, including Rosary and Mundelein Colleges in Chicago and the Colleges of St. Benedict and St. Catherine in Minnesota.

One of the magazine's best young contributing literary critics was Abigail Quigley McCarthy, a literature teacher at the College of St. Catherine in the late 1940s. McCarthy, like so many other post–1935 young American Catholic intellectuals, expressed special interest in European Catholic writers like Bernanos, Mauriac, Evelyn Waugh, and Graham Greene. In a number of essays in the late 1940s, McCarthy perceptively reviewed the work of both Bernanos and Greene, stressing their realistic protrayal of sin, evil, and man's relationship with God.[86] These widely read Europeans represented for McCarthy the mature integration of faith in fiction so eagerly sought in her own American Catholic writers.

Today, for its part, encouraged creative writing. It sponsored writing contests, conducted summer writing clinics, and published short stories by aspiring Catholic writers. The latter included Joseph Dever, Anthony Burn, Rosemary Entringer, and Edward Kennebeck. Many went on to write for other publications (Catholic or otherwise) or, like Dever (*No Lasting Home*, 1947), to write their own version of the modern Catholic novel. Cogley and O'Gara left *Today* in 1949—Cogley to join the editorial staff of the lay Catholic journal *Commonweal*, and O'Gara to serve as managing editor of the *Voice of St. Jude*. O'Gara joined *Commonweal* in 1952. *Today* ceased publication in 1971.

"It all came together," commented Marciniak in observing the concerns of his generation: a profound respect for the personal and corporate dynamics of the liturgy, a passion for social justice, and a deep interest in writing and literature as a way of influencing culture.[87] Marciniak, Cogley, Gallagher, Kuhl, McCarthy, and an influential number of other young lay Catholics took their faith seriously during the 1930s and 1940s. Without being sectarian, they saw their faith as the center and focal point of their lives, and the basis for thought and action. Combining an active intellectual life with a deep love for the principles of their Church, they sought to make their faith real to the modern world—on the picket line, in the novel, on the editorial page, and in their daily living. They were compelling examples of lay Christians functioning in society and addressing its deepest concerns.

8

Frank O'Malley: Thinker, Critic, Revivalist

Following the death of Notre Dame University English Professor Frank O'Malley in May 1974, one of his former students wrote:

I read in the June issue of *Notre Dame Magazine* that Frank O'Malley was dead. A likely story. . . . Frank O'Malley dead? Preposterous. Leon Bloy lives. So does Georges Bernanos, Charles Peguy, Karl Adam, Ignatio Saloni and Paul Claudel. . . . Shakespeare, Kierkegaard, Chaucer, Maritain dead? Ridiculous. . . . Frank O'Malley dead? I don't believe it. He was seen alive and well a few days ago, talking to "Mr. Blue."[1]

This touching tribute was but one of many paid to O'Malley by Notre Dame faculty, students, and alumni at the time, representing an outpouring of affection equaled, perhaps, only by the deep-felt sense of loss that accompanied the death of Notre Dame football coach Knute Rockne some forty years earlier. Indeed, on a campus almost overrun with legendary figures, some argue that the painfully shy, enigmatic, red-haired O'Malley stood second only to Rockne as an influence upon Notre Dame students in that school's history.

O'Malley is best remembered for the "Modern Catholic Writers" course he designed and taught for over thirty-five years at Notre Dame. It was by far the most popular course in the humanities ever offered at the university, and even attracted notice from *Time* magazine, where in 1962 O'Malley was described as Notre Dame's "most inspiring undergraduate teacher."[2]

"Modern Catholic Writers" began in 1936 and was similar in purpose and scope to the many other courses in "Modern Catholic Literature,"

"Newman," and "The Catholic Literary Revival" initiated at other Catholic colleges and universities at this time. O'Malley's intention was to expose Notre Dame students to the main currents of the European Catholic intellectual resurgence; but he also hoped, like many other American Catholic educators, literary critics, and cultural leaders between 1920 and 1950, that the European example would stimulate a similar revival of Catholic life and culture in the United States.

In this course O'Malley introduced his students to Bloy, Bernanos, Peguy, and Maritain, as well as the other major figures of the European Catholic revival—German-Italian liturgist and theologian Romano Guardini, French philosopher Etienne Gilson, Norwegian novelist Sigrid Undset, poets Paul Claudel and Gerard Manley Hopkins, and many others. O'Malley expanded his reading list in the 1940s and 1950s to keep up with the latest devlopments in post-World War II European Catholic theology and literature. French Catholic existentialist Gabriel Marcel was added, as were French "New Theologians" Henri de Lubac and Jean Danielou who, while not existentialists, frequently took account of existentialist themes in their work. English novelists Graham Greene and Evelyn Waugh, whose serious work in the 1940s and 1950s often projected strong Christian-Catholic themes, were also added. O'Malley also spoke on many of these same figures at Catholic colleges throughout the United States.

Through O'Malley—who was an electrifying lecturer—these Catholic thinkers took on a meaning and scope that was exciting to American Catholic college students of the era, many of whom were just awakening to the fact that Catholicism was a significant intellectual force operating within the modern world. Thus, while the eulogy that opened this chapter was intended by its student-author to praise O'Malley, it also illustrates the powerful influence that such thinkers as Bloy, Bernanos, Maritain, and other figures of the European Catholic revivals exercised over the generation of American Catholic college students who grew to maturity before Vatican II.

Historians often use representative figures to symbolize the intellectual and cultural currents of an age. In the history of the American Catholic experience, for example, Philip and Daniel Berrigan have been employed to illustrate the social activism among many Catholics during the Vietnam era.[3] The theme of this chapter is that the life, concerns, and thought of Frank O'Malley are representative of a significant intellectual pattern operating within the American Catholic cultural community during the 1940s and early 1950s. Centered primarily in Catholic colleges and universities, this pattern of thought was integral, Christian humanistic, and apostolic.[4] Directed primarily at the lay Catholic intellectual, it upheld the vision of a mental life unified and instructed as far as possible by the precepts of the Christian-Catholic faith. It urged Catholics not to separate their lives from their faith, but to be Christian in every dimension of thought and activity. So directed, Catholics, in the words of O'Malley, would "construct man, construct society, construct creation."[5]

The 1940s and 1950s were exciting times to be young, Catholic, and intellectual. It was a time of cult figures and quotable phrases, when many Catholics agreed with Guardini's celebrated dictum that "a religious process of incalculable importance has begun—the Church is coming to life in the souls of men." It was a time when a less legalistic generation of Catholics discovered with Paul Claudel that God writes straight with crooked lines; with Charles Peguy that the sinner lies at the very heart of Christianity; and with Graham Greene the dramatic action of divine grace upon "whiskey priests," murderers, and adulterous lovers. It was a time, moreover, when many zealous college-age Catholics quite literally believed with Leon Bloy that "there is but one sadness—not to be one of the saints."[6]

This intensification of Catholic life and faith during the 1940s and 1950s converged in the figure of Frank O'Malley. As a teacher at a major Catholic university, O'Malley worked to inspire his students with the vision of an "integrated Christian life" and the need to realize that vision "in the modern world."[7] As essayist, lecturer, literary critic, and Catholic intellectual, O'Malley constantly informed his own work with the principles of his faith. All the while, O'Malley drew upon the ideas and figures of the French and German Catholic revivals for his models, inspiration, and direction.

THE FORMATION OF AN AMERICAN CATHOLIC INTELLECTUAL

Francis J. O'Malley was born in Clinton, Massachusetts, in 1909 to working-class Irish-American parents. He enrolled at Notre Dame University in 1928, where he quickly distinguished himself as a serious Catholic and scholar. After graduating as valedictorian of the class of 1932, O'Malley remained at the university to earn a Master's degree in English. In 1933 he was hired as an instructor in English and history and the following year received a full-time appointment in the English department. At the time of his appointment, the twenty-four-year-old O'Malley was the youngest member of the Notre Dame faculty. O'Malley spent his entire professional adult life at Notre Dame, one of a small but influential cadre of "Bachelor Dons" (resident lay professors) who inhabited the campus during the school's history.[8]

Notre Dame during the 1930s was an inspiring place for a young Catholic intellectual to begin his professional career. Eager to improve the university's academic stature, its president, John F. O'Hara, C.S.C.

(1934–42), recruited a host of European "refugee scholars" to teach and lecture at the school, precipitating the "Notre Dame Renaissance" of the 1930s and 1940s. French neo-Thomist philosopher Yves Simon and German political thinkers Waldemar Gurian and F. A. Hermans all accepted permanent faculty positions between 1937 and 1940. French literary critic Charles DuBos's permanent appointment was cut short by his death in 1939.[9]

Maritain and Gilson were also notable campus visitors during the 1930s. Maritain, who held a lectureship at the University of Chicago in 1933–1934 and again in 1938, commuted regularly to Notre Dame, both to speak and to visit Gurian, who remained a lifelong patron and confidant. Gilson, who headed the prestigious Institute of Medieval Studies at the University of Toronto, also lectured at Notre Dame during the 1930s.[10]

O'Malley established social ties with Maritain through Gurian. Gurian was probably O'Malley's closest friend and associate during his early years at Notre Dame, and would often include his younger colleague in social affairs with Maritain and his wife Räissa. The Chicago home of John U. Nef, an economics professor at the University of Chicago and head of the school's Committee on Social Thought, was a favorite gathering place. Nef, University of Chicago Chancellor Robert M. Hutchins, neo-scholastic scholar Mortimer Adler, and other Chicago faculty shared an intellectual affinity with many Catholic thinkers at this time both in their concern over the vocationalization of the American college curricula, and in their desire to restore metaphysics as the unifying principle in modern university studies. The 1940s witticism that the University of Chicago was a place where "atheistic professors taught Catholic philosophy to Jewish students" underscored that kinship.[11]

O'Malley's interest in the role of the lay intellectual in the modern world grew from these professional relationships and out of his familiarity with the lives and thoughts of other European Catholics that he was beginning to encounter at this time: Gilson, Guardini, DuBos, Christopher Dawson, and others. All of the above, with the exception of Guardini, were laymen. Deeply and consciously religious, these men were in the vanguard of an immense effort on the part of European Catholic intellectuals between the wars to present Christian solutions to modern problems. Not merely philosophers, literary critics, historians, and political thinkers; they were *Christian* philosophers, literary critics, historians, and thinkers. Their membership in the Church determined their outlook and their religious faith was the integrating principle in their thought.

The concept of a Christian philosophy is crucial in placing O'Malley in proper intellectual context, but the idea itself had been widely debated by Catholic thinkers during the early 1930s.[12] "Christian philosophy" seemed a contradiction in terms to many. Modern philosophers since Descartes had maintained that philosophy and theology (reason and faith) belonged to completely independent orders. Philosophy was viewed as an autonomous science wherein the philosopher determined the first causes of things through the use of unaided human reason, wholly apart from divine revelation. This rational approach to experience dominated not only post-Cartesian thought systems, but also reigned within philosophical circles holding to the scholastic tradition. American Catholic colleges and universities before 1935, for example, were notorious for presenting scholasticism as a sort of "baptized Aristotelianism," with Aquinas's theology completely separated from his philosophy.

Proponents of a Christian philosophy in the 1930s and 1940s—principally Gilson, Maritain, and Guardini—challenged this outlook. Gilson, who devoted most of his career to the study of medieval philosophy and the historic roots of the scholastic tradition, became convinced in the early 1930s that the rationalistic Aristotelianism found in the scholastic manuals was not the real Aquinas. Aquinas and his medieval contemporaries did not separate their theology from their philosophy, Gilson first asserted in the 1931–1932 Gifford Lectures at the University of Aberdeen (published in 1936 as *The Spirit of Medieval Philosophy*).[13] They philosophized not as pagan Greeks—who had no conception of a loving personal God and the world as creation—but as believing Christians. Christian revelation, especially as it related to such basic theological concepts as creation, God as Pure Being, and the radically meaningful relationship of nature to grace, therefore exercised an unquestionable influence over the philosophizing of Aquinas and all the medieval schoolmen. Their philosophy, Gilson argued in convincing historic terms, was contained in their theology.

With its sources historically established in the authority of Aquinas, the idea of a Christian philosophy became prominent within some quarters of the Catholic international intellectual community and theology began to compete with philosophy as the integrating principle in the Catholic intellectual synthesis. Throughout the late 1930s and 1940s Gilson, Maritain, and Guardini maintained that it was a mistake to separate faith from reason, countering post-World War I neo-orthodox Protestant scholars influenced by Karl Barth whose theology excluded the possibility of reason elevated by grace. They contended instead that revelation illuminated and purified reason, just as, in Thomistic terms, grace transformed and completed nature. Most of the confusion in the world, they insisted, could be attributed to the abandonment of "religious knowledge."[14]

A new synthesis between faith and reason was particularly important, Gilson, Maritain, and Guardini maintained, when it came to questions dealing with the nature and destiny of man.[15] Any true philosophy of man must consider the "whole" person in his theological completeness: a finite creature possessing profound religious, existential, and spiritual depths. The progressive dehumanization of life by twentieth century statist regimes from which all these thinkers were forced to flee in the 1930s added urgency to their desire to promulgate a unified conception of man to the modern world. As Gurian wrote of Maritain's critique of modern political philosophy, "A purely natural political philosophy cannot know the ultimate end of man."[16] Thus, for Gurian, Maritain, Gilson, Guardini, and, ultimately, O'Malley, who patterned his thought after theirs, the concept of Christian philosophy became intimately linked with the concept of Christian humanism and the attempt, in O'Malley's words, to "integrate a true philosophy with the life of culture."[17]

O'MALLEY AND *THE REVIEW OF POLITICS*

O'Malley played out his role as a Christian philosopher in the modern world most effectively as a literary critic, but his interests were not confined solely to literature. The Notre Dame teacher, like the humanistic European Catholic thinkers he emulated, took an active interest in virtually every aspect of human culture, including literature, politics, philosophy, and education.

O'Malley, with Notre Dame philosophy professor Leo R. Ward, C.S.C., was instrumental in helping Gurian establish Notre Dame's *The Review of Politics* in 1939.[18] Blunt, opinionated, and "Catholic to the bone," Gurian (a convert from Judaism) had studied under German phenomenologist Max Scheler during the 1920s, an experience that left him with a deep distrust of materialist philosophies. As managing editor of *The Review* between 1939 and 1963, O'Malley worked closely with Gurian throughout the magazine's early history.

The Review reflected Gurian's intellectual orientation throughout most of the 1940s and 1950s. Deeply philosophical, the magazine's purpose, as articulated by O'Malley in its tenth anniversary issue in 1948, was "to bring to bear upon the special problems raised by modern culture, the illumination of a valid spiritual and philosophical tradition, an illumination best described as the Christian world-view."[19]

The Review drew upon a wide number of Judeo-Christian thinkers during the 1940s and 1950s who reflected that outlook: Italian Social Democrat Don Luigi Sturzo, Jewish political philosopher Hannah Arendt, Hans Barth, and neo-Thomists Dawson and Maritain were all contributors. Their broadly humanistic conception of mankind's nature and destiny established the identity of *The Review* that has lasted throughout its history. Maritain set the course for *The Review* in the lead article of the first issue when he advocated, in the fashion of Christian philosophy, an "integral humanism" that "considers man in the wholeness of his natural and supernatural being" as the only valid philosophical base for modern social, cultural, and political reconstruction.[20]

Most of O'Malley's own work appeared in *The Review*. He published eight full-length articles in the journal between 1941 and 1963, focusing mostly upon figures whose worldview reflected his own: Christian humanist thinkers like John Henry Newman, Maritain, Dawson, and Guardini, as well as nineteenth and twentieth century men of letters alienated from modern rational culture. The latter included such O'Malley favorites as Fyodor Dostoevksy, Søren Kierkegaard, D. H. Lawrence, William Blake, and Leon Bloy. O'Malley's identification with these cultural critics was so complete that it is sometimes difficult to ascertain where they end and he begins.

In sympathy with the anti-heroes, underground men, and "spiritual outcasts" from a triumphant "rationalist, materialist, irreligious civilization," O'Malley's essays, especially during the 1940s, denounced in apocalyptic tones the spiritual decay of modern life. "The enfeebling of religion and religious knowledge in the modern world is the most terribly tragic experience that the world knows," he wrote in his first full-length published work in 1942.[21] O'Malley's constant message was that the modern crisis was fundamentally a religious crisis and that the very survival of culture depended upon a new integration of religion and life.

It needs to be stressed that O'Malley presents something of a problem when subjected to traditional academic standards. He was not a particularly original thinker. His illustration of Blake and Lawrence as disaffected "religious minds" lurking "beneath the surface" of self-satisfied rationalist culture, for instance, was borrowed directly from two Dawson articles published in the London *Tablet* during the mid–1930s.[22] Much of O'Malley's other cultural criticism was merely a summation of ideas found in other works published by Dawson and Maritain between the wars.

Many of O'Malley's essays and speeches contained recycled materials. Twenty-five-line quotations were not uncommon in an O'Malley essay, followed by little substantive analysis. "Verbiage" was how one of his colleagues described O'Malley's writing. Neo-Thomist philosopher and Notre Dame colleague Yves Simon was even more critical. In a 1947 letter to Maritain he criticized O'Malley for lacking "rigorous thought" and, the worst of all possible scholastic sins, of harboring a "romantic" philosophical outlook.[23]

Moreover, O'Malley scorned the Ph.D. and regarded most research scholars as "cold, analytic, academic neutral[s]."[24] He associated them with the skepticism he abhorred and with what he considered to be the primary intellectual problem of modern times—the separation of religion from knowledge.

Like many great teachers, O'Malley was a dramatizer of ideas rather

than a creator of ideas. His strength lay in his ability to extract what
was important in a particular thinker, and then with passionate intensity
present it "as if he were discovering the work for the first time."[25] This
was most effective in the classroom and on the lecture platform. Here
O'Malley could step outside of his shyness and, in effect, become Leon
Bloy bellowing with brutal axe-edged words against Christian mediocrity, or Maritain and Dawson coolly analyzing the spiritual disintegration
of modern times, or Guardini movingly describing the liturgical character
of Christian existence.

The recurring references to Guardini in both his lectures and essays
illustrates the great influence that German thinker had over O'Malley
throughout his academic life. O'Malley could easily identify with Guardini. Priest, theologian, and literary critic, Guardini was Professor for
Philosophy of Religion and Catholic *Weltanschauung* at the University of
Berlin before and after World War II. Guardini also came out of the same
German phenomenological tradition as Gurian. By *Weltanschauung* Guardini meant a "world outlook, a vision and understanding of the world
from the standpoint of faith."[26] Perhaps no other Catholic thinker between 1930 and 1960 utilized the explanatory power of Christian revelation more effectively than Guardini in clarifying questions of modern
human existence.

Guardini grounded his own *Weltanschauung* in the liturgy of the
Church throughout his long life. In a number of popularly written theological works between 1930 and 1960 Guardini expressed the idea that
the Church contained the most profound expression of reality and thus
constituted the most fundamental basis of Christian living. By the
"Church" Guardini did not mean the juridical, institutional Church of
Rome. He meant instead the liturgical Church, the corporate community
of the faithful united with all other Christians in the Mystical Body of
Christ. Thus, in *The Church and the Catholic and the Spirit of the Liturgy*
(1935) Guardini urged modern Catholics to rediscover the dynamic sense
of this corporate Church and to live their lives within the fullness of its
liturgy. This meant an awareness of the theology of the Church and its
fundamental mysteries.

O'Malley devoured Guardini's ideas. Through all of O'Malley's
thought runs the same comprehensiveness regarding humanity, the
Church, and Christian life. Guardini's reforming spirit, his phenomenological appreciation for the person's total being, and his refusal to
draw a methodological division between philosophy and theology were
all important concepts to O'Malley. No less important was Guardini's
understanding of the organic inner life of the Church with Christ as its
center. O'Malley projected this same view of Christian life and the
Church in his own writing and in his "Modern Catholic Writers" course.

Appropriately, O'Malley began his course with a unit on "The Thinker in the Church" and a reflection upon Guardini's thought.[27]

CHRISTIAN HUMANIST AND CATHOLIC CRITIC

Is there a Christian-Catholic imagination? Is there a uniquely Catholic way of looking at the world? At man? At history? One of the central ideas that informed O'Malley's life as critic and teacher was that there existed a specifically Catholic imaginary dimension. It found its confirmation, he insisted, in the poets and prose writers of the European Catholic revival.

Sallie McFague TeSelle writes in *Literature and Christian Life* (1966) that there have been numerous attempts by twentieth century Christian critics to articulate a Christian philosophy of literature and to suggest guidelines for the literary imagination. Protestant critics, observes TeSelle, have operated from a "pre-Incarnational" imagination which, with a good deal of pessimism, dwells upon the doctrine of original sin and the tragic, limited vision of man it projects in literature and art. Catholic writers and critics, by contrast, work from an Incarnational perspective, writes TeSelle. "The theological criterion with which the Romans operate," she states, "is not original sin or Christology, but the Thomistic understanding of nature and grace." Unlike Protestants, Catholics, through the perspective of the Incarnation, believe that "grace operates through nature, not in spite of it."[28]

Twentieth century Christian humanist thought has been sustained by these same understandings. Humanism in general stresses the development and improvement of human personality. What distinguishes Christian humanism from the various secular, Marxist, and existentialist humanisms that gained twentieth century prominence is the former's assertion that man's existence and perfection is owed to God. While secular humanist thought since Renaissance times has made a virtue of free and autonomous man, the Christian humanist position, by contrast, stresses that man can never be fully human unless he is in relationship with God.

The Christian humanist thus looks at humanity in terms of wholeness and incompleteness, with wholeness lost in the Fall, but returned through the grace of Christ's Redemption. Consequently, many modern Catholic theologians look at the problem of sin as "broken harmony" between God and man, sometimes resulting in grave psychological disorder.

The most eloquent assertion of the twentieth century Catholic humanist position occurs in Maritain's *True Humanism* (1936). Writing to counter what he considered to be the disfigurement of humanity by

anthropocentric liberal and Marxist humanisms on the one hand, and
the antihumanism of post-World War I Protestant neo-orthodoxy (which
Maritain characterized as a theology of grace without freedom) on the
other, Maritain rhetorically asks, "What is man?" To which he poetically
replies:

[Man is] never simply his natural self. He is a being out of joint and wounded—
wounded by the devil with the wound of concupiscence and by God's wound
of love. On the one hand he carries the burden of original sin, he is born
dispossessed of the gifts of grace, not indeed corrupted in the substance of his
being, but wounded in his nature. On the one hand he is made for a supernatural
end . . . and if he does not turn against God his power of refusal he bears within
him here below the truly divine life or sanctifying grace and its gifts.[29]

These fundamental Thomistic understandings of fallen humanity and
wounded nature, on the one hand, and its restoration to divine life
through grace and the redemptive action of Christ, on the other, were
the elemental bases of Maritain's "integral humanism" or "the humanism of the Incarnation." Moreover, these same understandings provided
the fundamental framework through which twentieth century Catholic
humanists from O'Malley to writer Flannery O'Connor viewed the
world, humanity, and creation.

If one centers his imagination on the Incarnation and the idea of God-
Made-Man, O'Malley believed, a number of attitudes toward God, man,
and creation automatically follow. First, an Incarnational vision is an
integrated vision. "The knowledge of the Incarnation," O'Malley told a
group of Catholic literature teachers and critics in 1949, has brought
about an "astonishing transformation" over nature and "consequently
into the manner in which we must henceforth conceive it."[30] Here O'Malley joined such later Catholic critics as William F. Lynch, S. J. and writer
Flannery O'Conner in claiming that the Incarnation had resulted in "a
second and a new creation," demanding a new imaginative vision of all
created existences—no longer Manichean and divisive, but analogical
and integrative.[31] Through the perspective of the Word-Made-Flesh, the
finite was no longer separate from the infinite. The part contained the
whole. Human existence was a graced existence, and the way to the
infinite was through the concrete, the tangible, and the finite. O'Malley
believed that "the Catholic oneness of the universe, the unity of this
world with God's world" was best articulated in the poetry of English
Catholic Gerard Manley Hopkins where "the world is charged with the
grandeur of God" and "Christ plays in ten thousand places / Lovely in
limbs, and lovely in eyes not his."[32]

An Incarnational outlook, O'Malley believed, also affected the way
one viewed the nature and destiny of man. From the perspective of the

Incarnation, man is seen as a "tangled web," a complex creature of profound existential depths: fallen yet redeemed, sinful yet loved, rooted in nature, yet yearning to transcend nature, a spiritual being who is called to grace but as a free being includes the possibility of rejecting grace. Here again O'Malley's importance as a representative figure becomes clear, since he was only one of many twentieth century Catholic theologians, philosophers, and writers who turned to the Incarnation to supply depth and direction to both the individual and corporate life of mankind. It is interesting, for example, to compare O'Malley's theological development during this same period with that of Flannery O'Connor. Both Americans came to their understanding of Aquinas, in large part, through the writings of the same Europeans: Gilson, Maritain, Guardini, and German theologian Karl Adam. O'Connor, a serious Catholic layperson in the 1940s and 1950s, made no secret of the fact that her artistic technique and creative vision were shaped and defined by the Incarnation. She read and reviewed the published works of all of the above, regularly defended the notion of a Christian philosophy and the unity of all knowledge, and believed with other Thomists of the era that Christ's immersion into history had transformed the entire structure of being, investing all creation with radical new meaning.[33]

For O'Malley no less than Maritain, Flannery O'Connor and other Catholic thinkers between 1935 and 1950, the humanism of the Incarnation was both an optimistic and realistic philosophy of man. Realistic, because it addressed man as a concrete, existential being. Optimistic, because its view of creation was grounded in Christian revelation and Christian hope. It was this kind of "Christian realism" that informed O'Malley in his role as Christian philosopher and Catholic critic.

O'MALLEY AND THE REVIVAL

"It should be the belief of those responsible for a genuine philosophy of literature (involving a philosophy of art and a philosophy of man and culture)," O'Malley wrote in 1950, "that real standards and directions are provided in the classical and Christian traditions." The Christian tradition, he continued, "makes available concepts of man's being, man's destiny and man's art that are more secure and realistic, more universal and illuminating than those provided anywhere else."[34]

O'Malley cited a wide number of modern writers working within the Christian-Catholic tradition who confirmed this outlook: Poets Gerard Manley Hopkins, Francis Thompson and Charles Peguy, dramatist Paul Claudel, novelists Graham Greene, Francois Mauriac, Georges Bernanos, Sigrid Undset, and others. All of the above, with the exception of the Norwegian Undset, were associated with the English and French Catholic literary revivals in which a remarkable number of talented Cath-

olic writers (many of whom were converts), successfully integrated theological values into their works.

Graham Greene provides a good example of this integration while at
the same time illustrating for O'Malley some of the pitfalls of fusing
faith with fiction. Greene always disdained the designation "Catholic
novelist," but he nevertheless employed strong themes of sin, grace,
and redemption in several of his early serious novels. Many of Greene's
early protagonists are wounded by sin: Pinkie, the psychopathic killer
in *Brighton Rock* (1939) by pride in the knowledge of his own damnation;
the "whiskey priest" in *The Power and the Glory* (1940) by an unlived
faith; Sarah, the sensitive protagonist of *The End of the Affair* (1951), by
a self-destructive adultery.

Yet as wretched and as fallen as these characters are, each in his or
her own way maintains a relationship with God. Indeed, in most of
Greene's Catholic novels, God simply will not let go, as in the case of
the adulterous Sarah who is pulled toward grace even as she flees it.
Paradoxically, Sarah's affair becomes the very means of her redemption
as she realizes that sensual love cannot fill the emptiness created when
she rejected divine love.

O'Malley always appreciated Greene's Christian humanistic focus
upon man's relationship with God, but, as a Thomist, he believed that
the Englishman's Manichean-like attitude toward nature and grace constituted a failure of the Catholic imagination. Greene was always too
much of an Augustinian for O'Malley, whose own theological orientation
was centered in Aquinas. Greene created too great a "gap between this
world and God's world," observed O'Malley in 1950, and when grace
came it was too shattering and obtrusive.[35] It was the old Protestant-
Catholic problem of grace without freedom. Grace, in O'Malley's neo-
Thomistic view of creation, was a thing lived, not something one was
assaulted by. Greene's "muddled theology" during the 1940s and 1950s
was a concern of more than one Catholic critic.

Undset (1882–1949) succeeded for O'Malley where Greene failed. She
won the Nobel Prize for literature in 1928, one year after her best known
religious piece, *Kristin Lavransdatter*, was published in America.[36] The
Kristin trilogy (1920–1922) was written before Undset entered the Church
in 1925, but the work exercised considerable influence over the American
Catholic literary community during the early 1930s, especially among
Catholic college students and teachers who, like O'Malley, were hungry
for a new realism in Catholic fiction.

Briefly, *Kristin Lavransdatter* follows the life of its protagonist from
early adolescence through old age and death. The theme that dominates
the story is Kristin's lifelong willfulness, and how it estranges her from
her father (Lavrans), her lover and husband (Erland), and, most important, from her creator.

Throughout, Undset—in the best tradition of Henrik Ibsen and Scandinavian realism—is true to experience, whether she is treating Kristin's all-consuming passion for Erland, childbirth scenes, or the corrosive effect of sin upon Kristin's personality. Without moralizing, Undset shows how Kristin's stubborn refusal to relinquish earthly passions leads to a brooding disjointedness, further estranging her from those who love her. Only when Kristin learns late in life to cooperate with the will of God does she find the self-reconciliation that eluded her for so long.

For O'Malley, Undset's novel contained all the crucial elements of Christian realism: An Incarnational view of humanity that sees Kristin as a fallen creature who, aided by grace, engages in a lifelong struggle toward union with God; a moral attitude in literature that acknowledged that sin existed, that it was freely chosen, and that it resulted in "loss of being"; and finally, an imagination which assumed that every person carried on a relationship with his or her creator and that "this relationship is never lost, never diminished," no matter what the sin.[37]

Undset was a superb example for O'Malley of how belief could make a difference in literature. Theological values, insisted O'Malley in the manner of a Christian philosopher, "without affecting the autonomy of art," could "both illume art and illume our approach to art."[38] O'Malley consequently referred often to Undset and to many of the other writers of the French and English Catholic revivals as "true humanists, integral humanists," because they understood with Maritain "the real problem of man and his position as human creature before God."[39] This kind of realism was vitally important to O'Malley and many other American Catholic critics and teachers during an era when the novels of major writers like Ernest Hemingway, John Steinbeck, and James T. Farrell were projecting the limitations of human freedom and the absence of God.

Which conception of man "will permit or provide [the] greatest possibility of a really serious, human, tragic art?" asked O'Malley in 1948. "Maritain's or Hemingway's?"[40] Thus, through the example of Maritain, Undset, and the creative minds of the European Catholic resurgence, O'Malley maintained that Christian assumptions were relevant to the modern writer. Christian orthodoxy, he asserted, expanded rather than restricted the creative imagination, just as it had expanded the creative vision of Christian writers from Dante to Chaucer. Ironically, the modern writer could become more realistic not by rejecting religious knowledge but by embracing it.

To the twentieth century novelist, O'Malley thus posed the relevance of Christian humanism and the "integrating philosophy" of Maritain and Aquinas. To the modern poet, O'Malley posed the vision of the Incarnation and Claudel's and Hopkin's unitary view of creation. They suggested, argued the Notre Dame teacher and Christian philosopher, the concepts and channels for a new dimension in modern literature.

O'MALLEY AND AMERICAN CATHOLIC INTELLECTUAL LIFE, 1935–1955

Frank O'Malley's life and the segment of American Catholic intellectual life between 1935 and 1955 it represents is filled with a number of striking impressions. The strongest impression is the apostolic character of the Catholic laity during this period in the history of the American Church. Serious American Catholic lay intellectuals between 1935 and 1955 were quite sure that as practicing, instructed Christians, they could make an intellectual difference in the modern world. They especially believed that their faith had important things to say about the image of man to a materialistic and secularistic society.

Many American Catholic intellectuals, no less than O'Malley in the 1940s and 1950s, were convinced that incorrect conceptions of the nature and destiny of man were at the center of the political, social, and cultural crises of their age. The "proper understanding of man's nature is the beginning of cultural and all other reconstruction in our time," declared a standard American history textbook used in American Catholic high schools during the 1940s and 1950s. "It is the only basis for a proper education. The solution of the problem of peace depends upon it. The revival of art depends upon it."[41]

The same attitude was echoed by a spokeswoman for the Catholic Renascence Society (an organization of Catholic literature teachers devoted to the revival of Catholic letters) in 1949. "The bitter experiences of war," she argued "have convinced many . . . that the vacuum created by early twentieth century positivistic values must be filled with the cultural heritage of Christian civilization if we wish to save our humanistic way of life."[42]

Living during a period that emphasized such key theological concepts as Catholic Action and the "priesthood of the laity," educated, for the most part, at Catholic liberal arts colleges and universities which stressed the integration of faith and knowledge, and increasingly thrown into intellectual contact with a European Catholic lay intelligentsia that was actively engaged in world affairs, American Catholic lay intellectuals and college teachers between 1935 and 1955 felt—and transmitted to their students—a heavy responsibility to assert themselves intellectually as Catholics in the modern world. A strong "Incarnational" sensibility which stressed that grace operated through nature and that as members of Christ's Mystical Body all believers were called to complete his redemption on earth, heightened this sense of mission.

Many embraced the concept of a Christian philosophy in their determination to achieve a new synthesis between religion and life—perhaps not as literally as did O'Malley, but at least in its intellectual posture. Gilson's celebrated essay "The Intelligence in the Service of Christ the King" (1939), which urged Catholic intellectuals not to separate their Christianity from their lives as thinkers, scientists, and artists, but rather to "philosophize in the faith," thinking "as if they were Christian not as if they were not Christian," was well-known to serious Catholic collegians in the 1940s and 1950s and many acted upon its premises.[43]

What O'Malley attempted for American literature, a young Eugene McCarthy, for example, attempted to a lesser degree for American politics. McCarthy was a Catholic whose undergraduate education at Minnesota's St. John's University during the early 1930s was rooted in the same intellectual tradition as O'Malley. As a young Minnesota congressman during the 1950s, McCarthy wrote *Frontiers in American Democracy* (1960), where he drew upon the natural law social ethics of Maritain and Thomistic understandings of nature and grace to work out a Christian theory of politics.[44] "Is there a Christian politics?" McCarthy asked rhetorically in a 1954 *Commonweal* article. In language similar to O'Malley's, McCarthy emphasized that the Christian politician should reflect an awareness in his actions "of the great mystery of the Redemption and the sacred mystery and dignity of all men."[45]

McCarthy's personal life during the late 1930s and 1940s illustrates another less tangible but nonetheless definite cultural pattern operative within the Catholic lay community at this time. Simply stated, there was, as a close friend of McCarthy and his wife, Abigail, remembers, "a genuine desire for holiness" among many college-educated lay Catholics of their generation.[46]

Abigail Quigley McCarthy's autobiography *Private Faces/Public Places* (1972) provides a remarkable insight into this phenomenon. Recollecting a time in 1946 when a friend asked her why she married Eugene, she wrote: " 'Well, if you really want to know,' I said, 'because I think I have a better chance of becoming a saint that way.' "[47] This quest for personal sanctification found the McCarthys during the early years of their marriage setting up St. Anne's Farm, a distributist-style cooperative near St. John's where they attempted to revive the concept of Christian rural life, and, as "scholar farmers," to build a home life around the nightly Compline, the liturgy, and the Benedictine monastic ideal of mixed prayer and work.[48]

Personal holiness and sanctity appeared to be real options for at least some Catholics during the 1940s and early 1950s. Although difficult to measure, this impulse can be observed in such Catholic Action organizations as The Grail, an apostolate for young Catholic women whose "Program of Action" included a "total Christianity" where "every phase of individual and social activity—work, study, recreation, family life, even eating and sleeping"—was to be "lifted to the supernatural level of an organic Christian Life."[49] It can be observed in the *Integrity* magazine group, a collection of postwar Catholic idealists who were "dedicated to the task of discovering a new synthesis of RELIGION and LIFE for our times."[50] The immense popularity among college-age Catholics of Thomas Merton's spiritual autobiography *The Seven Storey Mountain* (1948) provides another indirect measure of this phenomenon.[51]

There was a culture of holiness and sanctity within the Catholic lay community during the 1940s and early 1950s, and the literature of the European Catholic revival played a significant role in its origin and operation. "Graham Greene and Evelyn Waugh," commented English Catholic critic and writer Bruce Marshall in 1950, "make me want to be holy."[52] Indeed, the novels and dramas of Greene, Bloy, Bernanos, and Claudel were filled with heroic saint-figures who were immensely attractive, from a personal standpoint, to O'Malley and his generation. These modern Catholic writers provided O'Malley's generation with models for the literary imagination, but they also provided it patterns for Christian living.

A more troublesome aspect of this phenomenon, however, was that the model of sanctity put forward by many of these writers often was fixed excruciatingly upon the Christian ideal of redemptive suffering. This was particularly true of the French writers advanced by O'Malley. Richard Griffiths has pointed out that the idea of suffering portrayed in the literature of the French revival "assumed an importance out of all proportion to other doctrines of the Church."[53]

Moreover, the theme of efficacious suffering in French Catholic literature was linked more often than not to the figure of woman. Bloy's self-denying Clotilde (*The Woman Who Was Poor*) suffers quietly through some of the worst abuses ever described in modern literature to expiate the sins of others. Bernanos's mystical Chantal (*Joy*) is misunderstood and finally murdered for her saintly innocence. Claudel's leper-saint Violaine (*The Tidings Brought to Mary*) surrenders to a life of self-sacrifice while serving as an instrument of grace for others.

Women scholars from a contemporary feminist perspective have criticized especially this idealization of feminine passivity and suffering.[54] O'Malley's wholly favorable critical discussions of these works unquestionably draws the same criticism. Yet, even as one acknowledges the merits of this judgment, it is important to remember that the lives of many of these characters—and, in some cases, of their creators—represented the heroic, total, self-surrendering ideal of Christian sainthood that was so appealing to young Catholic idealists at this time. Few American Catholic college teachers during the 1940s and 1950s were more adept than O'Malley at bringing this sense of total Christian existence to life, or of inspiring students to embrace the full consequences of their faith. Nor did any Catholic teacher attack more forcefully the unlived Christian life.[55]

The final theme that emerges from the life and times of Frank O'Malley is the reorientation of Catholic religious thought after 1935 toward a more dynamic and vital religious outlook. Developments in Christian philosophy under Gilson and other European Thomists illustrate some of the creative changes that occurred in neo-scholastic thought between 1935 and 1955. The idea of a Christian philosophy was not without its critics,[56] but it pumped new life into the neo-scholastic synthesis, investing it with an existential content and idiom that was missing from the closed conceptualism that characterized neo-scholastic thought following the Modernist crisis earlier in the century. The problems that concerned Gilson, Maritain, Guardini, and, ultimately, O'Malley between 1935 and 1955—questions of freedom and destiny, the contingencies of concrete human existence, and the strivings of man to transcend his own finitude—were questions central to modern minds.

Gilson and Maritain were Thomists in the 1930s and 1940s who were rediscovering, in the words of Gerald A. McCool, "the central place of the act of existence in St. Thomas's epistemology and metaphysics."[57] Aquinas's metaphysics of God was not Aristotle's changeless Pure Act, Gilson discovered. It was based rather on the Judeo-Christian theological understanding of God as Pure Being, signified by God's biblical name— I AM WHO AM. The supreme perfection of being thus was not form, but "esse" (the concrete act of existence). Existence was prior to essence.[58] For Frenchman Gabriel Marcel, American W. Norris Clarke, and other "existential Thomists" who came after Gilson in the 1950s and 1960s, this basic Thomistic insight shifted the focus in Catholic philosophical thought from form and essence—the preoccupation of Aristotle and traditional scholastic commentators—to existence itself.[59] This is another instance of how a revived Christian philosophy utilizing theological insights and categories was able to distance scholasticism from the static world of Aristotelian-Greek thought and project it into the concrete world of being. By 1960 there was no longer a single scholastic system but, as McCool observes, a diversity of systems: Gilson's historical Thomism; Maritain's traditional commentators' Thomism, enriched and enlivened by Christian philosophy; Frenchman Joseph Marechal's transcendental Thomism, using the insights of Kant and Hegel as its starting point; and an emergent post-World War II existential Thomism represented by Marcel and Clarke.[60]

It was this kind of pluralistic development within Catholic religious thought that freed post–1935 American Thomists like O'Malley from the essentialist categories of pre–1935 scholasticism and encouraged him to deal with the existential dilemma of modern man. The result was a richer, more restless intellectual outlook, perhaps less confident and unified

than the essentialist postures that characterized the 1920s but better able
to speak to the religious needs of the contemporary age.

European developments in the theology of the Church similarly enlivened the religious thought of educated American Catholics between
1935 and 1955. German theologians Guardini and Adam were examples
of Europeans in the 1920s and 1930s who were reorienting Catholic
thought toward the essential nature of the Church and its life in the
Mystical Body of Christ. This dynamic view of the Church as organic
sacramental community—as opposed to external institution and hierarchy—was further deepened in the 1940s when the liturgical movement
became linked to the names of Yves Congar and Henri de Lubac, who
as so-called "New Theologians" moved outside of scholastic categories
to seek ecclesiastical and theological renewal in biblical, patristic, and
liturgical sources. Under these thinkers, the Church was seen, in older
Pauline-patristic terms, as a sign and sacrament of Christ's presence in
the world. The Church was understood primarily as communion and
secondarily as institution, drawing its life and direction from Christ who
was present in its forms.[61]

The liturgical movement thus developed somewhat differently in Europe than in America after 1935. In America the movement's principal
spokesmen—Michel, Ellard, and Catholics within the orbit of *Orate
Fratres* and the Catholic Worker—stressed the central importance of the
Mystical Body in Catholic ecclesiology, but they were oriented more
toward the pragmatic social justice implications of the doctrine. This was
particularly true in the Depression years of the 1930s. In Europe, by
contrast, the liturgical movement from the start was much more broadly
theological and Christological, focusing upon the supernatural character
of the Church and its fundamental mystery and sacramentality. This
was the focus embraced by O'Malley, who, with Guardini, saw the
liturgy as the entire "culture of the Church," an embodiment of the
totality of Catholic belief, its pivotal dogmas and theology.[62]

O'Malley's own Christian theory of literature was connected intimately with the liturgy. The liturgy—broadly understood as the prayer
of the Church and its fundamental theology—represented the adult religious outlook that O'Malley believed was essential for lay Catholic
intellectual and cultural development in America. The liturgy would
integrate the Catholic imagination toward a more focused understanding
of the Incarnation, thereby allowing the believing artist to penetrate more
deeply into reality. The prayer of the liturgy, O'Malley pointed out, was
a constant reminder that man was creature, yet called by grace toward
wholeness through Christ. "This Incarnational awareness, this grasp of
the liturgical, factual reality of Christ-in-time, Christ-in-the-Universe,"
claimed O'Malley in 1949, "can enliven the poet's vision and illume,

inform his words." Claudel, Undset, and other major Catholic writers shared this "liturgical consciousness."[63]

O'Malley, like numerous other Catholic American cultural leaders of his generation, subsequently linked the American Catholic literary revival to the liturgical revival. He belonged to the Catholic Renascence Society and shared with other Catholic teachers and critics of his day an enthusiasm for the resurgence of Catholic letters abroad, but he never felt comfortable with the organizational aspects of the American movement. For the most part, he dismissed any organized efforts to stimulate a Catholic literary emergence in the United States as a self-conscious attempt by Catholic partisans to "manufacture Catholic literature."[64] Great Catholic literature, cautioned O'Malley, could never be "the product of meetings, conferences, or conventions, no matter how enthusiastic or fervid."[65]

A serious Catholic literature, insisted O'Malley, could "issue only from truly Christian persons, 'possessed' persons, those whose religious values have . . . 'turned to blood within.' "[66] In short, a new fusion of faith and reason was as essential for Catholic American literary development in O'Malley's view as it was for other areas of Catholic intellectual life. Catholics as thinkers would begin to influence modern thought and culture when they thought as adult Christians—which the liturgy implied—and not as if they were without identity as Christians.

Still, while O'Malley was surely correct in claiming that art cannot be coerced, his suggestion that Catholic letters must discover their power in liturgical models, and that knowledge of the liturgy would somehow make the writer a deeper artist (but not, O'Malley always stressed, a "better" artist) was overstated. At best, it was an aesthetic that was too closely tied to formalistic neo-scholastic theories of matter and form. At worst, it represented an attempt to tie the development of art to the spiritual growth of the artist. Moreover, aside from Claudel, there is little indication that the writers and poets of the French Catholic revival took their inspiration from the liturgy. Claudel was a great artist, but so were Farrell, Eugene O'Neill, and F. Scott Fitzgerald—all fallen-away Catholics.

O'Malley's preoccupation with the liturgy as the integrating component in the revival of Catholic art and culture only throws into sharper relief the total pattern of his life as an American Catholic intellectual of the 1940s and 1950s. The liturgy represented yet another attempt to achieve intellectual and personal wholeness through religious faith. It represented still another attempt at integration, synthesis, and unity. It found its counterpart in the idea of a Christian philosophy, the theology of nature and grace, and the cultivation of holiness and sanctity.

As much as any American Catholic intellectual of these years, O'Malley personified this quest for synthesis. It was a life that attempted to communicate a unified Christian vision, imagination, and philosophy to a troubled twentieth century and to have religious values assume a more prominent place in its literature, politics, and outlook.

Moreover, it was a life that looked toward some of the most progressive writers, philosophers, and theologians of Catholic Europe for its understanding of modern Catholic belief. In embracing Gilson's and Maritain's concrete existential regard for man, new understandings of the Church as organic community, and the new emphasis upon the priesthood of the laity, O'Malley, in significant ways, anticipated the reforms of Vatican II.

If the 1930s were an era when many Catholic Americans rediscovered their Catholic culture, the 1940s and the 1950s were a time when many rediscovered their Catholic faith. O'Malley contributed to that process. He offered the American Catholic cultural, literary, and collegiate community some impressive models for emulation, and in doing so contributed to the intellectual and cultural maturation of the American Church.

9

"Yes, We Have No Bernanos." The Search for the Great American Catholic Novel, II: Catholic Fiction During the Era of Transformation

It has been alleged that Catholics always seem to be fifty years behind the times. In matters of literary realism it was actually closer to twenty. Beginning in the mid–1930s, however, an increasing number of Catholic critics, writers, and college teachers began to demand that their fiction come to terms with the complexities of modern life.

"It is sheer nonsense," complained Fordham professor Francis X. Connolly in 1933, to insist that every Catholic character "should always be wearing a painted halo," or to suggest that Catholics had a monopoly on moral probity.[1] This kind of sterotypical characterization, Connolly warned, only would alienate the more discerning reader.

More significantly, Connolly joined Frank O'Malley and other Catholic critics in protesting that too much Catholic imaginative literature lacked devotion to truth. Literary "naturalists" like Theodore Dreiser, Frank Norris, and Ernest Hemingway "falsified reality" and created only caricatures of humanity, Catholics alleged; but many Catholic critics were painfully aware that these same criticisms applied equally to their own writers. "Little monsters of goodness" was how one 1943 critic described the pale characters who inhabited the novels typical of Lucille Papin Borden's genre.[2] Therefore, while Francis X. Talbot, Calvert Alexander, Daniel A. Lord, and the earlier proponents of an American Catholic literary emergence continued to pin their hopes on writers like Borden, Kathleen Norris, and Ethel Cook Eliot, a growing number of other Catholic teachers and critics viewed these same authors with an increasing sense of embarrassment.

No doubt these earlier novelists would have passed easily enough from the American scene as Catholics matured during the 1930s and

1940s. Hastening the process, however, was the impact made upon Catholic American literary culture by such European writers as Leon Bloy, Georges Bernanos, Francois Mauriac, and Graham Greene beginning in the mid–1930s. Their influence spread rapidly with translations of Mauriac's *Viper's Tangle* in 1933, Bernanos's *The Dairy of a Country Priest* in 1937, and Bloy's *The Woman Who Was Poor* in 1939. Greene's first major Catholic novel, *Brighton Rock,* was published in 1938. By the early 1940s, Greene, Bernanos, and Mauriac set the standards for Catholic fiction in the United States, at least in the more progressive circles of the Catholic literary establishment. An exception, of course, was O'Malley, who still adhered to Sigrid Undset as the model for the Catholic literary imagination.

Enthusiasm for the Europeans was especially strong in the Catholic colleges. When Abigail Quigly McCarthy returned to teach at her alma mater, the College of St. Catherine, in 1940, she found its literary quarterly filled with articles on the Europeans and their ideas in vogue "wherever the novel was seriously discussed."[3] In 1946 McCarthy helped establish a modest review, *Books Abounding,* to keep St. Catherine alumnae abreast of new developments in the Catholic novel and the Catholic literary revival.

The major Catholic reviews in the 1940s and early 1950s—*Commonweal, America* and the *Catholic World*—likewise shared a passion for the European. Greene, Bernanos, and Mauriac served as starting points for a long stream of articles on "Catholic realism" and formulas for the modern novel. In *Norms for the Novel* (1953), *America* literary editor Harold C. Gardiner, S. J. also used Greene's novels to educate an immature American Catholic reading public on the distinction between a modern literary naturalism that was indifferent to the concept of sin, and an emergent Christian "realism" in which characters were aware of the nature of their acts and made choices with full knowledge of good and evil.[4] Greene's American popularity was best underscored in 1952 when the Gallery of Living Catholic Authors, with Gardiner on its awards committee, selected Greene's *The End of the Affair* as the winner of its Annual Catholic Literary Award, given for literary excellence among current Catholic books.

But where was the American Greene? The American Bernanos? In the self-conscious world of Catholic American culture, these became increasingly persistent questions during the 1940s and in some (but not all) ways anticipated those posed by historian John Tracy Ellis and others during the Catholic intellectualism debate a decade later. Fewer Catholics by 1940 were willing to accept the customary argument that preoccupation with the brick-and-mortar stage of the Church's development had precluded serious Catholic cultural achievement. With over 200 colleges and universities, a number of publishing houses, and an active press, the American Catholic intellectual establishment seemed imposing indeed. England, France, and even Undset's Protestant Norway had produced their quota of important Catholic novelists. Why couldn't the American Church yield similar fruit? Throughout the 1940s and early 1950s, then, Catholic critics, teachers, and cultural leaders anxiously sought to encourage and develop a body of Catholic writers whose work could compare with the novelists of Europe.[5]

This post–1935 quest for the Great American Catholic Novel doubtless represents on one level the final chapter in the Catholic search for intellectual and cultural achievement. Again it invites comparison with the nineteenth century American literary experience when American writers were pressed to establish their own literary identity and tradition. Both episodes can be analyzed as indications of intellectual insecurity by emergent cultural groups.

But it is clear that the twentieth century American Catholic literary enterprise was motivated equally by apostolic concerns, especially when seen within the context of the entire revival. Even during the self-conscious and defensive 1920s, the Catholic literary revival in America aimed to reestablish the relationship between religion and culture. The Catholic novel was seen as a means toward that end. More than any other cultural group between 1920 and 1960, Catholics regarded literature as a significant cultural force capable of shaping the consciousness of society for good or for evil. Through the novel, Catholics would penetrate and change culture, leavening it with Christian truth. Thus, the critical interest in finding the American counterpart to Greene or Bernanos was complex and cannot be confined to attempts to offer relief from the Norrises and Bordens. Nor can it be seen merely as another effort to gain cultural status and prestige. As architects of a new culture, Catholic writers and critics between 1920 and 1960 believed they had an important redemptive mission to complete. The writing apostolate, or "Apostolate of the Pen," was an integral part of that plan.

TWO CRITICS IN SEARCH OF A NOVEL: RILEY HUGHES AND SISTER MARIELLA GABLE

"The fact is, of course," wrote Catholic literary critic and Georgetown University professor Riley Hughes in 1950, "that we are all in this together—Catholic writers, Catholic critics, Catholic readers."[6] Hughes was speaking of the search for the Great American Catholic Novel.

Virtually every critic during the hegemonic Greene-Bernanos-Mauriac era was eager to improve the quality of American Catholic fiction, but two stood out: Hughes and Sr. Mariella Gable, a Benedictine nun and head of the English department at the College of St. Benedict in St. Joseph, Minnesota. Gable and Hughes both were conspicuous figures on the Catholic literary scene during the 1940s and 1950s and shared a keen interest in developing American Catholic writers. Hughes was a member of the board of governors of the Gallery of Living Catholic Authors and a regular contributor to *Renascence* and *Books on Trial*, both organs of the Catholic revival. He also reviewed for the secular periodical press during the 1940s and 1950s, including the *Saturday Review*.

Gable wrote criticism for the *Catholic World* and the *Catholic Library World* during the late 1930s and 1940s. Her work as moderator of the *St. Benedict Quarterly* (the college's literary journal) and as literary advisor to *Today* magazine reflected Gable's professional interest in developing young Catholic writers. *Today's* strong literary focus during the 1940s and 1950s was attributable, in part, to Gable. She also edited three anthologies of short stories between 1942 and 1950. Published by Sheed and Ward, they included the work of a number of aspiring Catholic writers and were used in many Catholic high school and college literature classes of the era.

Gable was best known, however, for the literary "bull's-eye" she constructed for American Catholic writers and readers in her second anthology, *Our Father's House* (1945), using the novels of Georges Bernanos as her "target." Like so many other young critics in the 1940s, Gable was impressed by the Frenchman's realistic portrayal of the mystery of grace—and its deadly antithesis, spiritual mediocrity—in his early novels. Bernanos, like Greene and Mauriac in the 1930s and 1940s, had powerfully integrated the Christian mysteries of grace and redemption into some of his most notable works while assailing the spiritual emptiness of the French middle class. His *Diary of a Country Priest*, which focuses upon the life of a saintly young curé who clumsily but lovingly administers to the souls of his "dead parish," and *Joy* (1941), which tells the story of the saintly young mystic, Chantal, and the disquieting power of her faith over her spiritually inert bourgeois household, were especially popular among college-educated American Catholics in the 1940s.[7] Both novels represented the kind of Christian realism and mature handling of religious themes educated American Catholics were looking for.

Gable wanted American writers to follow Bernanos's lead. In *Our Father's House* and in a subsequent speech before the Catholic Library Association, she predicted that "the great Catholic novel will be the novel of grace." Catholic fiction "of the center," she urged, "will be about saints. . . . The greatest heroes are the saints. The greatest fiction will be about them." Only the novels of Bernanos, she said, "hit the punctual center of the bull's-eye."[8] Throughout her long career as teacher, essayist, and critic, Gable thus urged American Catholic writers to approximate the themes established by Bernanos and the Europeans: the mystery of grace, God's pursuit of the soul, sanctity, and redemption.

Gable's counterpart, Riley Hughes, focused on much the same concepts, albeit in slightly more sophisticated dress. While the Georgetown University professor frequently encouraged Catholic American writers to find their own idiom, and led an unsuccessful campaign to establish an American Catholic "little magazine" during the 1940s, Hughes just as often held his countrymen to European literary standards. In a 1948 *Renascence* review article, for example, Hughes characterized Mauriac as "the Catholic novelist *par excellence*," and stated that American writers could learn from the Frenchman's example.[9]

Gable and Hughes illustrate the ascendency that Greene, Bernanos, and Mauriac had over the American Catholic critical community after 1940; but like the English Catholic writers who influenced American Catholic letters during the pre–1935 era—Owen Francis Dudley, Robert Hugh Benson, Isabel C. Clarke, and others—these newer European novelists offered only limited guidance for the establishment of an American Catholic fictional tradition. Catholic American writers would have to work out their own idiom despite the advice of critics. This was illustrated nowhere more strongly than in the life and novels of Bostonian Joseph (Joe) Dever.

If there was a prototype of a young American Catholic writer in the 1940s, it was Joe Dever. A 1942 graduate of Jesuit-run Boston College, Dever was one of many young Catholic men and women who embarked upon literary careers in the 1940s and 1950s. Dever began by publishing short stories in the Boston College *Stylus*, which he edited between 1940 and 1941. By the mid–1940s, his stories were appearing in top Catholic journals like *Commonweal* and *America*. "Fifty Missions" (the story of an Air Force gunner who returns from the war only to find that his girlfriend has entered the convent) earned Dever second place in a 1945 Catholic Press Association short story contest and was subsequently published in Sister Gable's second anthology.

Dever published his first novel, *No Lasting Home*, in 1947.[10] It was, in Dever's words, a conscious attempt "to write what most critics theoretically believe[d] to be a Catholic novel."[11] Whether consciously following Gable's guidelines (he knew her personally) or influenced merely by the Greene–Bernanos–Mauriac hegemony of the era, the theme of sanctity was a recurrent element in the book. The story turns upon the life of Ed Creeden, the self-sacrificing eldest son of a second-generation Irish Boston working-class family who, in the absence of both parents, surrenders his own education, career, and personal happiness to see his younger brother, Gerry, successfully through college. With Gerry safely established in a literary career (he yearns for a Catholic literary revival), Ed becomes a Jesuit brother.

A major subtheme, structured around the apparent suicide of Ed's troubled wife, Barbara, is especially reminiscent of the early work of

Greene. "No one really knows the limit of God's mercy," comforts Father Boley, a close friend of Ed's, at Barbara's funeral; "The destination of her soul is for God in His infinite wisdom and mercy to decide."[12] This theme of God's unending mercy toward even the worst of sinners almost directly recalls Greene's 1939 *Brighton Rock*, in which, after the awful death of the psychopathic Pinkie, the old priest tells Pinkie's grieving girlfriend, Rose, "You can't conceive, my child, nor can I or anyone— the . . . appalling . . . strangeness of the mercy of God."[13]

The Catholic critical community nevertheless failed to see Dever as America's answer to either Greene or Bernanos. Most critics panned the book, including the indomitable Hughes, who wrote that Dever had awarded his characters denouements as "ill-fitting as paper hats."[14]

Shortly thereafter, Dever decided he had had his fill of the Catholic literary revival. In a 1951 article in *Books on Trial*, he blasted Hughes, Gable, the revival, and those critics who reflected its perspective. Greene, Bernanos, and Mauriac were outstanding Catholic novelists, Dever conceded, but they had little to say to American writers. How could a Bernanos, "or any other European Catholic writer," Dever asked, help him write about the Boston Irish—"my own people, my own home-town?" "Yes, we have no Bernanos," satirized Dever, "but we [do] have frail-to-strong human beings in droll, complex, colorful environments which are peculiarly American Catholic."[15] Dever announced henceforth he would write about them.

Dever's lesson might have come easier. Since the mid–1930s, the most successful American Catholic writers had demonstrated that they could find a rich imaginative world within their own uniquely American sub-culture: the world of Catholic ethnics and the Catholic working class, priests and laity, parish and rectory, the Catholic ghetto and the Church militant. Theirs was a parochial world, but unlike the American Catholic writers before them, it was a world they did not view uncritically. Indeed, self-criticism was the most distinguishing feature of American Catholic novels written after 1935.

Post–1935 American Catholic fiction thus owed more to the Europeans than Dever might admit, but not necessarily to the latter's preoccupation with the mysteries of sin, grace, and redemption. Rather, it was the more self-critical, "negative" side of the Europeans—their alienation from middle-class religiosity and "mediocrity"—that was most attractive to their American counterparts, especially during the socially conscious 1930s and 1940s. Gable and other critics may have wanted novels of grace;[16] they received instead novels of self-criticism and scrutiny of the Catholic ghetto. But in assailing their own Catholic subculture, post–1935 American Catholic writers affirmed at the same time the more positive patterns of thought and action emergent during this period. Bourgeois Christianity was the antithesis of social Christianity. Middle-class Christians were those who separated religion from life. Spiritual mediocrity was the opposite of full Christian living—of sanctity.

These more positive factors, more than any others, explain the self-critical themes of this era, and distinguish the anti-ghettoism of this period from that of the mid–1950s. When Catholic writers attacked ghetto Catholicism, mediocrity, and middle-class religiosity during the late 1930s and 1940s, they were simultaneously affirming a larger religious vision of apostolic faith and Christian spiritual renewal.

THE NOVELS OF HARRY SYLVESTER

In the numerous surveys and articles written between 1935 and 1960 about the hoped-for revival of Catholic fiction in America, the names most frequently mentioned were Joe Dever, Harry Sylvester, Richard Sullivan, Leo Brady, Hilary Leighton Barth, and J. F. Powers. Others received attention, but many produced only a single work and slipped quietly into obscurity. Notably missing from critics' lists during the early 1950s was Flannery O'Connor, whose stories about grace-smitten Southern fundamentalists (*Wise Blood*, 1952) defied easy categorization. O'Connor was not acknowledged as a serious Catholic writer until the mid–1950s, and by then the revival was all but over.

Harry Sylvester must begin any serious discussion of American Catholic fiction during the 1940s and early 1950s. Before the emergence of J. F. Powers, Sylvester was the best known and most widely discussed Catholic writer in America. Sylvester's influence upon his contemporaries was significant, and, in important ways, he set the agenda for Catholic writing in this country when Americans were struggling to find a middle way between themselves and the Europeans.

Sylvester was born in Brooklyn in 1908. His mixed parentage (Jewish father, Catholic mother) was a determining factor in Sylvester's life and left him with little patience for some of the exclusivist attitudes of his Catholic co-religionists. A 1930 Notre Dame graduate (he was a member of Knute Rockne's most legendary teams), Sylvester studied under several of the same progressive teachers as O'Malley: neo-Thomist philosopher Leo R. Ward, and literature professors John T. Frederick and Charles Phillips. A talented essayist and short story writer, by the mid–1930s Sylvester was featured in both the Catholic and secular press, where, according to one account, he was the "highest paid fiction writer on *Collier's* magazine since Damon Runyan."[17] Sylvester nevertheless, until he broke with the Church in the early 1950s, always considered himself foremost a Catholic writer, despite his often stormy relationship with Catholic critics.

Sylvester wrote four novels between 1942 and 1950—*Dearly Beloved* (1942), *Dayspring* (1945), *Moon Gaffney* (1947), and *A Golden Girl* (1950).[18]

Dearly Beloved and *Moon Gaffney* were his best, and illustrate how Sylvester, with other American Catholic writers, had assimilated the Catholic social thought concepts taught at many American Catholic colleges and universities during the post–1935 era.

In *Dearly Beloved* Sylvester confronted Catholics with the doctrine of the Mystical Body and its divorce from actual Catholic life. Set in Anne Arundel County, Maryland, one of the few regions in the United States where the Church, since colonial times, had enjoyed cultural dominance, the story is a catalogue of white Catholic bigotry. White prejudice forces blacks to the back of the church, wrecks a plan for a fishing cooperative, and causes the brutal death of a black man. "You'd think there wasn't any such thing as the doctrine of the Mystical Body," exclaims the weary Jesuit pastor, Father Kane, who, while impatient with the overt racism of his parishioners, nevertheless lacks sufficient courage to disrupt the status quo.[19]

Sylvester was best known for *Moon Gaffney*. Set in New York City during the early 1940s, it records the fall from political grace of Aloysius "Moon" Gaffney, a minor Tammany Hall functionary, whose bright political future ends when he loses favor with friends, Church, and political machine. In reality, though, *Moon Gaffney* is an indictment of ghetto Catholicism, with Sylvester's story filled with Jansenistic clergy, redbaiting prelates, and smugly parochial Catholic laity.

However, true to his intention of illustrating the "dichotomy between Catholic thought and Catholic practice,"[20] Sylvester contrasts the attitudes of this first group of ghetto Catholics with the activities and concerns of another group of young Catholic "radicals" toward whom Moon is irresistibly drawn. Inspired by the Catholic Worker movement and papal encyclicals on social justice, they work in the slums, teach in inner-city schools, and organize non-unionized workers. Alienated from the institutional Church, this latter group of young men and women nevertheless remain steadfast and serious Catholics. In the words of Ed Galvin, the independent-minded layman who edits the *Catholic Worker* in the story, they "like everything about the Church except the people who run it."[21] Moon's downfall comes when he, too, embraces the liberal, socially minded Catholicism of his radical friends. Shunned by Tammany and chancery powerbrokers, Moon becomes a labor lawyer, defending blacks and communists.

Sylvester's critical posture understandably aroused a good deal of controversy in the Catholic press, but his work signaled important changes in the temper of twentieth century American Catholic writing. Sylvester gave expression to two counterbalancing themes that characterized the bulk of Catholic American fiction from the mid–1930s to the late 1950s. The first, negative and self-critical, rebelled against the provincialism, legalism, and "bourgeois spirit" (in the phrase of the day) within the Church and laity. The second, positive and affirmative, stressed the fundamental correctness of Christian doctrine, apostolic as opposed to bourgeois Catholicism, and the necessity for Catholics everywhere to give literal witness to their faith in the modern world. These twin themes were prominent in most of the major as well as the minor Catholic writers of the day.

THE CATHOLIC NOVEL IN AMERICA, 1938–1958

Arthur Lovejoy has written that "it is in popular fiction that the tendencies of an age may appear most directly." Not in the writers of genius, "but in the sensitive, responsive souls of less creative power, current ideals record themselves with clearness."[22] This is certainly true of Sylvester, Dever, and the other writers of the post–1935 era. None of these writers, with the exception of J. F. Powers, made a lasting impression upon the literary world. Yet their novels provide a valuable record of the causes and concerns that inspired Catholic intellectuals and activists during the second third of the twentieth century, an era when the liturgical movement, Catholic Action, and the social doctrines of the Church found their American expression.

Like Sylvester, a number of other young Catholic writers during the 1930s and 1940s dealt with the themes of social justice and the rights of labor. In Hilary Barth's *Flesh Is Not Life* (1938), a novel suggestive of other proletarian fiction of the period, Harvey Sothoran, a communist-leaning labor organizer, bitterly complains about "stuff-shirted" priests who deny workers the use of their parishes as meeting places while calling the C.I.O. a "communist plague." Sothoran himself is a fallen-away Catholic, alienated from his faith after his legalistic pastor attempted to block his football scholarship to an "atheistic" non-Catholic university.[23]

In contrast to these parochial attitudes, however, stands Brendan Grover, a young Catholic activist who understands the responsibility of the Church in the modern world and its potential for social leadership. Intensely concerned about the rights of workers, Brendan takes his inspiration not from Karl Marx but from "the great labor encyclicals of our Church." "The Church has always been proletarian—of the people," Brendan argues before a group of workers, and its activities must center not around "buildings and money" but around social justice. "If the trained Catholic" and the institutional Church "do not make this latter, and all it implies, the supreme answer to the recent cry for proletarian freedom," Grover stammers, "it's—it's going to be just too bad."[24]

Here, as in other novels of the period, Catholic social teaching is often shown competing with communist ideology for the loyalty of young intellectuals and workers. In the same story, Tandra, a sensitive idealist with an ill-defined yearning for "oneness" and "completeness" falls in with Harvey and the Communist Party. She soon becomes troubled, however, with the Party's utilitarian ethics and class ideology. With the help of the ever-present Brendan, Tandra finds the solidarity and justice she craves in the radical fellowship of the Mystical Body and the social gospel of the Church.

The same theme is seen again in Dever's *Three Priests* (1958), a fictional portrait of Bernard J. Sheil, the progressive 1940s auxiliary archbishop of Chicago. In the story, Lucy, a fallen-away Catholic and leftist, returns to the Church after Fr. Vince Whelton (Sheil) exposes her to its social doctrines addressed to human dignity and the rights of labor. Lucy ends up teaching classes on Catholic social thought and the labor encyclicals to Chicago labor leaders at Whelton's adult school.[25]

The Catholic Worker movement, which had risen, in part, to counteract communist influence among workers and the unemployed during the 1930s, played a prominent role in many of the novels of the period. As in Sylvester's *Moon Gaffney*, characters based on the movement's co-founders, Peter Maurin and Dorothy Day, abound. In Dever's *Three Priests*, Day appears as Emily Winart, a friend of labor and skid-row bums. In *Moon Gaffney* she is simply "Dorothy." The implication is that the Catholic Worker is the cutting edge of an emergent, active, socially minded Catholicism, and an example for all modern Catholics to follow.

The characters of Emily, Brendan Grover, Tandra, and Moon Gaffney also illustrate another important change in the American Church during the 1930s and 1940s—the emergence of the laity as a growing social and cultural force. In a classic example of art imitating life, many Catholic protagonists, like so many actual lay Catholic idealists at this time, are apostolic and integral in their faith, read the Compline (the night prayer of the Church), ground their lives in the liturgy, often think independently of the Church's hierarchy, and regard their religion as a social and cultural force. They are impatient with the "bourgeois" element in the Church, and are convinced that a dedicated Catholic laity can make a vast difference in the modern world. Observing that perhaps only one-tenth of one percent of his co-religionists actually practice their faith, Grover comments: "Nothing's deader than a dead religion [and for that] our Catholic mediocres . . . are to blame." "It's long past time," he continued, that the laity "snapped out of their contented stupor and rolled up their sleeves and got down among the crowds to argue and fight as their vocation demands."[26]

Dever also stressed these new demands upon the laity in *A Certain Widow* (1951). Francis Ronayne, a sensitive young man of activist temper, is pressed by an overly ambitious mother into a vocation he does not want. He leaves the seminary only after he becomes convinced that as a committed layperson he would be in a better position to influence society. Francis's spiritual advisor, Father Carney, agrees. "There is so much you can do out there, Fran," the priest urges. "There's so much need for laymen who can be spiritual without being stuffy."[27] Ronayne becomes a crusading journalist, taking his place beside the multitude of encyclical-conscious Catholic labor leaders, social workers, teachers, and Catholic Actionists who populate the American Catholic novel between 1935 and 1958.

Though the concern for social issues began to fade by the early 1950s, the self-critical attitude in American Catholic fiction did not. This fact is illustrated in the novels of Leo Brady. A drama and speech professor at Catholic University and *Washington Post* movie critic, Brady wrote two novels during the early 1950s that were sharply critical of the Catholic middle class. His first, *The Edge of Doom* (1949), was consciously patterned after Greene's gangster thriller, *Brighton Rock,* and focuses on a young hoodlum and fallen-away Catholic, Martin Lynn, who, in a fit of rage, kills an aging priest with a single blow of a crucifix. Martin's crime sets in motion an exciting drama of flight and pursuit (from the law but also from the pull of grace) that ends in spiritual reconciliation and forgiveness.[28]

While the self-critical theme is less obtrusive, Brady, like Greene in many of his early Catholic novels, clearly prefers the outcast and sinner over the comfortably saved, whose religion trotted at their heels "like a pet dog, carefully groomed and fed, a well-mannered, characterless animal with no nasty habits."[29] Moreover, Brady's Greene-like theme of "The Hound of Heaven," stressing God's love for the worst of sinners, is a powerful affirmation of the spirit as opposed to the letter of Catholicism, and stands as an indictment against exclusivist notions of the past.

Taken together, the novels of Sylvester, Dever, Barth, and Brady are remarkable documents of social and cultural change, and stand in marked contrast to American Catholic novels of the previous age. Pre–1935 writers like Lucille Papin Borden, Ethel Cook Eliot, Frank Spearman, and Kathleen Norris identified closely with the institutional Church, wrote with ecclesiastical approval, and envisioned their literary apostolate in essentially moralistic-didactic terms. Later Catholic writers, by contrast, tended to relfect anger and alienation from significant dimensions of Catholic life and practice while nevertheless remaining steadfast and sincere Christians.

Similarly, while Catholic characters in the novels of the 1920s and early 1930s found self-definition by setting themselves apart from "pagan" society, the heroes and heroines of the latter era were eager to engage the world and reconstruct it according to Christian-Catholic principles. One traditional standard of Catholic identity—preoccupation with sexual morality—especially took a beating, as writers like Sylvester vehemently attacked sexual prudery within the clergy and laity.

Catholic villains in these post–1935 stories, on the other hand, tended to have many of the same qualities that characterized the heroes and heroines of the previous age. (Some, in fact, like Moon Gaffney's girl-friend, Rosemary Danaher, actually *read* the novels of Borden and Owen Francis Dudley.) Like Gaffney's lace-curtain Irish crowd, they are smug, self-righteous, and insular, certain of their own salvation and their status as God's chosen people. Lacking social consciousness, their faith is al-most entirely personal and devotional. Any religious activity centers around the self-enclosed parish: missions, novenas, Rosary Sodalities, Holy Name Societies, the Legion of Decency, and the more militant forms of Catholic Action.

A popular new antagonist was the "Big Catholic Layman." Dever's Nino Vanezzia (*Three Priests*) stands as an example. A Grand Knight of Malta, he gives liberally to the Church, but keeps his business ethics separated from his religious faith (he fires any worker engaged in union activity). Brady's Andrew Carnahan (*Signs and Wonders*, 1953), likewise, is a prominent businessman and communion breakfast speaker who combines a militant Catholicism (as a "Don Juan Legionaire" he pickets "indecent" films) with a mindless nationalism in holding the line against the enemies of God, Church, and country.[30]

Non-Catholic characters also took on new dimensions after 1935. Non-Catholics in most pre–1935 Catholic novels were inevitably presented in condescending or negative light. In these later stories, however, many non-Catholics actually outshine Catholics, especially when contrasted with the worst forms of Catholic insularity and chauvinism. Socially minded Jews, leftists, and union activists were especially popular. An example is Dever's Harry Brannick (*No Lasting Home*), whose effort "to-ward social justice and the workingman was perhaps more Catholic than many Catholics who went to mass every Sunday but lived as a pagan the rest of the week."[31]

One of the most dramatic shifts in characterization involved the image of the priest, a phenomenon already well-documented by Hugh D. Rank.[32] While this change will be examined more completely when we turn to J. F. Powers, it is sufficient to say that the Jansenistic, anti-Semitic, obscurantist clergy in Sylvester's and other novels of the post–1935 era represented a sharp break with the "Masterful Monk" and the priest-heroes of the past.

Breaking with the past, self-examination, and self-criticism were im-portant dimensions of post–1935 American Catholic fiction. The novels of Sylvester, Dever, Barth, and Brady reflect this mood. Still, what is notable about the fiction of this era is the positive affirmation of faith in the midst of all the criticism. For every smugly saved Andrew Carnahan there is a socially minded Brendan Grover, and for every "Don Juan Legionaire" there is a Catholic Worker. For every redbaiting prelate, there is a Father Whelton—a "labor priest" using *Rerum Novarum* and *Quadragesimo Anno* as a rationale for social action. American Catholic fiction thus affirmed important parts of Catholic American life between 1935 and 1958, as many young American Catholic writers—and fictional heroes and heroines—broke with the Catholic ghetto during this period. But true to the era, they did not break with their identity as Christians. Their faith was still their premise for action.

CRITICS AND WRITERS

Sylvester, Dever, Barth, and Brady chronicled important intellectual shifts in American Catholic life between 1935 and 1958, but the contemporary critical reception of these writers was mixed at best. Sylvester was surrounded by controversy throughout his career. Predictably, the Catholic critical evaluation of his work divided primarily along conservative-liberal lines. The conservative Catholic press—*America*, the *Catholic World*, *Books on Trial*—generally assumed a defensive attitude toward his novels. Reviewers in these magazines, for the most part, disregarded Sylvester's self-critical themes and complained that he misrepresented Catholics and the clergy.[33] Reviewers associated with the lay-edited *Commonweal* (for which Sylvester himself was a staff writer), by contrast, generally commended Sylvester for his "courage" and recognized his self-critical purpose. Indeed, many of the themes found in Sylvester's novels could also be found in *Commonweal* during the 1940s and 1950s as the magazine campaigned against Catholic insularity and other dimensions of ghetto culture. A 1947 *Commonweal* review of *Moon Gaffney* thus stressed that "many Catholics will abuse this book, but all Christians will be grateful for it."[34]

The two most visible proponents of American Catholic creative writing during this period, Georgetown University critic Riley Hughes and College of St. Benedict anthologist Sr. Mariella Gable, always maintained an uneasy relationship with Sylvester. In 1949 Hughes ranked Sylvester with Richard Sullivan and J. F. Powers as one of the top three Catholic writers in America. Nevertheless, he held deep reservations about Sylvester's future contribution to the revival. Novels like *Moon Gaffney* were probably a necessary corrective to the sectarianism of earlier writers like Borden and Dudley, conceded Hughes, but he believed that Sylvester's contemptuous attitude would prevent him from writing the true novels of grace that Catholic critics were looking for.[35]

Gable's relationship with Sylvester went from good to bad. The Benedictine nun, as was the case with a number of other writers, knew Sylvester personally. Gable corresponded with him about literary matters during the early 1940s, and in 1945 she included one of his short stories in her *Our Father's House* anthology. In 1942 the Gable-moderated *St. Benedict Quarterly* characterized Sylvester's *Dearly Beloved* as "the first top-ranking Catholic novel by an American."[36]

The relationship between critic and author grew increasingly strained toward the end of the 1940s, however, as Sylvester began to criticize the revival and its too-conscious attempts to encourage Catholic writing. A complete rupture came in 1948, after Sylvester, in an *Atlantic Monthly* article titled "Problems of the Catholic Writer," bitterly denounced the economic, psychological, and religious burdens placed upon Catholic writers by the American Catholic literary establishment; crudely mocked a Gable-inspired plan to subsidize married Catholic novelists; and, in effect, rejected the entire concept of Catholic writing as too parochial.[37] Sylvester, shortly thereafter, divorced his wife and left the Church.

The other writers mentioned in this survey—Barth, Dever, Sullivan, and Brady—all won brief but unsustained approval from Catholic critics. Barth, who was a sociology instructor at Chaminade College in Clayton, Missouri when he wrote his socially conscious *Flesh Is Not Life* in 1938, gained early recognition from Gable and Catholic collegians as representative of a "new realism" in American Catholic fiction.[38] But Barth was only a single-book author, and, like so many other social action novelists of the mid–1930s, quickly passed from the scene. The 1949 edition of the *American Catholic Who's Who* (the last year his name appears) lists Barth as a field director for the American Red Cross.

Few American Catholic writers between 1935 and 1960 surpassed Dever in sincerity and intention. Suddenly made aware of his own limitations as a Catholic writer after the crushing critical reviews of his first novel, *No Lasting Home* (1947), Dever quit trying to be the American answer to Greene or Bernanos. Given the regional focus of his later work, most Catholic critics thereafter acknowledged Dever for what he was: a "local color" Catholic writer who in such stories as *A Certain Widow* (1951) and *Three Priests* (1958) (probably the best single account of the American Catholic social revolution of the 1930s and 1940s) realistically recorded the lives and concerns of the generation of young Catholic intellectuals who grew to maturity between the Depression and World War II. Although *Three Priests* did achieve Catholic "best seller" status, Dever was never able to sustain a consistent living as a Catholic writer. He finished his career as a public relations assistant in the Massachusetts Department of Motor Vehicles.[39]

Richard Sullivan, as noted earlier, also received frequent mention by critics like Hughes as a Catholic writer "of promise" during the 1940s.[40] A Notre Dame English professor, Sullivan was best known for his realistic portrayals of lower middle-class Catholic family life. *Summer After Summer* (1942), for example, depicts the hopes and fears of a financially pressed young Catholic couple anxiously awaiting the birth of an un-planned second child.[41] Just as frequently, however, Sullivan's work was dismissed by Catholic critics as too sentimental. His significance to the 1940s and 1950s American Catholic literary effort, like Dever's, was seen in his contribution to the genre of "local color."[42]

Brady, in pure monetary terms, was probably the most successful Catholic writer before J. F. Powers. Samuel Goldwyn paid Brady $125,000 for the screen rights to *The Edge of Doom* and cast Farley Granger in the starring role. The book also won the Catholic Writers' Guild of America Golden Book Award for the best novel of 1949 and was generally praised by critics. Gable, in a 1949 review for *Today*, hailed Brady's work as yet another indication that "Catholic fiction is being born in Amer-ica."[43] His 1953 novel, *Signs and Wonders*, however, failed to win much acclaim. It proved to be his last.

J. F. POWERS AND AMERICAN CATHOLIC WRITING

There are volumes of literary analyses of James Farel Powers (b. 1917), but few which place him within the context of his times.[44] Yet, as with other Catholic writers of his age, to read Powers's short stories is to enter into the spirit of an era.

Powers's young adult life reads much like the manuscript of a post–1935 style Catholic novel: birth and boyhood in Illinois, Catholic edu-cated (Quincy College Academy, 1935), "anger at not being able to get a job, anger at the plight of the Negro, anger at other things I was just beginning to see,"[45] Depression-time links with the Chicago Catholic Worker (his first work appeared in the New York *Catholic Worker*), thir-teen months federal imprisonment for refusing induction into the armed services in 1943, impatience with the bourgeois element in the Church—all in all, a serious and committed young Catholic intellectual.

Eight of Powers's first ten short stories, published between 1943 and 1945, have strong social themes. Four deal with social injustice, mostly perpetrated by Catholics toward blacks. A fifth, "Renner," treats the problem of Catholic anti-Semitism.[46] Though lacking in the subtlety and skill that typifies his later work, these stories, nevertheless, are expres-sive of the apostolic, socially minded Catholicism that marked Powers's early career. In "Blessing" (1945), Catholic segregationists drive a black family from their parish. Dismayed by the behavior of his co-religionists, Father Blair, a young curate who has befriended the family, emotionally pleads for an end to the "cautious," "cowardly," and "worldly" Ca-tholicism infecting his parish. Blair calls, instead, for a faith that is "frankly unwise, incautious and imprudent," one that dares "to take Christ literally" and is committed to a program of social action based upon his Mystical Body.[47]

"Blessing" and several of Powers's other early works bear the mark of a Catholic integralist and a commitment to a literal, total, apostolic faith. The concept of sainthood and sanctity is striking in both Power's early and mature work. He returned to this theme again and again. In "Saint on the Air" (1943), for example, an unnamed "Saint," as a guest on a radio talk show, declares, "a saint is not an abnormal person. He is simply a mature Christian. Anyone who is not a saint is spiritually undersized—the world is full of spiritual midgets." *Morte d'Urban* (1962), Powers's first novel, represents a less obtrusive and more powerful handling of this same theme. It is a searching story of a worldly priest who finally transcends his secularity when grace suddenly enters his life after he is knocked unconscious by an errant golf ball.[48]

Literary critic Naomi Lebowitz asserts that it is this "sign of contra-diction," the tension between sanctity and mediocrity, "secularism and divinity, the letter and the spirit . . . the actual and the ideal that lies at the heart of Powers' best stories."[49] At first hard and uncompromising, Powers treated this theme with increasing wit, irony, and compassion. This explains, in part, why he focused on the clergy in so many of his stories. As he observed in a 1964 interview, "I write about priests for the reasons of irony, comedy, and philosophy. They officially are com-mitted to both worlds [secular and spiritual] in a way most people are not. This makes for strong beer."[50]

Powers was thus concerned, with other writers of this period, about the discrepancy between Catholic faith and Catholic practice. Unlike most of his contemporaries, however, Powers's technique was not merely to juxtapose obviously ghetto Catholics against equally obvious apostolic Catholics. Rather, as he did in "Prince of Darkness," "Lions, Harts, Leaping Does," and so many of his other clerical stories, Powers subtley confronted worldly, self-satisfied, all-too-human clergy with the uncompromising standards of their faith.

In Fr. Ernest Burner ("Prince of Darkness," 1946) Powers presented his fullest portrait of priestly compromise.[51] A living personification of the "seven deadly sins," incongruity, and dichotomy mark the slovenly Burner's every move. He takes mornings off for flying lessons, practices putting golf balls into his soiled clerical collar (while dreaming of news photos showing "Rev. Ernest 'Boomer' Burner, par-shattering padre, blasting out of a trap"), and contemplates an annuity for his old age. Dominated by thoughts of worldly security, Burner's chief priestly goal is to obtain, after seventeen years as a lowly assistant, a parish of his own.

Burner lives mentally in the Catholic ghetto. Gossipy, triumphalistic, and judgmental, distrustful of Protestants and "interfaith nonsense," he feels threatened by an aggressive laity and wonders if there might be some way to terminate perpetual novenas. Stunted in his apostolate and painfully aware of it, his life is without synthesis and integration. Burner, by all standards, is a bourgeois Christian.

Yet, as is usual in Powers's fiction, the vision is affirmed. "I can't call to mind a single Saint Ernest, Father. Can you help me?" asks the saintly archbishop of Burner in the evocative final scene. When Burner also fails to recall a saint with his namesake, the archbishop, in assigning Burner not to his own parish but to still another curateship, responds: "Well, Father, it looks as if you have a clear field."[52] As with all Christians, sanctity is the standard by which Burner's life is ultimately to be judged.

Grace thus comes in Powers's stories. It arrives in strange and unsettling ways, but it always arrives. For the worldly Burner, it is the humbling experience of yet another assistantship. For Didymus, the aging friar of "Lions, Harts, Leaping Does" (1943), it comes via a crippling stroke that forces him finally to confront the meaninglessness of his life and ministry.[53]

In his attention to the mystery of grace and the essential Christian dogmas of the Incarnation, the Resurrection, and Redemption, Powers constructed some of his best short stories from the same imaginative universe as many of the finest European Catholic writers. Nevertheless, he remained a distinctively American Catholic writer. In his self-critical motif, assault upon ghetto Catholicism and middle-class religiosity, and insistence that Christians must not live dichotomously but in union with their faith, Powers's outlook coincided with some of the most frequently expressed American Catholic views of the day. In Powers, then, progressive sectors of the pre-Vatican II American Catholic intellectual and cultural community believed they had found a formidable writer and spokesman.

Abigail Quigley McCarthy in her 1972 autobiography recalls that Powers during the 1940s "brought to near perfection . . . what we thought of as truly Catholic themes." Not only had Powers equalled the Europeans in realistic portrayals of sin, grace, and redemption, she argued, but he had done so within an American idiom. "He was, for the moment," wrote McCarthy, "our American Mauriac or Bernanos."[54]

Powers shared an interesting relationship with McCarthy, Sylvester, Gable, and other Catholic literary figures of the era. McCarthy (then Abigail Quigley), herself a struggling young Catholic writer in the early 1940s, was first contacted by Powers in 1945 while he was working as a hospital orderly in St. Paul shortly after being paroled from Minnesota's Sandstone Prison. They became close friends, unified by their common faith and interest in literature.

Sylvester, an established older writer, also took a special interest in Powers. When critics and reviewers in the early 1940s seemed to be ignoring Powers, Sylvester praised him in a letter to *Commonweal*, and described "Lions, Harts, Leaping Does" as "the first profound and distinguished short story written by an American Catholic."[55] Sylvester also sent a copy of the story (first published in *Accent*) to Sister Gable, portraying Powers as "the great white hope" of American Catholic fiction.

Gable agreed; indeed, she did more than any other Catholic critic to bring Powers to the attention of the Catholic American reading public. She published "Lions, Harts, Leaping Does" and another of Powers's short stories in *Our Father's House,* and characterized the former as the first true story of grace by an American Catholic writer. A close personal relationship developed between Gable and Powers at the same time. Gable (who Powers first met on a visit to the College of St. Benedict in the autumn of 1945) introduced Powers to his future wife, Betty Wahl, herself an aspiring writer and one of Gable's top students. They were married five months later, with Sylvester as part of the wedding party. Powers thereafter settled near Collegeville, Minnesota, where he wrote and taught part time at St. John's University.

With the 1947 publication of *Prince of Darkness* (a collection of short stories with "Prince of Darkness" as its title piece), Powers assumed a dominant position in Catholic American fiction and Catholic literary culture. Most Catholic reviewers hailed the book despite some resistance to Powers's "anticlericalism" in conservative circles. Hughes called it "the finest achievement of anyone who has ever written as a Catholic in America."[56] Gable claimed that it marked "a milestone in American Catholic letters." At last, she rejoiced, "we have an indication that we can produce a fiction comparable to the great European Catholic fiction."[57] Gable, like other critics, looked forward to Powers's first novel with considerable interest. They would wait for fifteen years.

Part III

DISSOLUTION, THE 1950s
AND AFTER

10

"Ought There to Be a Catholic Criticism?" The 1950s and the End of the Revival

Had J. F. Powers's first novel *Morte d'Urban* (the winner of the 1962 National Book Award) appeared in 1950, it might have effectively ended the search for the Great American Catholic Novel, although this quest, like all quixotic ventures, may have been doomed to go on forever. But it came in 1962, and by then few critics were interested in finding the great Catholic novel. Fewer still were interested in the Catholic literary revival, the "New Christendom," or Catholic culture. By the mid–1950s such concerns, in the jargon of the day, seemed too "ghettoish."

The Catholic literary revival always mirrored the relationship between Catholicism and American society and culture. During the first half of the twentieth century that relationship was marked by a good deal of tension (much of it creative) as Catholics, likening themselves to a prophetic minority, denounced modern unbelief and proposed religious solutions to modern problems. Most Catholic cultural leaders (Francis X. Talbot, Daniel A. Lord, and Frank O'Malley included) never doubted that Catholics, and especially Catholic intellectuals, were a distinctive cultural group whose particular vision and outlook brought an added dimension to the nation's philosophy, literature, and social thought. Smugly triumphalistic in the 1920s, the focus of American Catholic intellectual and cultural life became increasingly apostolic as Catholics after 1935 spoke of the Church's historic mission in the world and the necessity of lay Christians to reach out to every dimension of thought and culture. Hence the Catholic literary revival, O'Malley's Christian philosophy of literature, the Catholic Worker movement, and the more progressive forms of Catholic mobilization and Catholic Action. All were inspired, in large part, by this vision of faith integrated with life. American Catholic novels written during this same era repeated that focus.

Similarly, much of Catholic self-criticism between 1935 and 1955 focused upon the Church turned inward—in short, upon ghetto Catholicism. The novels and stories of Harry Sylvester, J. F. Powers, and Leo Brady that criticized the privatization of religious life on the part of the middle-class Catholic laity and clergy thus found their post–1935 counterpart in thinkers like O'Malley, Jacques Maritian, and Etienne Gilson, who likewise criticized the failure of modern Catholic intellectuals to assert themselves as Christians within the modern world. Sr. Mariella Gable and other integral-minded literary critics chastised Catholic imaginative writers for similar reasons.

During the early 1950s, however, the focus of Catholic anti-ghettoism began to change and with it the dynamics of American Catholic intellectual and cultural life. These changes were subtle; but the anti-ghettoism of the 1950s was a much different phenomenon from that of the previous era.

Anti-ghettoism during the 1930s and 1940s was linked directly to Catholic mobilization and the goal of Christian cultural renewal. Outward-looking and apostolic, it attacked Catholic mediocrity, isolationism, and exclusiveness while urging Catholics to exert an influence upon society and culture at large.

Philip Gleason has observed that 1950s anti-ghettoism, by contrast, was in part a "reaction against" many aspects of this same mobilization. The 1950s saw renewed Protestant-Catholic conflict over the school issue, censorship, and Church-State relations. Many young Catholic liberals anxious over the accepted place of Catholicism in American life reacted negatively to these events by rejecting Catholic parochialism in whatever form. Instead, they hailed the virtues of pluralism and urged fellow Catholics to "mix indiscriminantly as 'Americans.' " Nineteen-fifties anti-ghettoism thus had a distinctively Americanist emphasis as its liberal proponents embraced the American cultural mainstream.[1] Gleason writes that much of this was valid, but adds that the most notable aspect of the debate was the degree to which these 1950s critics "overlooked (or were unaware of) the apostolic purpose that Catholic mobilization presumed."[2] Whatever its intention, the effect of such criticism was to throw on the defensive the entire idea of Catholic cultural distinctiveness and the Catholic intra-group associations and structures that supported Catholic mobilization to begin with.

Typical was John Cogley. During the 1930s and 1940s Cogley—first as Catholic Worker and then as one of the founding editors of *Today*—had been in the forefront of Catholic social action and Catholic cultural renewal. By 1951, however, Cogley (who was now assistant editor at *Commonweal*) was publically disassociating himself from his fellow "integralists" and their attempts to "theologize the secular milieu."[3] "Too much talk of a Catholic Literary Revival," further editorialized Cogley's *Commonweal* in 1952, had the effect of cutting Catholics off from the larger literary world and in isolating Catholics from the genuine existential insights of modern secular literature.[4] It did not occur to Cogley— as it did to O'Malley and Flannery O'Connor, for example—that literature written from an orthodox Christian perspective might hold its own existential insights. Cogley is thus representative of what Gleason writes of many Catholic liberals in the 1950s: They believed that the proper way for Catholics to influence secular culture was not through self-isolating "ghetto organizations" (in 1952 *Commonweal* characterized the Catholic literary revival as "a culture within a culture") but through joining forces with "pluralistic" organizations distinguished by function "rather than by denominational commitment."[5]

After 1955 anti-ghettoism flowed into the Catholic intellectualism issue as scores of Catholic scholars followed Catholic historian John Tracy Ellis in blaming the lack of American Catholic cultural achievement on the Church's "self-imposed ghetto mentality."[6] Again, the effect of such criticism was to call into question the entire intellectual apparatus of American Catholicism.

As understood by O'Malley, O'Connor, Maritain, Gilson, Christopher Dawson, and other Catholic thinkers during the 1940s, scholarly enterprise did not preclude serious religious commitment. On the contrary, they believed that religious orthodoxy enhanced understanding through a fuller disclosure of reality. But as Catholic scholars in the 1950s (many by now educated at secular graduate schools) sought intellectual standing within their profession, they began to define their role in increasingly secular terms. Ellis still spoke of "the exalted mission" of the Catholic scholar, but more self-conscious Catholic specialists were more likely to caution that the whole concept of an intellectual apostolate raised serious questions about "intellectual honesty," objectivity, and professionalism. By the mid–1960s, some Catholic scholars were characterizing a Catholic intellectual apostolate as a contradiction in terms which threatened "to subvert the intellectual and turn him into a holy panderer for the Catholic Church."[7]

Thus, if the focus of Catholic self-criticism in the 1930s and 1940s was that Catholics were not Catholic enough, that of the 1950s implied that Catholics, at least as intellectuals, could be *too* Catholic. Catholic intellectuals went from questioning their religious commitment to questioning whether they, as intellectuals, should be committed at all. By the late 1950s, the question that most troubled the Catholic intellectual community was not the apostolic one of, "Where is the American Bernanos?" Rather, it was the more self-conscious one of, "Where are the Catholic Salks, Oppenheimers, Einsteins?"[8] The first was primarily faith-centered. The second reflected mere embarrassment and long held concern about intellectual status and prestige. This second question, asked in 1957 by Notre Dame president John J. Cavanaugh, C.S.C., while comparing the American Catholic and Jewish immigrant experience, expressed anxiety not over the Church's intellectual mission within American society but over the Church's image within that society. Reminiscent of the 1920s, Cavanaugh's question implied a quest not for Catholic intellectuals but for intellectuals who happened to be Catholic.

With this as a background, it is easier to understand what happened to the Catholic literary revival in the 1950s and early 1960s. The terms "Catholic literature" and the "Catholic novel"—unlike "Catholic sociology"[9]—were not annihilated by the intellectual reorientation of the mid–1950s (indeed, they remain meaningful concepts in our own age), but the Catholic literary community was influenced deeply by the anti-ghettoism and intellectualism debates of that era.

As happened in so many other areas of Catholic intellectual and cultural life (including the issue of parochial schools) after 1950, pluralistic-minded critics increasingly questioned the desirability or necessity of a separate Catholic literature or literary establishment. In 1954 *Commonweal* contributor Henry Rago (a Catholic scholar who taught humanities at the University of Chicago) thus dismissed the entire idea of a Catholic literary revival as "largely irrelevant, except as it would induce more Catholics to read." Again overlooking the apostolic purpose the revival presumed, Rago thought the term "Catholic literature" (he was reluctant to use the term at all) represented an interference with the autonomy of literature, and an attempt to "claim" it for partisan purposes. In Rago's view, this even included works that justified themselves by presenting "a Christian concept of man." Rago himself favored "pure-minded" reading of literature, which he believed could be received only at non-Catholic universities.[10]

American Catholic commentator Dan Herr wondered where all this self-criticism would end. As director of the Catholic Press Association and a columnist for the Catholic periodical *Critic*, Herr had long maintained an active interest in developing aspiring Catholic writers. Now, complained Herr in 1953, "to listen to some Catholics you would think it a social error that we admit such categories as Catholic books and Catholic writers." Within the prevailing flight-from-the-ghetto atmosphere, it seemed to Herr that Catholics were saying there was no such thing as a Catholic book, "or if there is there should not be."[11]

Herr was not far from the mark. By 1959 some academic critics like LaSalle University professor Rev. John Simons were advising their co-religionists that it would be "good literary diplomacy" to avoid the expression "Catholic novel" altogether because it smacked too much of sectarianism.[12]

Apart from questions concerning the desirability of Catholic literature and the Catholic novel, Catholic critics themselves began to question their own right to exist by the early 1960s. "Ought there to be [a Catholic criticism]?"[13] was not an uncommon question in the preconciliar era as Catholic critics pondered whether their professional focus should be any different from others in their field. O'Malley and other likeminded Catholic critics still held out for a Christian philosophy of literature in the early 1960s, but they were the exceptions. Most Catholic critics after 1955 began to take their literary standards from the secular literary establishment. This trend was underscored by Fordham University teacher and critic Justin J. Kelly, S. J., when he wrote approvingly in 1962 that "each year it becomes less easy to distinguish a Catholic literary periodical from its secular counterpart."[14]

The fate of the Catholic Renascence Society and its literary journal *Renascence* during the 1950s and early 1960s further illustrates this trend. The organization, as previously noted, was founded in 1939 during the height of the Catholic cultural movement in the United States. Frankly apostolic, the society's membership (composed primarily of Catholic college literature and modern language teachers) pledged itself to a renewal of twentieth century literature through "the cultural heritage of Christian civilization."[15]

Accordingly, the society sought during the 1940s "to stimulate and encourage an interest in the Catholic Renascence of letters and to recognize and advance scholarship" in the field.[16] Talks on the works of Jacques Maritain, Paul Claudel, Georges Bernanos, and Francois Mauriac delivered by Catholic critics and philosophers like Wallace Fowlie and Yves Simon dominated its annual symposia. Refugee German theologian Dietrick von Hildebrand, whose *Liturgy and Personality* (1943) was popular among American Catholic intellectuals during the 1940s and early 1950s, delivered three lectures on "Religion and Culture" at the society's third annual meeting in 1942. The organization peaked in the late 1940s with the 1949 publication of *Renascence* and its Tenth Anniversary Meeting that same year. Over 500 Catholic educators gathered at New York City's Manhattanville College to hear O'Malley and others discuss "The Catholic Renaissance in a Distintegrating World."[17]

The society's focus, however, changed noticeably during the early 1950s. Critical evaluations of the writers and thinkers of the French and English Catholic literary revivals no longer prevailed at the group's spring meetings. Instead, beginning in 1953, the society began to focus upon a wide range of literary topics: the revolt against Puritanism (1953), symbolism and existentialism (1954), literary theory (1955), modern poetry (1958), and other less parochial subjects. Speakers and panelists also changed; academic critics such as Walter J. Ong, S. J., W. K. Wimsatt, and Marshall McLuhan, all of whom were influenced by the New

Criticism, displaced earlier ones like O'Malley and Simon, whose religious-philosophical outlook was central to their critical vision. By 1959 the Catholic Renascence Society's assimilation into American literary culture was virtually complete—symbolized by its meeting that year in conjunction with the annual meeting of the Modern Language Association.

Renascence underwent similar changes during the 1950s. Like its parent organization, the magazine's early issues during the late 1940s focused almost entirely upon the writers, poets, and novelists of the European Catholic revival. The magazine's Spring 1949 issue, for example, was an extended symposium on the novels of Graham Greene. Employing a distinctly theological perspective, critics like Jesuit Harold C. Gardiner hailed Greene as an "eschatological author" who wrote of "the things that finally and eternally matter."[18] In addition, a regular feature in the magazine's early issues were reports from European correspondents on the progress of the revival in France, England, Holland, Belgium, and elsewhere.

By 1954, however, *Renascence* was exploring a wide circle of novelists and poets—Catholic as well as non-Catholic. Existentialist writers were especially popular during the mid–1950s, reflecting the postwar impact of existentialist philosophy upon American Catholic colleges and universities. A single 1954 issue, for example, contained extended analyses of Simon Weil and Franz Kafka.[19] At the same time, the New Criticism made deep inroads into the magazine's earlier philosophical-theological format, as articles like "Hopkins' Imagery" and "Symbolism in *Brighton Rock*" focused on issues of language, symbol, and metaphor.[20] The New Criticism thus stressed that the meaning of a creative work inhered in its formal structure, apart from its broader philosophical or theological aspects.

These changes were made principally at the urging of *Renascence* editor John Pick, a Gerard Manley Hopkins scholar who had studied under Helen C. White at the University of Wisconsin during the mid–1930s. While Pick was justifiably reacting against an excessive moralism in Catholic criticism, his position, like that of other Catholic scholars during the 1950s, was clearly influenced by the intellectualism debate of that decade and by concerns about how Catholics were perceived outside their own literary community. Pick's editorials during the early 1950s thus worried about the "provincialism in Catholic letters" while warning Catholic critics that to "win the respect of intelligent readers" they must "concentrate upon the work of art itself."[21] The New Criticism, in Pick's view, accomplished this. It was a way, he later recalled, of demonstrating that Catholics "were capble of purely literary criticism," of showing that Catholics "were culturally [and] literarily respectable."[22] Pluralistic, "catholic," and detached, and marked by an ever-increasing tendency to view literature on its own terms rather than for what it said about the nature of God, humanity, or the universe, *Renascence* during the 1950s spoke less and less of a Catholic literary revival or Catholic cultural renewal.

When does a movement die? When it loses its vision? When the historical forces that summoned it no longer prevail? When its leadership fades or increasingly accepts the norms, standards, and values of the culture it had set out to change? When it increasingly begins to doubt itself and the certainty of its goals?

All of these things happened to the Catholic literary revival in America between 1950 and 1960. There are many reasons why the revival ended when it did, but the most important is that by 1960 the American Catholic literary community had lost, for the most part, the cultural consciousness that had been the driving force behind the entire movement. The cultural conditions that had given rise to the revival and the impulse to promote, to defend, and to redeem simply did not exist by 1960. Self-promotion was an important element in the intellectualism issue, but it was to take secular, not Catholic, forms. Unlike the 1920s, an organized Catholic literary revival or "emergence" would have been a source of embarrassment for most American Catholic intellectuals in 1960.

Moreover, Catholics during the immediate preconciliar era could hardly think of themselves any longer as a beleaguered, disadvantaged minority. A 1957 study illustrated that both socially and economically, the Catholic population had pulled even with the rest of American society.[23] Anti-Catholic bigotry had not entirely vanished from American life, but the worst forms of it, along with the American Protective Association, were largely things of the past. By 1955 sociologist Will Herberg (*Protestant-Catholic-Jew*) emphasized that Catholicism, as one of the "three great faiths" of American society, stood with Protestantism and Judaism as equally respected forms of religious expression.[24] Any doubts about Catholic assimilation into the mainstream of American life seemed settled with the election of John F. Kennedy as president in 1960.

Catholic Americans by 1960 thus were no longer outsiders. They no longer felt rebuffed, ridiculed, and misunderstood, or surrounded as they were in the 1920s by external adversaries against whom they must defend. Intellectually, culturally, and philosophically, there were fewer enemies to react against. Still, it was this very sense of apartness and difference that had given the revival, at least during its early stages, its creative edge. Already dated by the 1930s, controversialists like G. K. Chesterton, Hilaire Belloc, and Owen Francis Dudley were as out of place in the 1950s as were their antagonists—H. G. Wells, George Bernard Shaw, and the sinister Julian Verrers—and fated to go the same way as The Catholic Truth Society, Catholic study clubs, and *The Masterful Monk*.

But if the conditions that had given rise to Catholic defensiveness (and cohesiveness) faded by the 1960s, so too did the historical forces behind the more positive idea of the lay apostolate. Even apart from the intellectualism debate, the idea of an intellectual apostolate and a Catholic cultural movement seemed less and less relevant after 1950. The apostolate had arisen during a time of acute social, economic, cultural, and political necessity. The world during the 1930s and 1940s really did seem in urgent need of redemption, and Catholics of that era believed that they would be in the vanguard of new world reconstruction. This gave many educated Catholic Americans an earnestness and certainty about their faith unequalled in modern times.

But the complacent Eisenhower years were not a good time for new beginnings and cultural crusades. Even the apocalyptic Frank O'Malley found it hard to keep the vision alive. As Notre Dame became increasingly secular during the 1960s, O'Malley dreamed of founding "Christ's College" ("a specifically Catholic college, a college ordered and vivified by theological wisdom"[25]) while slipping more deeply into the alcoholism that would eventually take his life. O'Malley continued to teach his "Modern Catholic Writers" course (most Catholic schools had dropped theirs by the late 1960s), but he wrote nothing after 1963.

The others who had given meaning and direction to the revival also faded from view. Daniel A. Lord, Francis X. Talbot, and Calvert Alexander belonged to another place and time. Even the indefatigable Sr. Mariella Gable, out of her depth among the new academic critics, published her last anthology in 1950. Riley Hughes was captured by the New Criticism. By 1960 the revival was over. The crisis had passed, it seemed, and with it the excitement, conviction, and urgency that characterized American Catholic intellectual and cultural life during the critical years of the twentieth century.

Endnotes

INTRODUCTION

1. Wilfrid Ward, *William George Ward and the Catholic Revival* (London: Macmillan, 1893); Abbè Jean Calvet, *Le Renouveau Catholique dans La Literature Contemporaine* (Paris: F. Lanone, 1927).

2. Twenties and thirties American Catholic cultural leaders like Francis X. Talbot, S. J., sometimes pointed out that it was a misnomer to characterize any American Catholic literary movement as a revival because in the Protestant-dominated United States there was no Catholic cultural past to be reborn. Instead, Talbot preferred to characterize the American phase of the modern Catholic literary movement as an "emergence." Nevertheless, the majority of Catholics associated with the movement between 1920 and 1960 preferred to use the word "revival."

3. Philip Gleason makes brief reference to the "leadership," "prestige," and "missionary" themes in American Catholicism in a 1969 study of the Catholic intellectualism debate of the 1950s. Gleason's study, however, does not discuss the twentieth century development of these themes. Like most historians, Gleason sees the Catholic intellectualism issue emerging only in the mid–1950s. This study shows its roots in the post-World War I era. See Gleason, "The Crisis of Americanization," in Gleason, ed., *Contemporary Catholicism in the United States* (Notre Dame, Ind.: University of Notre Dame Press, 1969), pp. 18–27.

4. William Halsey, *The Survival of American Innocence: American Catholicism in an Era of Disillusionment, 1920–1940* (Notre Dame, Ind.: University of Notre Dame Press, 1980).

5. Ibid., chaps. 8–9. Gleason, "In Search of Unity: American Catholic Thought, 1920–1960," *Catholic Historical Review* 65 (April 1979): 185–205; "Neoscholasticism as Preconciliar Ideology," *U.S. Catholic Historian* 7 (Fall 1988): 401–11.

6. See Mel Piehl, *Breaking Bread, The Catholic Worker and the Origins of Catholic Radicalism in America* (Philadelphia: Temple University Press, 1982). While limited

mainly to social thought, Piehl's work stands as the best current analysis of the transmigration of European Catholic thought to America during the fruitful 1930s and 1940s.

7. Calvert Alexander, S. J., "Humanism in Saint Louis," *Fleur de Lis* (March 1932): 9.

8. Andrew Greeley in "Catholicism Midwest Style," *America* 114 (12 February 1966): 222–23; *The Hesitant Pilgrim, American Catholicism after the Council* (New York: Sheed and Ward, 1966), pp. xvi-xvii.

9. Francis X. Talbot, "The Prospect of Catholic Literature," in John A. O'Brien, ed., *Catholics and Scholarship. A Symposium on the Development of Scholars* (Huntington, Ind.: Our Sunday Visitor Press, 1938), p. 206.

CHAPTER 1: THE 1920s: A TIME OF TROUBLES

1. Richard M. Griffiths, *The Reactionary Revolution: The Catholic Revival in French Literature, 1870–1914* (London: Constable and Company, 1966), p. 14. For a brief account of the Catholic literary revival in Europe see the *New Catholic Encyclopedia*, 1967 ed., s.v. "Literary Revival, Catholic" by W. Grenzmann. On the French revival see Gene Kellogg, *The Vital Tradition: The Catholic Novel in a Period of Convergence* (Chicago: Loyola University Press, 1970), pp. 7–37.

2. Griffiths, *Reactionary Revolution*, p. 14.

3. Ibid., p. 8.

4. Sr. M. J. Fiecke, O.S.F., *The Revival of Catholic Literature in Twentieth Century Germany* (Milwaukee: Bruce Publishing Company, 1944), p. 337.

5. Ibid., p. 338.

6. Smith actively sought the Democratic nomination for president in 1924. He was nominated in 1928. The most thorough study of the religious issue in the 1924 and 1928 campaigns is found in Allen J. Lichtman, *Prejudice and the Old Politics. The Presidential Election of 1928* (Chapel Hill: University of North Carolina Press, 1979) and David Burner, *The Politics of Provincialism. The Democratic Party in Transition, 1918–1932* (New York: Alfred A. Knopf, 1968).

7. Morton White, *Social Thought in America: The Revolt against Formalism* (Boston: Beacon Press, 1957).

8. Catholic public militancy in the 1920s is covered in James J. Hennesey, *American Catholicism: A History of the Roman Catholic Community in the United States* (New York: Oxford University Press, 1981), pp. 234–53, and Lynn Duimenil, "The Tribal Twenties: The Catholic Response to Anti-Catholicism" (Paper delivered at the Cushwa Center for the Study of American Catholicism, University of Notre Dame, Spring 1988).

9. See "The Pope and the Presidency," *Current History* 27 (March 1928): 767–800; "Catholicism and Politics in America," *Living Age* 333 (15 September 1927): 486–87; "America and Roman Catholicism," *Forum* 73 (March 1925): 289; and "The Catholic Church and the Modern Mind," *Atlantic Monthly* 141 (January-March-May 1928): 12–21, 385–402, 539–40, 664–75.

10. Editorial, *Christian Register* (20 January 1927); "Catholics and the Presidency," *Christian Century* 44 (14 April 1927): 456; George Washington Williams, in "Symposium Correspondence," *Forum* 74 (August 1925): 305.

11. Charles C. Marshall, "An Open Letter to the Honorable Alfred E. Smith," *Atlantic Monthly* 139 (April 1927): 548.

12. "The Paramont Issues," *Christian Century* 45 (1 November 1928): 1315–17.

13. David J. O'Brien, *American Catholics and Social Reform: The New Deal Years* (New York: Oxford University Press, 1968), p. 45.

14. W.I.L., review of *The Roman Catholic Church and the Modern State*, by Charles C. Marshall, *America* 39 (28 April 1928): 70.

15. "Another Exploiter of the 'Catholic Question,'" *America* 38 (10 March 1928): 525.

16. Quoted in "Noted Speakers and Religious Prejudice," *Catholic Historical Review* 8 (January 1929): 633.

17. Quoted in Roger Van Allen, *The Commonweal and American Catholicism* (Philadelphia: Fortress Press, 1974), pp. 15–16.

18. John Jay Chapman, "Strike at the Source," *Forum* 73 (April 1925): 449–57.

19. Lichtman, *Prejudice and the Old Politics*, p. 76.

20. Edmund A. Moore, *A Catholic Runs for President* (New York: The Ronald Press Company, 1956), p. 200.

21. James H. Smylie, "The Roman Catholic Church, The State, and Al Smith," *Church History* 29 (September 1960): 321–43; Burner, *The Politics of Provincialism*, pp. 206–214.

22. John E. Hattery, "The Presidential Election Campaigns of 1928 and 1960: A Comparison of *The Christian Century* and *America*," *Journal of Church and State* 9 (1967): 49.

23. "A Catholic in the White House," *America* 37 (7 May 1927): 78; "Crabites, Smith and the Constitution," *America* 37 (27 August 1927): 463.

24. "R.C. No. 61," *America* 38 (21 January 1928): 358.

25. "Dr. Ryan and *Current History*," *America* 38 (24 March 1928): 574.

26. Chapman, "Strike at the Source," p. 449.

27. Sumerfield Baldwin, "The Crucifixion of the Catholic Mind," *Atlantic Monthly* 140 (August 1927): 178–82.

28. William MacDonald, "Catholics in the United States," review of *The Roman Catholic Church and the Modern State*, by Charles C. Marshall, *Current History* 28 (July 1928): 616.

29. Henry F. May, *The End of American Innocence* (New York: Alfred A. Knopf, 1959).

30. Bertrand Russell, "What I Believe," *Forum* 82 (September 1929): 134.

31. See Frederick J. Hoffman, *The Twenties* (New York: Collier Books, 1949), p. 282, and White, *Social Thought in America: The Revolt against Formalism*.

32. "Next Month," *Forum* 82 (August 1929): iv.

33. H. L. Mencken, "What I Believe," *Forum* 84 (September 1930): 139; Albert Einstein, "What I Believe," *Forum* 84 (October 1930): 194; John Dewey, "What I Believe," *Forum* 83 (March 1930): 177.

34. George E. G. Catlin, "What I Believe," *Nation* 135 (26 October 1932): 398.

35. Edmund Wilson, "What I Believe," *Nation* 134 (27 January 1932): 98.

36. Wilson, "T. S. Eliot and the Church of England," *New Republic* 58 (24 April 1929): 283.

37. Wilson, "The Church and Intellectuals." *New Republic* 50 (15 May 1929): 361.

38. "Resolutions," *Proceedings of the National Catholic Education Association* 30 (November 1933): 72.

39. Dan W. Gilbert, "Is Secular Education Anti-Religious?" *Catholic World* 137 (August 1933): 523.

40. Ibid., pp. 520–23; "Atheism in the Colleges," *America* 46 (17 October 1931): 30.

41. "The Elimination of Conscience," *America* 27 (2 September 1922): 471; Mark O. Shriver, "The Catholic Inferiority Complex," *America* 43 (16 August 1930): 451–52; Ruth K. Burns, "Liberals on the Campus," *Commonweal* 16 (14 September 1932): 469–70.

42. "That Critical Attitude," *America* 44 (14 March 1931): 543.

43. Edmund A. Booth Young, " 'He Stopped Thinking,' " *America* 48 (10 December 1932): 231.

44. William M. Stinson, S. J., "Literary Effects and Catholic Apathy," *America* 45 (6 June 1931): 211–12.

45. Harvey C. Lehman and Paul A. Witty, "Scientific Eminence and Church Membership," *Scientific Monthly* 33 (December 1931): 544–49. In another 1927 study social researcher William S. Ament crudely correlated intellectual distinction with inclusion in *Who's Who in America*. The data showed that Unitarians had "222.7 times the chances of a Catholic of appearing in *Who's Who.*" "Religion, Education, and Distinction," *School and Society* 26 (24 September 1927): 401. See also Ellsworth Huntington and Leon F. Whitney, "Religion and 'Who's Who,' " *American Mercury* 11 (August 1927): 12–18.

46. "Some Additional Catholic Scholars," *America* 47 (16 July 1932): 338.

47. Sr. Mary Eleanore, C.S.C., "Discussion: The Writing Apostolate," *Proceedings of the National Catholic Education Association* 27 (November 1930): 161.

48. Wilfrid A. Parsons, S. J., "Catholic Literature's Dilemma," *America* 42 (11 January 1930): 339.

49. Francis X. Talbot, S. J., "On Literary Self-Complacency," *America* 32 (11 April 1925): 616–18; Parsons, "Literature's Dilemma," p. 340.

50. Muriel Nolan Delaney, "The Collegians on Catholic Books," *America* 51 (19 May 1934): 137.

51. Parsons, "Literature's Dilemma," p. 339.

52. George N. Shuster, "Have We No Scholars?" *America* 33 (15 August 1925): 418–19.

53. Shuster, *The Catholic Spirit in America* (New York: Dial Press, 1927), pp. 167–71.

54. Shuster, "Soldiers of France," *Catholic World* 111 (April 1920): 10–19; "Catholic Literature as a World-Force," *Catholic World* (July 1920): 454–62. There is no substantive study of Shuster's long career. Useful beginnings include: Vincent P. Lannie, ed., *On the Side of Truth: George N. Shuster, An Evaluation of Readings* (Notre Dame, Ind.: University of Notre Dame Press, 1974); William M. Halsey, *The Survival of American Innocence: American Catholicism in an Era of Disillusionment, 1920–1940* (Notre Dame: University of Notre Dame Press, 1980), pp. 84–98; and Thomas E. Blantz, C.S.C. "George N. Shuster and American Catholic Intellectual Life," in Robert F. Trisco, ed., *Studies in Catholic History in Honor of John Tracy Ellis* (Wilmington, Del.: Michael Glazier Publisher, 1985).

55. Shuster, *The Catholic Spirit in Modern English Literature* (New York: Macmillan Company, 1922), pp. 294, 312.

56. Shuster comments on his isolation in Lannie, *On the Side of Truth*, pp. 223–25.

57. Daniel A. Lord, S. J., "War to the Death," *America* 47 (1 October 1932): 610.

58. Lord, "Too Easy to Write," *Queen's Work* 21 (January 1929): 4; "The Criminal As Author," *Queen's Work* 21 (March 1930): 4.

59. Lord, "Editor talks with an Objector," *Queen's Work* 24 (March 1932): 8.

60. Jack English, "Can a Catholic Write a Novel?" *American Mercury* 31 (January 1934): 90–95.

CHAPTER 2: FRANCIS X. TALBOT AND THE CATHOLIC LITERARY "EMERGENCE"

1. Calvert Alexander, *The Catholic Literary Revival: Three Phases in its Development from 1845 to the Present* (Milwaukee: Bruce Publishing Company, 1935).

2. William J. McGucken, S. J., *The Jesuits and Education* (Milwaukee: Bruce Publishing Company, 1932).

3. See John LaFarge, S. J., "The Jesuit Reviews," *America* 51 (14 April 1934): 7.

4. Mary Kiley, "The Talbot Club—New Senior High School Book Club," *Catholic Bookman* 4 (March–April 1942): 114.

5. *New Catholic Encyclopedia*, 1967 ed., s.v. "Talbot, Francis X.," by H. C. Gardiner. See also Halsey, *Survival of American Innocence*, pp. 108–9.

6. Francis X. Talbot, "Catholicism in America," in Harold E. Stearns, ed., *America Now: An Inquiry into Civilization in the United States* (New York: Charles Scribner's Sons, 1938), pp. 528–42.

7. On Talbot's references to "conciliationists" see Talbot, "Catholicism in America," p. 534; Shuster recounts his dispute with Talbot in Vincent P. Lannie, ed., *On the Side of Truth: George N. Shuster, an Evaluation of Readings* (Notre Dame, Ind.: University of Notre Dame Press, 1974), pp. 223–25.

8. Talbot, "The Catholic Spirit in Literature," review of *The Catholic Spirit in Modern English Literature*, by George N. Shuster, *America* 27 (15 July 1922): 304–5. See also Halsey, *Survival of American Innocence*, p. 195.

9. Talbot, "Catholic Spirit," pp. 304–5.

10. Talbot, "The Prospect of Catholic Literature," in John A. O'Brien, ed., *Catholics and Scholarship. A Symposium on the Development of Scholars* (Huntington, Ind.: Our Sunday Visitor Press, 1938), p. 209.

11. Talbot, "That Dangerous Reading Habit," *America* 42 (15 March 1930): 556.

12. Talbot, "On Literary Self-Complacency," *America* 32 (11 April 1925): 616–18.

13. Ibid.

14. Talbot, ed., *Fiction by Its Makers* (New York: The America Press, 1928), p. 5.

15. Talbot, "What Are the Best Ten Catholic Books?" *America* 29 (6 October 1923): 509; "The Catholic Best Ten," *America* 29 (6 October 1923): 592.

16. Talbot, "Cast Your Vote," *America* 54 (19 October 1935): 40–42.

17. Sr. Mary Joseph, S.L., "Twenty Gallery Years," *Living Catholic Authors Bulletin* (February 1952): 4.

18. A selected list of other members of the board of governors includes: Katherine Bregy, critic and lecturer; Ursula Clinton, editor of the *Horizon* (Melbourne, Australia); Denis Gwynn, editor of the *Dublin Review* (London); and Blanche Mary Kelly, literary critic and English professor at Brooklyn College.

19. Talbot, "Cast your Vote," p. 41. Talbot similarly ruled in the 1923 Best Books contest that "Catholic authors alone are to be on the roster." "The Catholic Best Ten," p. 593.

20. Talbot, "The Best Catholic Books," *America* 30 (19 January 1924): 332–33.

21. Talbot, "Results of Voting on Catholic Authors," *America* 56 (10 October 1936): 18–19.

22. Knox's most acclaimed work, *Enthusiasm*, was published in 1950. American Catholics in the 1920s and 1930s regarded Knox primarily as a Church defender.

23. F. T. Marsh, review of *Out of the Whirlwind*, by William Thomas Walsh, *New York Times Book Review*, 26 May 1935, p. 6.

24. Review of *A Watch in the Night*, by Helen C. White, *Christian Century* 50 (10 May 1933): 629.

25. Talbot, "The Best Catholic Books," p. 332.

26. Talbot, "Reflections on the Plebiscite," *America* 54 (21 March 1936): 573.

27. For Coughlin's nomination, see "The Role Call of American Catholic Authors," *America* 54 (4 January 1936): 304. Coughlin presumably was nominated for *Eight Lectures on Labor, Capital, and Justice* (Royal Oak, Mich.: The Radio League of the Little Flower, 1934).

28. Talbot, "The Sheed and Ward Imprint," *America* 48 (4 March 1933): 532–33.

29. Advertisement for the Catholic Book Club, *Commonweal* 22 (27 September 1935): 533.

30. Talbot, "A Poetic Five-Year Span," *America* 55 (18 April 1936): 40–42; "The Tenth Anniversary," in *The Catholic Poetry Society of America Tenth Anniversary Celebration, The Congress Papers* (Fordham University, 27 April 1941), pp. 9–10.

31. Emmett Lavery, "The Catholic Theatre, New Thought on Old Dream," *America* 56 (5 December 1936): 198.

32. Lavery, "The Catholic Theatre," *Catholic Worker* 4 (March 1937): 3.

33. James J. Donohue, "Contemporary Catholic Authors: Emmett Lavery, Leading Catholic Dramatist," *Catholic Library World* 14 (November 1942): 35–42. For a short history of the Catholic Theatre movement see the *New Catholic Encyclopedia*, 1967 ed., s.v. "Catholic Theatre Movement," by Leo Brady.

34. Robert E. Spiller, ed., *The Roots of National Culture, American Literature to 1830* (New York: The Macmillan Company, 1949), p. 18.

35. Charles Jared Ingersoll, "Discourse Concerning the Influence of America on the Mind," in Robert E. Spiller, ed., *The American Literary Revolution, 1783–1837* (New York: New York University Press, 1967), p. 246, 247.

36. Talbot, "Catholic Book Conference," *America* 51 (21 April 1934): 28–29.

37. Cecelia Mary Young, "First Book Fair," *America* 51 (26 April 1934): 165.

38. Talbot, ed., *Novels and Tales by Catholic Writers* (New York: The American Press, 1930), pp. iii, vii.

39. Daniel A. Lord, "The Great American Catholic Women Overlooked," *Queen's Work* 25 (February 1933): 2.

40. Mary H. Kennedy, "This is an Advertising Age," *America* 34 (14 July 1928): 327.

41. Sara K. Diethelm, "Why Not Catholic Best Sellers," *America* 33 (4 July 1925): 284.

42. Brother Jogues, C.F.X., "How to Meet the Menace of Immoral Literature," *Proceedings of the National Catholic Education Association* 32 (May 1936): 324–33.

CHAPTER 3: A REVIVAL IS ORGANIZED: DANIEL A. LORD AND THE SODALITY LITERARY CAMPAIGN

1. Alexander, *Catholic Literary Revival*.

2. Daniel A. Lord, "Editor's Note," *Queen's Work* 25 (January 1933): 1.

3. Alexander's articles, all in volume 25 of the *Queen's Work*, include the following: "The Call to a Crusade of Truth" (January 1933), "Visit to the English Catholic Poetry Society" (February 1933), "The Church, the Mother of Dogma and Song" (March 1933), "Newman Prepares on Ark of Safety Against the Deluge of Decadence" (April 1933), "Arousing Catholic Action with a Song" (May 1933), and "A Catholic Cultural Revival in America Promises" (June 1933); "A Catholic Cultural Revival Promises," pp. 3, 9–11.

4. See Alexander, "The Oxford Centenary in America," *America* 49 (26 August 1933): 496–87.

5. Lord, "Training Youth for Authorship," in John A. O'Brien, ed., *Catholics and Scholarship, A Symposium on the Development of Scholars* (Huntington, Ind.: Our Sunday Visitor Press, 1938), pp. 243–44.

6. Lord, "Editor's Note," p. 1; Alexander, "The Call," p. 10.

7. Lord, "Training Youth," p. 248.

8. On Lord's long association with the Sodality and the *Queen's Work* see: Joseph T. McGloin, S.J., *Backstage Missionary, Father Dan Lord, S.J.* (New York: Pageant Press, 1958), and William B. Faherty, S.J., "A Half-Century with the Queen's Work," *Woodstock Letters* 92 (1963): 99–114.

9. Lord, *Played by Ear* (Chicago: Loyola University Press, 1956), pp. 4–24, 43–44. Other biographical data on Father Lord includes: *New Catholic Encyclopedia*, 1967 ed., s.v. "Lord Daniel Aloysius," by J. T. McGloin; C.M.N., "Reverend Daniel Aloysius Lord, S.J.," in Matthew Hoehn, ed., *Catholic Authors, Contemporary Biographical Sketches, 1930–1947* (New Jersey: St. Mary's Abbey, 1947), pp. 436–37; and Rev. John B. McDonald, "Contemporary Catholic Authors: Daniel A. Lord, S. J., Defender of Youth," *Catholic Library World* 13 (April 1942): 195–202.

10. In *The Church Is Out of Date* (St. Louis, Mo.: The Queen's Work Press, 1955), for example, Lord dealt with the problem of the existence of God and the reality of the soul. Nearly all of Lord's pamphlets carried the impression that the Church possessed a solution to every current problem. Most of Lord's pamphlets have been microfilmed and are available through the St. Louis University library.

11. Faherty, "A Half-Century," p. 107.

12. Lord, *Played by Ear*, p. 200.

13. Lord, "Sodalities in America and Catholic Action," *Studies* 22 (June 1933): 199. According to McGloin, even the regular subscribers to the *Queen's Work* "hardly ever read it." Many had taken the magazine to receive the attractive premiums offered by some of its unscrupulous agents. One enterprising sales-man, unknown to the editors, had promised each new subscriber burial rights in a Jesuit cemetery, complete with Jesuit habit. See McGloin, *Backstage Missionary*, p. 68.

14. Pius XI, *Ubi Arcano Dei Consilio*. Encyclical of Pope Pius XI on the Peace of Christ in the Kingdom of Christ (December 23, 1922), in Claudia Carlen, I.H.M., ed., *The Papal Encyclicals* (Raleigh, N.C.: McGrath Publishing, 1981), pp. 225–38; " 'Catholic Action' Defined by Pope Pius XI," *National Catholic Welfare Conference Bulletin* 10 (March 1932): 9–10. See also *New Catholic Encyclopedia*, 1967 ed., s.v. "Catholic Action," by D. J. Geaney. On Catholic Action in fascist Italy see: Anthony Rhodes, *The Vatican in the Age of the Dictators, 1922–1945* (London: Hodder and Stoughton, 1973), pp. 31–33; and Michael De La Bedoyere, "The Policy of Pius XI," *Fortnightly Review* 146 (1936): 193–97.

15. A good study of the Catholic Worker movement is Mel Piehl, *Breaking Bread*. Another fine account is William D. Miller, *A Harsh and Dreadful Love: Dorthy Day and the Catholic Worker Movement* (New York: Liveright, 1973).

16. On the problems of specialized Catholic Action, see Dennis M. Robb, "Specialized Catholic Action in the United States, 1936–1949: Ideology, Leadership, and Organization" (Ph.D. dissertation: University of Minnesota, 1972).

17. Lord, "Schools of Catholic Action," *Studies* 22 (1933): 455, 456.

18. Lord, *Religion and Leadership* (Milwaukee: Bruce Publishing Company, 1933), p. 4.

19. Ibid., 193–95. The *Queen's Work* during the 1920s and early 1930s bristled with "question and answer" departments in which Lord raised all possible arguments and objections toward the Church, and provided his Sodalists with fact and answer. In 1925 and 1926, "What Shall I Answer When Asked?" and "How Much Do You Know About Your Church?" were introduced as two regular features. But while the *Queen's Work* claimed to deal with "all the big questions of the day," Lord's answers frequently lacked substance. Often an attack upon a Catholic abuse (the Inquisition) was dismissed with an attack upon a Protestant abuse, such as the English penal laws. In answer to the criticism that the Church discouraged scientific research, Lord resorted to the now tiresome tactic of Catholic cataloguing, with scores of famous Catholics listed as proof that the Church did not discourage scientific endeavor. For the most part, questions were answered in an authoritative, dogmatic manner, which would ill-prepare Catholic youth sincerely interested in enlightening the non-Catholic public. For representative question and answer selections see: "What Shall I Answer When Asked?" *Queen's Work* 17 (June 1925): 144; "How Much Do You Know About Your Church?" *Queen's Work* 18 (May 1926): 125; *Queen's Work* 19 (January 1928): 14. Lord also included a chapter on "Great Catholics" in *Religion and Leadership*, a religion textbook for Catholic College freshmen.

20. Lord, "Sodalities in America," p. 204.

21. Faherty, "A Half-Century," p. 108.

22. Lord, "Schools of Catholic Action," pp. 454–68; McGloin, *Backstage Missionary*, p. 80.

23. Lillian M. Howard, "Catholic Youth and Catholic Action," *America* 47 (24 September 1932): 587–88.

24. Lord, *I Can Read Anything* (St. Louis: The Queen's Work Press, 1933), pp. 18–19; Lord, *Played by Ear*, pp. 101–103.

25. Pius XI, *Rappresentanti in terra*. Encyclical of Pope Pius XI on the Christian Education of Youth (December 31, 1929), in Carlen, ed., *The Papal Encyclicals*, pp. 366–67.

26. Alexander, "The Oxford Centenary in America," p. 487.

27. Alexander, "The Call to a Crusade of Truth," pp. 1, 10.

28. Alexander, "Visit to the English Catholic Poetry Society," p. 3.

29. Alexander, "Arousing Catholic Action with a Song," p. 2.

30. Alexander, "A Catholic Cultural Revival Promises," pp. 3, 9, 11.

31. Alexander, *The Catholic Literary Revival*, pp. 242–43.

32. William Halsey, *The Survival of American Innocence: American Catholicism in an Era of Disillusionment, 1920–1940* (Notre Dame, Ind.: University of Notre Dame Press, 1980), p. 11.

33. Alexander, *The Catholic Literary Revival*, p. 308.

34. Celestian J. Steiner, S.J., "The Seminar Idea," *Modern Schoolman* 1 (January 1925), p. 1, 4.

35. Alexander, "A Catholic Cultural Revival Promises," p. 3.

36. The activities at the College of St. Benedict, a Catholic woman's school in St. Joseph, Minnesota, were representative. A Sodality-sponsored Catholic Students Reader's Guild was organized in 1933. Its purpose was to give members "a keener appreciation of Catholic literature, past and present." A Graduate Writers Guild also operated at the college, with members pledged to submit a Catholic short story twice a year. The Gerard Manley Hopkins Unit of the Catholic Poetry Society also operated at St. Benedict's during the 1930s, encouraging aspiring Catholic poets. See *St. Benedict Quarterly* 8 (Feburary 1933): 34; *College of St. Benedict Bulletin*, 1935–1936.

37. Sodality-sponsored Writers' Guilds were established in 1932. Herbert O'H. Walker, S.J., of the Sodality central office headed the project. "Sodality Sponsors Writers Training Guilds," *Queen's Work* 25 (November 1932): 2.

38. Talbot[?], "Comment," *America* 56 (6 March 1937): 506.

39. Borden is quoted by John T. Loftus, O.F.M., "The Apostolate of the Book, Author's Viewpoint," in *Franciscan Educational Conference. Report of the Twenty-Second Annual Meeting, Detroit, Michigan, June 24–26, 1940*. vol. 22 (December 1940), p. 20.

40. Michael Williams, "Ecclesiastical Thought in Popular Language," *Queen's Work* 25 (March 1933): 3.

41. Alexander, "The Apostolate of Publicity," *America* 41 (18 May 1929): 129.

42. Hilary Barth, *Flesh Is not Life* (Milwaukee: Bruce Publishing Company, 1938), p. 226.

43. Sr. Mary Joseph, S.L., "Twenty Gallery Years," *Living Catholic Authors Bulletin* (February 1952): 4; "The Gallery of Living Catholic Authors," *Catholic Library World* 11 (January 1940): 111. On the Gallery of Living Catholic Authors see: Sr. M. Lilliana Owens, S.L., "Without Benefit of Tombstones," *Catholic*

Library World 29 (October 1957): 11–18; Catherine M. Neale, "The Gallery of Living Catholic Authors Celebrates Tenth Anniversary," *Catholic Bookman* 4 (July-August 1942): 164–65; and "The Gallery of Living Catholic Authors," *Catholic World* 165 (September 1947): 547–51.

44. "Over 200 Hear Catholic Literary Emergence Expounded at Chicago," *Catholic Library World* 8 (15 January 1937): 3; *St. John's Record,* 21 February 1939, p. 2; Talbot [?], "Catholic Book Conference," *America* 51 (21 April 1934): 28.

45. Benjamin L. Masse, "The Literary Front," *Queen's Work* (June 1936): 4.

46. See Talbot, "The Sheed and Ward Imprint," *America* 48 (4 March 1933): 532–33; and C.M.N. "Maisie Ward," in Hoehn, ed., *Catholic Authors,* p. 774.

47. C.M.N. "Maisie Ward," pp. 774–75.

48. See "Dr. Francis J. Sheed Speaks Sunday Night," *Notre Dame Scholastic,* 19 October 1934, p. 3; "Mrs. Maisie Ward Sheed Claims Big Audience," *Notre Dame Scholastic,* 30 November 1934; Maisie Ward Sheed, "The World We Live In," *Ariston* (December 1941): 17.

49. "Greets Catholic Revival," *Queen's Work* 26 (January 1934): 7.

50. Talbot[?], "Denver's Literary Experiment," *America* 50 (18 November 1933): 148.

51. Smith, O'Ryan, and Lord are quoted in Gerald Ellard, S.J., "The Denver Literary Congress," *American Ecclesiastical Review* 90 (April 1934): 407–18. All subsequent information on the Denver congress comes from this report.

52. Ibid.

53. James T. Farrell, *A Note on Literary Criticism* (New York: The Vanguard Press, 1936), p. 24.

54. See Gerald Rabkin, *Drama and Commitment: Politics in the American Theatre of the Thirties* (Bloomington: Indiana University Press, 1964).

55. On the attraction of communism for American writers during the 1930s see: Daniel Aaron, *Writers on the Left* (New York: Avon Books, 1961), Chaps. 6–11; Walter B. Rideout, *The Radical Novel in the United States, 1900–1954: Some Interpretations of Literature and Society* (New York: Hill and Wang, 1956), Chaps. 6–8; and Richard H. Pells, *Radical Visions and American Dreams: Culture and Social Thought in the Depression Years* (New York: Harper and Row, 1973).

56. Lord, "Communism's Appeal to Youth," *Proceedings of the National Catholic Education Association* 33 (February 1937): 238–46. See also: "Catholicity and Communism," *Irish Monthly* 64 (October 1936): 658–59; "Thanks to the Communists," *Irish Monthly* 66 (March 1938): 169–181.

57. Alexander, "Fall Operations on the Literary Front," *America* 54 (12 October 1935): 17–18.

58. Talbot, "Reflections on the Plebiscite," *America* 54 (21 March 1936): 573–74.

59. Lord, "Open Letter Inviting You to Niche Left by Chesterton," *Queen's Work* 29 (April 1937): 1.

60. Owen Francis Dudley, *The Masterful Monk* (London: Longmans, Green and Company, 1929).

61. Dorothy J. Willmann, "Owen Francis Dudley—Priest and Novelist," *Queen's Work* 23 (January 1931): 1. Other contemporary accounts of Dudley include: Alice Louise Le Fevre, "Contemporary Catholic Authors: Owen Francis Dudley and the Philosophical Novel," *Catholic Library World* 14 (April 1943): 195–

200; and "Very Reverend Owen Francis Dudley," in Walter Romig, ed., *The Book of Catholic Authors*, 2d series (Detroit, Mich.: Walter Romig and Sons, 1943): 82–87.

62. Muriel Delaney, "The Collegians on Catholic Books," *America* 51 (19 May 1934): 137–38.

63. Besides Calvert Alexander's accounts of the writers of the English Catholic literary revival, the *Queen's Work* ran features on the following American writers: Novelist James B. Connolly, best known for New England sea adventures like *Glouchestermen* (1901) and *Out of Glouchester* (1902); playwright John Steven McGrouthy, author of the *Mission Play*, recounting the life of California Fransiscan missionary Fr. Junipero Serra; and poetess Vera Tracy, who integrated spiritual themes into works like "Incense" and "Burnished Chalice." Like Alexander's accounts of the English, these articles were not meant to be substantive analyses of these writers. Rather, Lord's intention was to briefly identify their work as illustrations of Catholics who were making an impact upon modern literature, drama, and poetry. Lord's selections of "great Catholics" were similarly designed to boost confidence and present a roll-call of Catholics making an impact upon contemporary life. Lord also began his campaign to select "The Twelve Greatest Catholic Women" in America during this period.

64. "Catholics the Victims Not the Authors of Persecution," *Queen's Work* 25 (April 1933): 2.

65. See "A Catholic Discusses Persecution with a Methodist," *Queen's Work* 25 (June 1933): 1, and "Do Non-Catholics Really Try to Understand Catholicism, Catholics Not Narrowminded," *Queen's Work* 25 (Feburary 1933): 1.

66. Lord, "The Battle of the Books—Style 1935," *Queen's Work* 27 (February 1935): 15–16.

67. See Halsey, *The Survival of American Innocence*, pp. 119–20. For the Sodality's involvement in the Legion of Decency campaign see M. Milan, "Student Looks at Catholic Action," *America* 53 (20 April 1935): 37–38; "The Legion of Decency Marches On," *America* 51 (7 July 1934): 289.

CHAPTER 4: THE REVIVAL AS REACTION, I: CATHOLICS AGAINST MODERNITY

1. Alexander, *Catholic Literary Revival*, p. 4.

2. Alexander, "The Call to a Crusade of Truth," *Queen's Work* 25 (January 1933): 10.

3. Owen Francis Dudley's *Masterful Monk* series (1926–1948) is representative.

4. Thomas Merton, *The Seven Storey Mountain* (New York: Harcourt, Brace, 1948).

5. Halsey, *Survival of American Innocence*.

6. Ibid., p. 2.

7. Ibid., pp. 3–4.

8. Ibid. See, especially, chaps. 8 and 9.

9. Alexander's *Catholic Literary Revival* thus described the prewar world "in which men have ceased today to believe" as beginning "at the Renaissance." *Catholic Literary Revival*, p. 11. Jacques Maritain's *Three Reformers: Luther-Descartes-*

Rousseau (London: Sheed and Ward, 1920) traced the spiritual crisis of the West to Luther, Descartes, and Rousseau. Jesuit historian Demitrius Zema's *The Thoughtlessness of Modern Thought* similarly began with the Reformation. *The Thoughtlessness of Modern Thought* (New York: Fordham University Press, 1934), p. 42. Finally, Daniel A. Lord, in assessing the modern philosophical heritage left by Darwin, listed the post-Darwinian "Materialist Group" of "Huxley, Spencer, and Haeckel" as the Church's "modern enemies." *Religion and Leadership*, p. 68.

10. A very popular book among Catholics during the 1920s and early 1930s was James J. Walsh's *The Thirteenth, Greatest of Centuries* (New York: Catholic Summer School Press, 1907).

11. Carlton B. Hayes, *A Generation of Materialism, 1871–1900* (New York: Harper and Brothers, 1941).

12. Martin E. Marty, *The Modern Schism, Three Paths to the Secular* (New York: Harper & Row, 1969), p. 22.

13. Ibid. p. 12.

14. The papacy of Pius IX (1846–1878) was symbolic of the rupture between the Church and nineteenth century culture. The besieged pontiff's *Syllabus of Errors* (1864), issued in the face of the threatened loss of the papal states to the forces of nineteenth century liberalism, appeared to declare war on the nineteenth century. Condemning all the post-Renaissance "isms" which threatened to obliterate the temporal and ecclesiastical authority of the Church, Pius IX concluded his famous bull with the injunction that the papacy need not reconcile itself to "progress, Liberalism, and modern civilization." Pius IX, *Quanta Cura*. Encyclical of Pope Pius IX Condeming Current Errors (December 8, 1864), in Claudia Carlen, I.H.M., ed., *The Papal Encyclicals* (Raleigh, N.C.: McGrath Publishing, 1981), pp. 381–85.

15. Gerald N. Grob and Robert N. Beck, eds., *American Ideas; Source Readings in the Intellectual History of the United States* (New York: Free Press of Glencoe, 1963), pp. 48, 49, 51.

16. On Dewey's utilitarian ethics see Edward A. White, *Science and Religion in American Thought, the Impact of Naturalism* (Stanford, Ca.: Stanford University Press, 1952), pp. 90–109.

17. On the dual tendencies of materialism, see Carlton B. Hayes, *A Political and Cultural History of Modern Europe, vol. 2* (New York: Macmillan Company, 1933–1937), p. 365.

18. Theodore Dreiser, *A Book about Myself* (New York: Boni and Liveright, 1922), p. 459.

19. John Tracy Ellis, "The Formation of the American Priest: An Historical Perspective," in Ellis, ed., *The Catholic Priest in the United States, Historical Investigations* (Collegeville, Minn.: St. John's University Press, 1971), p. 61.

20. Two exceptions are Michael V. Gannon, "Before and After Modernism: The Intellectual Isolation of the American Priest," in Ellis, *The Catholic Priest*, pp. 308–56 and Jay P. Dolan, "American Catholicism and Modernity," *Cross Currents* 31 (Summer 1981): 150–62. The primary concern of both studies, however, is to delineate the negative theological, as opposed to the broader philosophical and intellectual implications of the anti-Modernist campaign.

21. Henceforth, Modernism, in the upper case, refers to the specific theolog-

ical crisis in the early twentieth century Church. The broader lower case designation—modernism—will be used in describing new philosophical and literary forms commonly associated with the term.

22. Pius X, *Pascendi Dominici Gregis*. Encyclical of Pope Pius X on the Doctrines of the Modernists (September 8, 1907), in Carlen, ed., *The Papal Encyclicals*, pp. 71–96.

23. For a concise history of the Modernist crisis see Alec R. Vidler, *The Modernist Movement in the Roman Church, Its Origins and Outcome* (Cambridge, England: University Press, 1934). There were few American Modernists, but there has been increased recent interest in linking Modernism with the late nineteenth century problem of Americanism, which, like Modernism, took an accommodating posture toward the modern world. See M. Scott Appleby, "Modernism as the final phase of Americanism," *Harvard Theological Review* 81 (1988): 171–92.

24. Ellis, "The Formation of the American Priest," p. 65.

25. The anti-Modernist oath read in part: "I hold most certainly, and sincerely profess that faith is not a blind sense of religion welling up from the hiding places of the subconscious . . . but it is an assent of the intellect to truth extrinsically from hearing." Recorded in Bakewell Morrison, S.J., *Revelation and the Modern Mind* (Milwaukee, Wis.: Bruce Publishing Company, 1936), p. 13.

26. The following works colorfully describe "manualist" pedagogy as it existed in American Catholic seminaries into the 1950s: Gannon, "Before and After Modernism," pp. 296, 351–52; Robert I. Gannon, *Up to the Present: The Story of Fordham* (New York: Fordham University Press, 1967), pp. 108–09; and Raymond Schroth, S.J., review of *The Survival of American Innocence*, by Willaim Halsey, *Cross Currents* 32 (Summer 1982): 247. Examples of the most widely used manuals include M. Shallo, S. J., *Lessons in Scholastic Philosophy* (Philadelphia: Peter Reilly Company, 1908) and Charles R. Buschab, *A Manual of Neo-Scholastic Philosophy* (St. Louis, Mo.: B. Herder Company, 1923).

27. Talbot was less outspoken against Modernism and modernity than Lord or Alexander. Nevertheless, his reviews of non-Catholic religious and philosophical works often revealed an anti-Modernist bias. See Talbot's reviews of the following: *Every Man's Bible*, by William R. Inge, *America* 46 (February 6, 1932): 439; *Religion in the Making*, by Alfred North Whitehead, *America* 30 (January 19, 1924): 336; and, *Meanwhile*, *America*, by H. G. Wells, *America* 38 (November 5, 1928): 94. Alexander's views will be more fully explored in chapter 5.

28. See *America*, Volume 18, October 13, 1917 to March 2, 1918. The series was later collected into book form and published as *Armchair Philosophy* (New York: The America Press, 1918). Lord explains his intentions in his autobiography where he also reports important detail about his philosophical training at St. Louis University. See Lord, *Played by Ear*, pp. 96, 213–15.

29. Lord, "Our Futuristic Senses," *America* 18 (17 November 1917): 128; "Necessary Egotism," *America* 18 (1 December 1917): p. 179; "Beyond the Realm of Sense," *America* 18 (24 November 1917): 158–59; "Whence They Came?" *America* 18 (5 January 1918): 316–17.

30. Lord, "The World of Sight and Other Senses," *America* 18 (10 November 1917): 105; "Intellectual Harakiri," *America* 18 (3 November 1917): 82–83; "Dynamiting the Moral World," *America* 18 (15 December 1917): 229–30.

31. Gerald A. McCool, S.J., "Twentieth Century Scholasticism" *Journal of Religion* (1978 Supplement): S206.

32. This practical approach to religious studies is described in John D. Garvey, "Theology in the American Catholic College: An Historical Overview," *Numen Vitae* 33 (1978): 367–76. Jesuit catechistic reform efforts grew out of the 1932 Conference of Jesuit Directors of Religion from the Chicago and Missouri Provinces. Father Morrison, who attended the conference, describes its focus in "An Interpretation of the Work of the Convention of Religious Teachers," *Jesuit Educational Quarterly* 1 (October 1938): 17–26. See also William J. McGucken, S.J., *The Jesuits and Education* (Milwaukee: Bruce Publishing Company, 1930).

33. Lord, *Religion and Leadership*.

34. Bakewell Morrison, S.J., *The Catholic Church and the Modern Mind* (Milwaukee: Bruce Publishing Company, 1933); *Revelation and the Modern Mind*.

35. Morrison, *Revelation and the Modern Mind*, pp. x, 12–22.

36. Gannon, "Before and After Modernism," p. 350.

CHAPTER 5: THE REVIVAL AS REACTION, II: NEWMAN, CHESTERTON, AND BABBITT, CATHOLIC REVIVALISTS

1. Newman's influence over Vatican II is noted in Edward E. Kelly, S.J., "Newman, Vatican I and II and the Church Today," *Catholic World* 202 (February 1966): 291–97. On Newman as a pioneering ecumenist, see Webster J. Patterson, S.J., *Newman: Pioneer for the Layman* (Washington, D.C.: Corpus Books, 1968), and John Tracy Ellis, "John Henry Newman, A Bridge for Men of Good Will," *Catholic Historical Review* 56 (April 1970): 1–24.

2. Garry Wills, *Chesterton, Man and Mask* (New York: Sheed and Ward, 1961), p. 169.

3. Quoted in Wilfred Ward, *The Life of John Henry Cardinal Newman*, Vol. 2 (London: Longmans, Green and Company, 1912), p. 460. Newman discusses nineteenth century liberalism in David J. DeLaura, ed., *Apologia Pro Vita Sua* (New York: W. W. Norton and Company, 1968), p. 218.

4. G. K. Chesterton, *The Man Who Was Thursday, A Nightmare* (New York: Dodd, Mead and Company, 1936), p. 58.

5. Good studies of Newman are: Meriol Trevor, *Newman, The Pillar of the Cloud* (London: Mcmillan and Company, 1962) and Charles F. Harrold, *John Henry Newman* (London: Longmans, Green and Company, 1945).

6. Biographical information on O'Connell is found in Paul A. Fitzgerald, S.J., *The Governance of Jesuit Colleges in the United States, 1920–1970* (Notre Dame, Ind.: University of Notre Dame Press, 1984), pp. 39–40.

7. Daniel M. O'Connell, "Newman and Catholic Colleges," *America* 30 (29 December 1923): 265–66; "A Newman Centenary," *American Ecclesiastical Review* 80 (1929): pp. 391–402. See also "Teaching Newman," *America* 30 (9 February 1924): 409. O'Connell promoted Newman studies into the 1940s. See O'Connell's "For the Modern Reader" in John K. Ryan, ed., *American Essays for the Newman Centennial* (Washington, D.C.: Catholic University Press, 1947), pp. 104–111.

8. Fitzgerald, *The Governance*, pp. 6–39.

9. *Bulletin of St. Louis University, College of Arts and Sciences, 1928–1929*, p. 88; *Bulletin of Loyola University of Chicago, Illinois, 1923–1924*, p. 53.

10. *Bulletin of St. Louis University, College of Arts and Sciences, 1933–1934*, p. 94; English Department Minutes, Loyola University of Chicago, 11 October 1933. Loyola University Archives, Chicago, Illinois.

11. Edwin Ryan, D. D., *A College Handbook to Newman* (Washington, D.C.: Catholic Education Press, 1930), pp. 44, 85.

12. Edward E. Kelly writes that Newman's non-scholastic developmental approach to religious dogma "made him suspect for the Rome-trained theologians" for three decades after *Pascendi*'s condemnation of Modernism in 1907. "Newman, Wilfrid Ward, and the Modernist Crisis," *Thought* 68 (Winter 1973): 517. See also Mary Jo Weaver, ed., *Newman and the Modernists* (Washington, D.C.: University Press of America, 1985).

13. Raymond Corrigan, S. J., *The Church in the Nineteenth Century* (Milwaukee: Bruce Publishing Company, 1938); Bakewell Morrison, S. J., and Stephen J. Rueve, S. J., *Think and Live* (Milwaukee: Bruce Publishing Company, 1937); Alexander, *Catholic Literary Revival*.

14. Joseph Husslein, S. J., "The Science and Culture Series," *Catholic Bookman* 1 (December 1937): 122–25; *Woodstock Letters* 51 (1932): 487; *Woodstock Letters* 63 (1934): 135.

15. Morrison, *Think and Live*, pp. 16–17.

16. Corrigan, *The Church*, pp. 27–29, 151, 291, 306.

17. Quoted in Ward, *Life of Newman*, p. 416.

18. Quoted in Roger E. Bacon, "Shall America Have a Catholic Revival?" *Fleur de Lis* 33 (March 1934): 58.

19. Newman, *The Idea of a University*, Daniel M. O'Connell, S. J., ed., (New York: The American Press, 1941), pp. 338–40.

20. Ibid., pp. 114–40.

21. Newman, *Apologia*, p. 218.

22. Alexander, *The Catholic Literary Revival*, p. 30.

23. Ibid.

24. Ibid., p. 26.

25. Ibid., p. 34.

26. Ibid., p. 35.

27. Francis X. Talbot, review of *The Catholic Spirit in Modern English Literature*, by George Shuster, *America* 27 (15 July 1922): 304.

28. O'Connell, "Newman and Catholic Colleges," p. 266.

29. Talbot, "The Best Catholic Books," *America* 30 (19 January 1924): 332–33. Sr. Mary Louise, S. L., *Over the Bent World* (New York: Sheed and Ward, 1939).

30. Alfred G. Brickel, S. J., "Cardinal Newman and Gilbert K. Chesterton," *Catholic World* 109 (1919): 746.

31. Alexander, *Catholic Literary Revival*, p. 242.

32. Chesterton, *Man Who Was Thursday*, p. 188.

33. Chesterton, *Heretics* (London: John Lane, 1905), pp. 12–13, 81.

34. Ibid., pp. 13, 31.

35. Ibid., p. 131.

36. Chesterton, *Manalive* (Bristol: J. W. Arrowsmith Ltd., 1921), p. 160.

37. Chesterton, *Heretics* p. 302.

38. Chesterton, *Orthodoxy* (New York: Dodd, Mead and Company, 1908), p. 32.

39. Ibid., p. 29.

40. Ibid., p. 58.

41. Chesterton, *The Napoleon of Notting Hill* (London: John Lane, 1904), p. 33.

42. Chesterton, *Orthodoxy*, p. 53.

43. Ibid., pp. 53–55, 61–62; *Heretics*, pp. 35–36.

44. Chesterton, *Orthodoxy*, p. 249.

45. Chesterton, *Heretics*, p. 36.

46. Chesterton, *The Collected Poems of G. K. Chesterton* (New York: Dodd, Mead and Company, 1932).

47. Ibid., pp. 294–95.

48. Ibid., p. 296.

49. Chesterton, *Orthodoxy*, p. 186.

50. Fulton J. Sheen, *God and Intelligence in the Modern World* (London: Longmans, Green and Company, 1925), pp. vii–ix.

51. Daniel A. Lord, "The Greatest of Natural Gifts," *Fleur de Lis* 36 (1936): 14.

52. Victor Hermann, O.F.M., "Literature from the Catholic Viewpoint," *Franciscan Educational Conference. Report of the Twenty-Second Annual Meeting, Detroit, Michigan, June 24–26, 1940*, vol. 22 (December 1940), p. 174.

53. Harry Wilson, "Between Chesterton and Me," *Fleur de Lis* 35 (December 1935): 16.

54. "New Academic Prize is Memorial to Chesterton," *Notre Dame Scholastic*, 22 January 1937, p. 5.

55. Alexander, "Chesterton as Fighter," *Catholic School Journal* 37 (May 1937): 150.

56. A good account of the New Humanism is J. David Hoeveler's *The New Humanism, A Critique of Modern America, 1900–1940* (Charlottesville: University Press of Virginia, 1977). For an account of the Catholic-New Humanist Alliance, see Donald Romito, "Catholics and Humanists: Aspects of the Debate in Twentieth-Century American Criticism" (Ph.D. dissertation, Emory University, 1976).

57. Nineteen thirty is generally seen as the "pinnacle" of the New Humanist movement. That year saw the publication of the movement's manifesto, the Norman Foerster edited *Humanism and America: Essays on the Outlook of Modern Civilization* and the most outspoken attack upon it in Harley Gratten, ed., *The Critique of Humanism: A Symposium*. See Hoeveler, *The New Humanism*, p. 25.

58. Talbot, "Humanism is Against," *America* 43 (12 April 1930): 44–45.

59. Ibid.

60. Alexander, "Humanism in St. Louis," *Fleur de Lis* (31 March 1932): 9.

61. Benjamin L. Masse, "The Passing of Babbitt," *Fleur de Lis* (March 1934): 18.

62. Irving Babbitt, *Rousseau and Romanticism* (Boston: Houghton Mifflin Company, 1919), p. 155. Hoeveler, *The New Humanism*, p. 45.

63. Hoeveler, *The New Humanism*, pp. 34–36, 152–58; George A. Paniches, "Babbitt and Religion," in George A. Paniches and Claes G. Ryn, eds., *Irving Babbitt in Our Time* (Washington, D.C.: University Press of America, 1986), pp. 32–34.

64. Masse, "The Passing of Babbitt," p. 19.

65. Alexander, "Humanism in St. Louis," p. 9.

66. Alexander, "Scholasticism and the New Humanism," *Modern Schoolman* 6 (January 1930): 26.

67. Alexander, "Humanists and Humanists," *Modern Schoolman* 6 (May 1930): 68–69.

68. T. S. Eliot, "Second Thoughts About Humanism," *Hound and Horn* 2 (1929): 343. Eliot's embrace and later repudiation of the New Humanism is recorded in James W. Tuttleton, "T. S. Eliot and the Crisis of the Modern," *Modern Age* (Summer/Fall, 1988): 275–83.

69. "No Via Media," *Modern Schoolman* 11 (November 1932): 5.

70. Camile McCole, "Humanism's Challenge to Catholicism," *America* 43 (24 May 1930): 164. A similar opinion was expressed by Calvert Alexander in 1930. The New Humanism, wrote Alexander, was a challenge to Catholic critics "to exercise the kind of leadership, at least among Catholics, that Mr. Babbitt and his followers are carrying on for the benefit of non-Catholic literateurs." "Scholasticism and the New Humanism," p. 26.

71. Alexander, "Scholasticism and the New Humanism," p. 27.

CHAPTER 6: THE SEARCH FOR THE GREAT AMERICAN CATHOLIC NOVEL, I: CATHOLIC FICTION TO 1935

1. James Albano, "The Catholic Novel," *Georgetown Journal* (April 1936): 405.

2. All the writers discussed in this chapter appeared on recommended reading lists for Catholic high schoolers and collegians during the 1920s and early 1930s. While some of the novels discussed here were written before 1920 (marking the chronological beginning of this book) they nevertheless were read and valued by Catholic readers, teachers, and critics throughout the pre–1935 era. Francis X. Talbot similarly featured a number of these same writers in *Fiction by Its Makers* (New York: The America Press, 1920), which was a symposium on the art of modern Catholic fiction.

3. Paul R. Messbarger, *Fiction with a Parochial Purpose: Social Uses of American Catholic Literature, 1884–1900* (Boston: Boston University Press, 1971), p. 114.

4. C.M.N., "Frank Spearman," in Matthew Hoehn, ed., *Catholic Authors, Contemporary Biographical Sketches, 1930–1947* (New Jersey: St. Mary's Abbey, 1947), pp. 700–701.

5. Frank H. Spearman, *Robert Kimberly* (New York: Grosset and Dunlap, 1911); *The Marriage Verdict* (New York: Charles Scribner's Sons, 1923).

6. Kathleen Norris to Francis X. Talbot, S.J., circa 1926. Francis X. Talbot Papers, Georgetown University Archives, Washington, D.C.

7. Ibid., Norris to Talbot, October, 1929. See also Norris, *Noon, an Autobiographical Sketch* (New York: Doubleday, Page and Company, 1925), pp. 14–15.

8. Norris, *Little Ships* (New York: Doubleday, Page and Company, 1925).

9. Lucille Papin Borden, "Lucille Papin Borden," in Walter Romig, ed., *The Book of Catholic Authors*, 3d series (Detroit, Mich.: Walter Romig Publishers, 1945), p. 13.

10. Borden, *The Candlestick Makers* (New York: Macmillan Company, 1923); *Gentlemen Riches* (New York: Macmillan Company, 1925); *From Out Magdala* (New York: Macmillan Company, 1927); *Silver Trumpets Calling* (New York: Macmillan Company, 1931).

11. Norris, *Mother* (New York: Macmillan Company, 1911), pp. 178–81, 194–95.

12. Norris, *Margaret Yorke* (New York: A. L. Burt, 1930).

13. Borden, *Silver Trumpets*, p. 107.

14. Norris, *The Lucky Lawrences* (New York: Doubleday, Doran and Company, 1930), 110.

15. Ibid., pp. 119, 116.

16. Spearman, *Robert Kimberly*, p. 376.

17. Isabel C. Clarke, *Fine Clay* (New York: Benziger Brothers, 1914), pp. 156–57, 174.

18. Ethel Cook Eliot, *Her Soul to Keep* (New York: Macmillan Company, 1935), pp. 108–109.

19. Borden, *Candlestick Makers*, pp. 12–14.

20. Eliot, *Her Soul to Keep*, p. 216.

21. Borden, *Candlestick Makers*, p. 15.

22. Norris, *Little Ships*, p. 29.

23. Dudley, *The Masterful Monk*, pp. 131, 159.

24. See chapter 3, pp. 47–48.

25. Benson's most popular novels were *By What Authority?* (London: Burns Publishing, 1904) and *Come Rack! Come Rope!* (London: Hutchinson and Company, 1912). See E. E. Reynolds, "The Historical Novels of Robert Hugh Benson," *Dublin Review* 233 (Autumn 1959): 272–78.

26. Talbot, "The Best Catholic Books," *America* 30 (19 January 1924): 332–33; Dorothy J. Willmann, "Owen Francis Dudley—Priest and Novelist," *Queen's Work* 23 (January 1931): 1. A 1936 poll asked Notre Dame students, "What one piece of literature has most influenced your life?" *The Masterful Monk* ranked second, preceded only by the catechism.

27. On the English Catholic experience, see: David Mathew, *Catholicism in England, 1535–1935; Portrait of a Minority, Its Culture and Tradition* (London: Longmans, Green and Company, 1936), and Bernard Bergonzi, "The English Catholics," *Encounter* 24 (January 1965): 19–30.

28. R. Laurence Moore, *Religious Outsiders and the Making of Americans* (New York: Oxford University Press, 1986).

29. See Gordon S. Wood, *The Creation of the American Republic, 1776–1787* (Chapel Hill: University of North Carolina Press, 1969), pp. 46–124, and Cushing Strout, "The Shadowy Grandeurs of the Past: Irving and Longfellow," in Strout, ed., *Intellectual History in America*, I (New York: Harper and Row, 1968), pp. 131–40.

30. Talbot, "Catholicism in America," in Harold E. Stearns, ed., *America Now; An Enquiry into Civilization in the United States* (New York: Charles Scribner's Sons, 1938), p. 533.

31. Ibid.

CHAPTER 7: THE TRANSFORMATION OF THE CATHOLIC LITERARY REVIVAL IN THE AMERICAN CATHOLIC COLLEGE DURING THE 1930s AND 1940s

1. See Philip Gleason, "Neoscholasticism as Preconciliar Ideology," *U.S. Catholic Historian* 7 (Fall 1988): 401–11.

2. The fact that more and more Catholic philosophers after 1935 were designating themselves as neo-Thomists as opposed to neo-scholastics underscores this change.

3. Joachim Daleiden, O.F.M., "Discussion," *Franciscan Educational Conference. Report on the Twenty-Second Annual Meeting Detroit Michigan, June 24–26, 1940,* vol. 22 (December 1940), p. 397.

4. Ibid., pp. 397–98.

5. This chapter specifically addresses the impact of the Catholic literary revival at selected midwestern schools, but it is important to note that other Catholic colleges throughout the country also underwent similar development. The nationwide 1940 Franciscan Educational Conference survey underscores this point. Boston College, for example, introduced a course on the "Catholic Literary Revival" in 1936. Beginning in the mid–1930s Fordham University's student literary quarterly (*The Fordham Monthly*) was similarly filled with editorials urging an American Catholic revival based upon European models. Courses in Catholic social thought were also introduced nationwide in the mid–1930s.

6. *Bulletin of Loyola University of Chicago, Illinois, 1924,* p. 54.

7. *Bulletin of Marquette University, Milwaukee, Wisonsin, 1931–132,* p. 49; *Bulletin of Marquette University, Milwaukee, Wisconsin, Teachers' Courses Announcements, 1935–1936,* p. 20.

8. Report on the English Department from 1890 to 1950. St. John's University Archives, Collegeville, Minnesota.

9. See chapter 5, pp. 65–66.

10. Gleason, "A Historical Perspective," in Robert Hassenger, ed., *The Shape of Catholic Higher Education* (Chicago: University of Chicago Press, 1967), pp. 42–53.

11. Victor Herman, O.F.M., "Literature From the Catholic Viewpoint," *Franciscan Educational Conference,* p. 171; "Report of the Committee on Resolutions," ibid., p. 416.

12. *Proceedings of the National Catholic Education Association* 30 (1933): 72. Intensifying the movement toward a more fully integrated Catholic college curriculum after 1930 was the model of Catholic education set forth by Pius XI. In his encyclical *The Christian Education of Youth* (1929) Pius declared that the ultimate end of all Catholic education should be the formation of "the true and perfect Christian." Pius XI thus directed every Catholic school to organize its "teachers, syllabus, and textbooks in every branch" around "the Christian spirit" so that religion became "the foundation and crown of youth's entire training." Pius XI, *Rappresentanti in terra,* in Claudia Carlen, ed., *The Papal Encyclicals,* p. 365.

13. *Bulletin of Marquette University, Teachers' Courses Announcements, 1935–1936,* p. 20.

14. *Bulletin of the College of St. Benedict, St. Joseph, Minnesota, 1936–1937,* p. 53.

15. *Bulletin of the College of St. Catherine, 1942*, p. 31.

16. Alexander, *Catholic Literary Revival.*

17. Sr. Mary Louise, S.L., ed., *Over the Bent World* (New York: Sheed and Ward, 1939).

18. Francis B. Thornton, ed., *Return to Tradition, A Directive Anthology* (Milwaukee: Bruce Publishing Company, 1947).

19. Gleason, "In Search of Unity," p. 191.

20. An excellent account of the role that Dawson and Maritain played in American Catholic life before the Second Vatican Council is in James Hitchcock, "Postmortem on a Rebirth, the Catholic Intellectual Renaissance," *American Scholar* 49 (Spring 1980): 211–25.

21. The only full-length scholarly treatment of Dawson is Bruno Schlesinger, *Christopher Dawson and the Modern Political Crisis* (Notre Dame, Ind., 1949). Collected papers of the annual conferences of the Society for Christian Culture are also helpful. See Peter J. Cataldo, ed. *Essays on Dawsonian Themes* (New York: University Press of America, 1984). Dawson's daughter, Christina Scott, strikes a personal note in *A Historian and His World. A Life of Christopher Dawson 1889–1970* (London: Sheed and Ward, 1984).

22. Räissa Maritain's autobiographical *We Have Been Friends Together*, trans. Julie Kernan (New York: Longmans, Green and Company, 1942) is very good at placing the young Maritains within the context of the pre-World War I era. A good introduction to Jacques Maritain's life and thought is Donald and Idella Gallagher, eds., *A Maritain Reader* (New York: Image Books, 1966).

23. The standard work on Michel and the liturgical movement is Paul Marx, O.S.B., *Virgil Michel and the Liturgical Movement* (Collegeville, Minn.: Liturgical Press, 1957). A more recent work is R. W. Franklin and Robert L. Spaeth, *Virgil Michel: American Catholic* (Collegeville, Minn.: Liturgical Press, 1988).

24. Gerald Ellard, S.J., *Christian Life and Worship* (Milwaukee: Bruce Publishing Company, 1933); John Leo Klein, S.J., "The Role of Gerald Ellard (1894–1963) in the Development of the Contemporary American Liturgical Movement" (Ph.D. dissertation, Fordham University, 1971).

25. Christopher Dawson, "General Introduction" in Dawson, ed., *Essays in Order* (New York: Macmillan Company, 1931), p. v.

26. See C. J. Eustace, "Jacques Maritain, Philosopher of Our Age," *Catholic World* 162 (March 1946): 500.

27. Marx, *Virgil Michel*, p. 7.

28. Quoted in Dawson, "General Introduction," p. xvi.

29. Dawson, *Enquiries into Religion and Culture* (London: Sheed and Ward, 1934), p. 115.

30. Dawson, *The Modern Dilemma, The Problem of European Unity* (London: Sheed and Ward, 1932), p. 47.

31. Dawson, *The Making of Europe* (London: Sheed and Ward, 1932).

32. Maritain, "Religion and Culture," in Dawson, ed., *Essays In Order*, pp. 3–61; *True Humanism* (New York: Charles Scribner's Sons, 1938).

33. Dawson, *Progress and Religion*, chap. 7; *Enquiries into Religion and Culture* (New York: Sheed and Ward, 1933), pp. 295–96. Maritain, *True Humanism*, pp. xv, 8.

34. Dawson, *The Modern Dilemma*, p. 113.

35. Dawson, *Progress and Religion*, p. 260; Maritain, *True Humanism*, p. 156.

36. Quoted by Marx, *Virgil Michel*, p. 261.

37. Ellard, *Christian Life and Worship*, p. xi.

38. Marx, *Virgil Michel*, p. 179.

39. Dawson, *Religion and the Modern State* (London: Sheed and Ward, 1935), p. 150.

40. Maritain, *True Humanism*, pp. 114–15, 86.

41. Michel, "Christian Culture," *Orate Fratres* 13 (14 May 1939): 296–304.

42. Hitchcock, "Postmortem," p. 220.

43. See Gerald A. McCool, "Twentieth Century Scholasticism," *Journal of Religion* (1978 Supplement): S209–211.

44. "Jacques Maritain, Noted Philosopher, Is Guest of Paper," *Catholic Worker* 3 (January 1936): 1.

45. Peter Maurin, "Catholicism and the Bourgeois Mind," *Catholic Worker* 3 (January 1936): 2.

46. Mel Piehl, *Breaking Bread*, p. 85.

47. Course in Catholic Backgrounds and Current Social Theory, Third and Fourth Semesters, 1937–1938, St. John's University Archives, Collegeville, Minnesota. Mimeo.

48. Paul Hanley Furfey, *Fire on the Earth* (New York: Macmillan Company, 1936), pp. 6–7, 92.

49. Piehl, *Breaking Bread*, p. 126.

50. *Bulletin of Marquette University, Milwaukee, Wisconsin, Summer Session, 1936*, p. 27.

51. A good account of both encyclicals is given in Thomas Bokenkotter, *A Concise History of the Catholic Church* (New York: Image Books, 1979), pp. 341–42, 354, 391–93.

52. Joseph Reiner, S.J., *A Program for Catholic Social Action* (St. Louis, Mo.: The Queen's Work Press, 1935), p. 8.

53. Sidney Hook, *Reason, Social Myths, and Democracy* (New York: Humanities Press, 1940), p. 78.

54. James Hennessey, S.J. *American Catholics: A History of the Roman Catholic Community in the United States* (New York: Oxford University Press, 1981), pp. 255–57.

55. William J. McGucken, S.J., "The Renascence of Religion Teaching in American Catholic Schools," in Roy J. Deferrari, ed., *Essays on Catholic Education in the United States* (Washington, D.C.: The Catholic University of American Press, 1942), pp. 331–32.

56. Ibid.

57. Bernard J. Sheil, "The Catholic Graduate and the World Today," *Today* (20 May 1947): 9–10.

58. Donald A. Gallagher, interview with author, Milwaukee, Wis., 1 April 1985.

59. Richard A. Finnegan, "Editorial Notes," *Fleur de Lis* 33 (December 1933): 5.

60. Ibid., p. 6.

61. Cyril T. Echele, "The Bourgeois Spirit in America," *Fleur de Lis* (March 1934): 34–38.

62. Finnegan, "The Catholic Literary Revival, its Need in the United States," *Fleur de Lis* (March 1934): 57–58.

63. Donald A. Gallagher, "Go To Thomas," *Fleur de Lis* 35 (March 1936): 5–10.

64. Cyril Echele, "Catholic Youth Finds a Cause," *Catholic Worker* (June 1958): 3.

65. Ibid., pp. 4, 5.

66. Ibid., p. 5.

67. The fullest development of Maritain's practical philosophy for the achievement of a "New Christendom" appears in *True Humanism*. See especially pp. 290–92. Maritain's endorsement of a pluralistic society that was at once "personalist" and "communitarian" is also found in *The Rights of Man* (1943), *Christianity and Democracy* (1944) and *Man and the State* (1954).

68. Scholarly treatment of Maritain's political philosophy is abundant. See Paul E. Sigmund, "Maritain in Politics," in Deal W. Hudson and Matthew J. Mancini, eds., *Understanding Maritain: Philosopher and Friend* (Macon, Ga.: Mercer University Press, 1987), pp. 153–70; and John W. Cooper, *The Theology of Freedom: The Legacy of Jacques Maritain and Reinhold Niebuhr* (Macon, Ga.: Mercer University Press, 1985). A critique of Maritain's New Christendom can be found in Gustavo Gutierrez, *A Theology of Liberation, History, Politics and Salvation*, trans. John Eagleson (Maryknoll, N.Y.: Orbis Books, 1973). Gutierrez writes that Maritain's distinction between Christians as individuals and Christians as Church members is "ambiguous" and "timid" (pp. 56–57). Sidney Hook, *Reason, Social Myths, and Democracy*, on the other hand, considers the New Christendom dangerous to pluralistic democracy (pp. 78–91).

69. On Maritain's specific impact upon American Catholicism see Ralph McInerny, "Jacques Maritain In and On America," *This World* 18 (Summer 1987): 75–83; Kenneth L. Woodward, "Jacques Maritain and American Intellectual Life," *Critic* 21 (Feburary-March 1963): 30–34; and Leo R. Ward, "Meeting Jacques Maritain," *Review of Politics* 44 (October 1982): 483–88. Maritain's distinction between "anthropocentric" and "theocentric" humanism was particularly meaningful to Donald Gallagher. See Gallagher, "The Legacy of Jacques Maritain's Christian Philosophy" in Victor Brezik, C.S.B., ed., *One Hundred Years of Thomism: Aeterni Patris and Afterwards, A Symposium* (Houston: Center for Thomistic Studies), pp. 45–59.

70. Gallagher, 1985 interview.

71. Arthur Kuhl, *Royal Road* (New York: Sheed and Ward, 1941).

72. Quoted in Piehl, *Breaking Bread,* p. 150. The history of the Chicago Catholic Worker is treated most fully in Frank Sicius, "The Chicago Catholic Worker Movement, 1936 to the Present." (Ph.D. dissertation, Loyola University of Chicago, 1979). I am indebted to Sicius and Piehl for much of the factual information about the Chicago Catholic Worker contained in this chapter.

73. Ed Marciniak, interview with author, Chicago, Ill., 14 February 1985.

74. "The Story of an Idea," *Today* (May 1946): 16.

75. R. C. Hartnett, S.J., Unpublished paper. Community Conference on the Late Rev. Joseph Reiner, S.J., 1881–1934, Loyola University Archives, Chicago, Illinois.

76. Telephone interview with Joan Smith O'Gara, 2 February 1985.

77. Piehl, *Breaking Bread,* p. 150.

78. "Catholic Labor Theatre Underway," *Chicago Catholic Worker* 1 (March 1939): 3.

79. Daniel A. Lord, *Storm-Tossed. If Communists Had the Truth or Catholics Had the Zeal* (St. Louis, Mo.: The Queen's Work Press, 1936).

80. Lord, *Our Part in the Mystical Body* (St. Louis: The Queen's Work Press, 1935). Lord's Jesuit confrere Benjamin L. Masse underwent similar growth. See Masse, *Justice for All: An Introduction to the Social Teachings of the Church* (Milwaukee: Bruce Publishing Company, 1964).

81. Lord, *Storm-Tossed,* p. 100.

82. "Catholic Labor Theatre," p. 3.

83. John Cogley, "C.I.O. Organizer Pays Us a Visit," *Chicago Catholic Worker* 1 (July 1938): 1; "To Catholic Unionists," *Chicago Catholic Worker* (October 1938): 1.

84. *Today,* 1–3 (1946–1948). See Piehl, *Breaking Bread,* p. 169.

85. Cogley, "Christianizing the World," *Today* (15 May 1947): 2; "Christians in the World," *Today* (1 November 1947): 2.

86. Abigail Quigley McCarthy, "Darkness, Death, and Relentless Light," *Today* (1 February 1948): 13; "The Novels of Bernanos," *Today* (15 October 1947): 14; "Catholic Literature—and Two Irishman," *Today* (Christmas 1947): 16.

87. Marciniak, 1985 interview.

CHAPTER 8: FRANK O'MALLEY: THINKER, CRITIC, REVIVALIST

1. The quotation is from a letter by Charles F. Russ, Jr. (Class of 1949) published in the Notre Dame alumni magazine shortly after O'Malley's death. "The Last Hurrah," *Notre Dame Magazine* 3 (October 1974): 32. "Mr. Blue" refers to the loveable eccentric of Myles Connolly's *Mr. Blue* (New York: Macmillan Company, 1928). The book, which went through thirty-one printings, was a popular item among Catholic collegians in the 1930s. Its last words, spoken by a friend upon hearing of Blue's premature death, read: "You can't make me believe that Blue is dead" (p. 119).

2. "God and Man at Notre Dame," *Time* (9 February 1962): 48–54. Novelist Edwin O'Connor, a 1950 Notre Dame graduate, claimed that O'Malley was "the single greatest help for me in college." As a Notre Dame freshman, O'Connor was encouraged by O'Malley to pursue a literary as opposed to a journalistic career. Their friendship endured beyond O'Connor's graduation with the latter periodically returning to Notre Dame to lecture in O'Malley's classes. O'Connor dedicated *The Edge of Sadness* (1961) to O'Malley. O'Connor is quoted in Hugh Rank, *Edwin O'Connor* (New York: Twayne Publishers, 1974), pp. 19–20.

3. See Gary Wills, *Bare Ruined Choirs: Doubt, Prophecy, and Radical Religion* (New York: Doubleday, 1972), pp. 230–50.

4. The integral Christianity that is written about here should not be confused with its nineteenth century meaning, a theological attitude that prevailed in many European Churches which insisted that "everything must be formally and explicitly Christian before it is good." Richard P. McBrien, *Catholicism,* vol. 1

(Minneapolis: Winston Press, 1980), p. xiv. Under this view the Church was seen as a "perfect society," a divine institution immune to time, process, and history. A good discussion of this attitude is in Jay Dolan, *The American Catholic Experience: A History from Colonial Times to the Present* (Garden City, N.Y.: Doubleday, 1985), pp. 303–5. The meaning of the term to O'Malley's generation was quite the opposite. It encouraged Catholics to embrace the modern world as integrated persons—as believing Christians within secular culture.

5. Frank O'Malley, "The Literature of this Century," Francis J. O'Malley Papers, University of Notre Dame Archives, Notre Dame, Indiana.

6. Romano Guardini, *The Church and the Catholic and the Spirit of the Liturgy,* trans. Ada Lane (London: Sheed and Ward, 1935), p. 11; Leon Bloy, *The Woman Who Was Poor,* trans. I. J. Collins (New York: Sheed and Ward, 1947), p. 356.

7. Introductory to Frank O'Malley, "The Restlessness of Our Time," in *Program of Action. A Suggested Outline for the Lay Apostolate of Young Women,* part 1 (Grailville, Ohio: 1946).

8. See Thomas Stritch, "A Lost Breed," *Notre Dame Magazine* 10 (February 1981): 21. Professor Stritch was a friend and English Department colleague of O'Malley. A 1981 interview with Professor Stritch was especially useful in helping me to begin the process of reconstructing the O'Malley years at Notre Dame. I am also indebted to Professor Stritch for his other fine studies of Notre Dame in the 1940s and 1950s.

9. On O'Hara's efforts see Stritch, "The Foreign Legion of Father O'Hara," *Notre Dame Magazine* 10 (October 1981): 23–27.

10. Maritain gave a series of seven lectures at Notre Dame during a three-week period in 1938. He was repeatedly reinvited to campus, sometimes lecturing twice a year. Gilson was a less frequent visitor. The *Notre Dame Scholastic* (the university's student newspaper) records three separate Gilson lecture series between 1930 and 1935. On Maritain's visits see Leo R. Ward, "Meeting Jacques Maritain," *Review of Politics* 44 (October 1982): 483–84, and Julie Kernan, *Our Friend Jacques Maritain: A Personal Memoir* (Garden City, N.Y.: Doubleday, 1975), pp. 89–95.

11. Quoted in James Hitchcock, "Postmortem on a Rebirth, the Catholic Intellectual Renaissance," *American Scholar* 49 (Spring 1980): 211–25. Hutchins makes his case for metaphysics in the college curriculum in *The Higher Learning in America* (New Haven, Ct.: Yale University Press, 1936).

12. The best discussion of the Christian philosophy debate is Maurice Nedoncelle, *Is There a Christian Philosophy?* trans. Iltyd Trethowan (New York: Hawthorn Books, 1960).

13. Etienne Gilson, *The Spirit of Medieval Philosophy,* trans. A.H.C. Downes (New York: Charles Scribner's Sons, 1936).

14. See Gilson, *Christianity and Philosophy* (New York: Sheed and Ward, 1939); Romano Guardini, *Freedom, Grace, and Destiny* (New York: Sheed and Ward, 1954), pp. 8–10, and Jacques Maritain, *An Essay on Christian Philosophy,* trans. Edward H. Flannert (New York: Philosophy Library, 1955). Maritain's Christian philosophy was the subject of at least one advanced Notre Dame study, Frank L. Keegan's "The Development of Jacques Maritain's Conception of Christian Philosophy, 1910–1929." (Ph.D. dissertation, University of Notre Dame, 1959).

15. The question of "man," according to Franklin L. Baumer, has been "at the center of twentieth century thought." *Modern European Thought: Continuity and Change in Ideas 1600–1950* (New York: Macmillan Company, 1977), p. 417.

16. Waldemar Gurian, "On Maritain's Political Philosophy," *Thomist* 35 (January 1943): 10.

17. O'Malley, "The Literature of this Century."

18. On Gurian's role in establishing *The Review of Politics* see Stritch, "After Forty Years: Notre Dame and *The Review of Politics*," *Review of Politics* 40 (October 1978): 437–46.

19. O'Malley, "The Image of Man: Ten Years of *The Review of Politics*," *Review of Politics* 10 (October 1948): 395–96.

20. Jacques Maritain, "Integral Humanism and the Crisis of Modern Times," *Review of Politics* 1 (January 1939): 1–17.

21. O'Malley, "Religion and the Modern Mind," *Review of Politics* 4 (October 1942): 502.

22. See Christopher Dawson, "Religion and the Age of Revolution, III: William Blake and the Religion of Romanticism." *Tablet* 168 (12 September 1936): 336–38.

23. Letter, Yves Simon to Jacques Maritain, 3 September 1948. Personal copy obtained from Leo R. Ward, C.S.C.

24. O'Malley, "The Passion of Leon Bloy," *Review of Politics* 10 (January 1948): 112. O'Malley criticizes the Ph.D. and articulates his own view of teaching in "The Education of Man," *Review of Politics* 6 (1944): 14–15.

25. Pat Sweeny, "The Last Hurrah," p. 32.

26. Guardini, *Freedom, Grace, and Destiny*, p. 11.

27. On Guardini's impact upon O'Malley see: O'Malley, "The Culture of the Church," *Review of Politics* 16 (1954): 131–154; and "Thinker in the Church II: The Urgencies of Romano Guardini," *Review of Politics* 25 (1963): 451–59.

28. Sallie McFague TeSelle, *Literature and Christian Life* (New Haven, Ct.: Yale University Press, 1966), p. 29.

29. Jacques Maritain, *True Humanism* (New York: Charles Scribner's Sons, 1938), pp. 2–3. Historians to date have not sufficiently appreciated the creative dialogue that occurred between Protestant neo-orthodox and Thomistic Catholic theologies in the 1920s and 1930s. The relationship between the natural and supernatural orders was a central question of discussion in the crisis atmosphere that permeated the European churches following World War I. Barthian neo-orthodox "crisis" theology, which radically restated the Reformation doctrines of Justification by Faith and the corruption of fallen nature in its essence, forced continental Catholic theologians and philosophers to rethink their own position on the relationship of the natural to the supernatural.

Maritain's statements above were representative of the Catholic response. The Catholic position was to reaffirm the analogy of being between creator and creation, to stress that gracae does not destroy nature but elevates and perfects it, and to reassert the instrumentality of the person in his or her own salvation. Catholics appreciated Barth's critique of prewar immamentistic theologies but they believed he oversimplified the division between transcendent God and finite, fallen man. The Christian philosophy debate insofar as it addressed Protestantism by reasserting the Thomistic position of reason elevated by grace was part of this larger theological discussion.

Protestant-Catholic dialogue concerning the supernatural was especially substantive in Karl Barth's Germany where the post-World War I religious crisis ran the deepest, and where, under the German university system, Catholics and Protestants shared the same faculty. The result was a Catholic theology that was more Christocentric, Incarnational, and existential. Romano Guardini with University of Tübingen priest and theologian Karl Adam wrote a number of popular christological works in the 1920s and 1930s which placed the Incarnation at the very center of Christian understanding of creation, history, the Church, and human society. Christ, in answer to the postwar Barthians, was portrayed as Savior and Redeemer, a "mediator" between fallen man and transcendent God. The universe was a "synthesis" between finite and infinite and the Incarnation was the central event of human history. Catholics, no less than Protestants, were returning to the basics.

Liturgical theology was deepened subsequently by these discussions as the Church was seen as the Sacrament of Christ giving witness to his continued presence in the world. It is not surprising that Germany was the most creative center for liturgical studies following World War I, with Guardini and Adams playing central roles. Serious Catholic laypersons like O'Malley were familiar with the works of both scholars, many of which were available in translation through Sheed and Ward publishers. See Karl Adam, *The Spirit of Catholicism*, trans. Dom Justin McCann, O.S.B. (London: Sheed and Ward, 1929); *Christ Our Brother*, trans. Dom Justin McCann (London: Sheed and Ward, 1931), and Guardini, *Sacred Signs* (London: Sheed and Ward, 1937); *The Church and the Catholic and the Spirit of the Liturgy*.

30. O'Malley, "The Renascence of the Novelist and the Poet," in Norman Weyand, S.J., ed., *The Catholic Renascence in a Disintegrating World* (Chicago: Loyola University Press, 1951), p. 79.

31. William F. Lynch, S.J. *Christ and Apollo, the Dimensions of the Literary Imagination* (Notre Dame, Ind.: University of Notre Dame Press, 1960), p. 189.

32. Hopkins is quoted in O'Malley, "The Renascence of the Novelist and the Poet," pp. 67–68.

33. In 1957 O'Connor wrote, "I see from the standpoint of Christian orthodoxy. This means that for me the meaning of life is central in our Redemption by Christ and what I see in the world I see in its relation to that." "The Fiction Writer in His Country," in Granville Hicks, ed., *The Living Novel, A Symposium* (New York: Macmillan Company, 1957), p. 162. O'Connor's correspondence in the 1950s acknowledged her debt to Maritain, Guardini, Adam, and Gilson. See Robert and Sally Fitzgerald, eds., *The Habit of Being; Letters of Flannery O'Connor* (New York: Farrar, Straus, Giroux, 1979), pp. 74, 230–31, 296. See also Ralph C. Wood, "The Heterdoxy of Flannery O'Connor's Book Reviews," *Flannery O'Connor Bulletin* 5 (Autumn 1976): 3–15. The best recent work to place O'Connor within her theological milieu is John F. Desmond, *Risen Sons: Flannery O'Connor's Vision of History* (Athens: University of Georgia Press, 1987).

34. O'Malley, "The Faustianism of John Milton," in *Proceedings of the American Catholic Philosophical Association* 24 (1950): 123.

35. O'Malley, "The Renascence of the Novelist and the Poet," p. 59.

36. Sigrid Undset, *Kristin Lavransdatter* (New York: Alfred A. Knopf, 1928).

37. O'Malley, "Sigrid Undset and the Christian Aesthetic," O'Malley Papers.

38. O'Malley, "A Note on Education and Literary Study," O'Malley Papers. O'Malley is quoting an article written by one of his students: J. H. Johnsten, "Philosophy of Literature," *Concord* 2 (May-June 1949): 28–29. It was common for O'Malley to integrate papers, articles, and materials written by his students into his class lectures.

39. O'Malley, "Religion and the Modern Mind," pp. 540–45.

40. O'Malley, "Introduction," in Francis B. Thornton, ed., *Return to Tradition, A Directive Anthology*, p. vii.

41. M. A. Fitzsimons, et. al., *Christianity and Civilization* (New York: W. H. Sadlier Company, 1947), pp. 794–95.

42. Mother Grace, O.S.B., "The Catholic Renascence Society. Its Past and Future," *Renascence* 1 (Autumn 1948): 3.

43. Etienne Gilson, "The Intelligence in the Service of Christ the King," in *Christianity and Philosophy*, pp. 118–25.

44. "It is absurd to hold that religion and politics can be kept wholly apart when they meet in the conscience of one man," wrote McCarthy. "If a man is religious and if he is in politics, one fact will relate to the other if indeed he is a whole man." Eugene J. McCarthy, *Frontiers in Democracy* (Cleveland, Ohio: World Publishing Company, 1960), p. 57.

45. McCarthy, "The Christian in Politics," *Commonweal* 60 (1 October 1954): 626–28.

46. Arleen Hynes, interview with author, College of St. Benedict, 15 November 1980.

47. Abigail Quigley McCarthy, *Private Faces, Public Places* (New York: Doubleday, 1972), p. 107.

48. Ibid., p. 118.

49. *Program of Action. A Suggested Outline for the Lay Apostolate of Young Women*, part 1 (Grailville, Ohio: 1946), p. 47.

50. *Integrity* 1 (October 1946): 1.

51. The theme of sanctity and sainthood even found its way into the sociology of Fr. Andrew Greeley during the pre-Vatican II years. "Can an organization man be a saint?" asked Greeley in *Strangers in the House: Catholic Youth in America* (New York: Sheed and Ward, 1960). Yes, Greeley answered, if he attended retreats, became contemplative, and lived the charity of the Mystical Body (p. 147).

Greeley's comment recalls the general revival in American religious life following World War II. Post-World War II American Catholic cultural values thus mirror in interesting ways the larger American cultural progression from social awareness in the 1930s to an emphasis upon personal religious values in the 1950s. But the match is not perfect. 1950s-style religiosity, emphasizing love of God, family, and country, in fact, was the very antithesis of the kind of religious values that many of the Catholic activists involved in this work stood for. It represented the comfortable "bourgeois" Catholicism they abhorred.

52. Bruce Marshall, "Graham Greene and Evelyn Waugh," *Commonweal* 51 (3 March 1950): 533.

53. Richard Griffiths, *Reactionary Revolution*, p. 157.

54. See Elsie Brien, "The Catholic Revival Revisited," *Commonweal* 106 (21 December 1979): 714–16.

55. Consequently, Leon Bloy ("The Pilgrim of the Absolute") always enjoyed a special place in O'Malley's literary pantheon. Bloy's fulminations against complacent, well-fed, "pharisaical" Christians were legendary. O'Malley appropriated them all. For O'Malley, no less than Bloy, "bourgeois" Christians were Christians who failed to live integrated lives, neutral Christians who would "not take the chances of heroes and saints." See O'Malley, "The Evangelism of Georges Bernanos," *Review of Politics* 6 (October 1944): 407.

56. A balanced critique of Christian philosophy is found in Anton C. Pegis, *Christian Philosophy and Intellectual Freedom* (Milwaukee: Bruce Publishing Company, 1955).

57. Gerald A. McCool, S.J., "An Alert and Independent Thomist: William Norris Clarke, S.J.," in McCool, ed., *The Universe as Journey: Conversations with W. Norris Clarke, S.J.* (New York: Fordham University Press, 1988), pp. 13–23.

58. McCool traces these important developments in Aquinas's thought under Gilson in "Twentieth Century Scholasticism," *Journal of Religion* (1978 Supplement): S198–221; and "The Tradition of Saint Thomas in North America: At 50 Years," *Modern Schoolman* 65 (March 1988): 185–206.

59. W. Norris Clarke comments upon how he found his way to existentialism through Gilson in "Fifty Years of Metaphysical Reflection: The Universe as Journey," in McCool, ed., *The Universe as Journey*, pp. 57–62.

60. McCool, "Twentieth Century Scholasticism," p. S215. Patrick Carey also briefly comments upon twentieth century Thomistic development in *American Catholic Religious Thought* (New Jersey: Paulist Press), pp. 46–52.

61. This view of the Church, stressing its organic as opposed to its institutional forms, was confirmed at the Second Vatican Council in the Dogmatic Constitution of the Church and the Constitution on the Liturgy. On Congar's role in these developments see Richard McBrien, "Church and Ministry: The Achievements of Yves Congar," *Theology Digest* 32 (Fall 1985): 203–11, and Bernard Laurey, ed., *Fifty Years of Catholic Theology. Conversations with Yves Congar* (Philadelphia: Fortress Press, 1988).

62. O'Malley, "The Culture of the Church," *Review of Politics* 16 (1954): 131–150.

63. O'Malley, "The Renascence of the Novelist and the Poet," pp. 65, 42.

64. O'Malley, "The Catholic and Literature," O'Malley Papers.

65. O'Malley, "The Renascence of the Novelist and the Poet," pp. 84–85.

66. Ibid.

CHAPTER 9: "YES, WE HAVE NO BERNANOS." THE SEARCH FOR THE GREAT AMERICAN CATHOLIC NOVEL, II: CATHOLIC FICTION DURING THE ERA OF TRANSFORMATION

1. Francis X. Connolly, "The Catholic Theme," *America* 50 (December 1933): 234.

2. Kevin Sullivan, "Two Party Lines," *America* 69 (17 July 1943): 410.

3. McCarthy, *Private Faces, Public Places*, pp. 76, 101.

4. Harold C. Gardiner, S.J., *Norms for the Novel* (New York: The America Press, 1935).

5. In 1947 this search took on major proportions with the Christophers offering $15,000 (the largest non-commercial literary prize to date in 1947) for the best written "Christian" novel. The Christophers were founded by Fr. James Keller, M.M. in 1945 to encourage Christians to accept personal responsibility in bringing the Christian message to all areas of modern life. Specific areas of focus were government, education, literature, and entertainment. The winner of the contest was George Howe's *Call It Treason* (1949). Chosen from over two thousand manuscripts, the story focuses upon three Germans during World War II who volunteer to spy for the United States: one for riches, one for adventure, and one "from the heart." Because of its muted religious theme, most Catholic reviewers were disappointed in its selection. See *Books on Trial* 8 (September 1949): 78.

6. Riley Hughes, "But Why Write About It?" *Books on Trial* 9 (March 1951): 250.

7. Georges Bernanos, *The Diary of a Country Priest*, trans. Pamela Morris (New York: Macmillan Company, 1938); *Joy*, trans. Louise Varese (New York: Pantheon Books, 1946).

8. Sr. Mariella Gable, O.S.B., *Our Father's House* (New York: Sheed and Ward, 1945), pp. xiv–xv; "Arrows at the Center," *Catholic Library World* 18 (April 1947): 219–24; "Catholic Fiction," *Catholic World* 152 (December, 1940): 297.

9. Hughes, review of *The Edge of Doom*, by Leo Brady and *The Young McDermott*, by Edward McSorley, *Renascence* 1 (Autumn 1948): 78–80.

10. Joseph Dever, *No Lasting Home* (Milwaukee, Wis.: Bruce Publishing Company, 1947).

11. Dever, "The Catholic Novel-Pitfalls," *Today* (1 October 1947): 15.

12. Dever, *No Lasting Home*, p. 421.

13. Graham Greene, *Brighton Rock* (New York: The Viking Press, 1938), pp. 356–57.

14. Hughes, review of *No Lasting Home*, by Joseph Dever, *Commonweal* 46 (5 September 1947): 507. For another critical review see *America* 77 (27 September 1947): 721–22.

15. Dever, "Yes, We Have No Bernanos," *Books on Trial* 9 (March 1951): 248, 250, 276.

16. As elsewhere in this study, I have employed Gable and Hughes as representative figures. The impact of Greene, Mauriac, Bernanos, and, in some cases, Evelyn Waugh upon American Catholic readers and critics during the 1940s and early 1950s is well documented. Contrasting "new and old Catholic novels," Harry Sebastian, a St. John's University student, observed in 1941 that since the coming of Greene, Mauriac, Bernanos, and Leon Bloy upon the Catholic literary scene, "the influence of these French novelists has spread and the standards set by them have become the criteria for judging all Catholic novels." "The Catholic Novel Then and Now," *St. John's Quarterly* 4 (March 1941): 9.

It was common in progressive Catholic American literary circles during the 1940s to contrast the realistic treatment of sin by the Europeans with the self-conscious piety of American Catholic writing. Commenting upon the cultural immaturity among Catholics in this country, Marquette University literature teacher Kevin Sullivan feared that "if a Waugh or Bernanos were to appear in America now, they would be hounded into obscurity." "Nose-Led Authors," *America* 70 (9 October 1943): 17. Another college literature teacher, Sr. Joseph Immaculata, C.S.J., of St. Joseph College in Brooklyn, New York, was also grateful for the changes brought by the Europeans. In 1952, she wrote that "because of men like Leon Bloy, Mauriac, Bernanos, and Graham Greene," Catholic literature was "no longer narrowly dogmatic, sentimentally pietistic, or merely apologetic." Instead, it was now "truly Catholic, in the best sense of that term." "The Catholic Novelist as Apostle," *Catholic Library World* 23 (May 1952): 247.

By the early 1950s, some Catholic literary leaders were beginning to regret the dominance of the Europeans over the American Catholic literary community. Norman Weyand, S.J., the president of the Catholic Renascence Society and a Loyola University of Chicago literature teacher, warned in 1951 that American Catholic critics "tend too much to look to the French writers and artists for guidance and to use them as a standard of comparison." Weyand was convinced that "this attitude, natural as it is, presents a danger" because it discouraged the development of a truly American Catholic idiom. "The Catholic Renascence, An Unexplored Horizon," *Catholic Library World* 23 (October 1951): 7–9. Charles A. Brady, a professor of English at Canisius College, had similar misgivings. Catholic critics in this country, he wrote "have too much tendency" to the somber. "There are moments," continued Brady, "when one almost regrets that the present ascendancy of Waugh and Greene is so absolute and so seductive." "A Brief Survey of Catholic Fiction," *Books on Trial* 12 (January-February 1954): 159.

17. M. H., "Harry Sylvester," in Matthew Hoehn, ed., *Catholic Authors, Contemporary Biographical Sketches, 1930–1947* (New Jersey: St. Mary's Abbey, 1947), p. 723.

18. Harry Sylvester, *Dearly Beloved* (New York: Duel, Sloan, and Pierce, 1942); *Dayspring* (New York: D. Appleton-Century Company, 1945); *Moon Gaffney* (New York: Holt and Company, 1947); *A Golden Girl* (New York: Harcourt, Brace, and Company, 1950). *Dayspring* and *A Golden Girl*, with their emphases upon the mystery of grace and spiritual renewal, are probably closest to the European Catholic prototype. The first is the story of an amoral anthropologist who poses as a Catholic to gain admission to the religious rites of the New Mexico Penetentes and encounters the first real spiritual insight of his life. *A Golden Girl*, on the other hand, is an Ernest Hemingway-like story set in Lima whose main character is a deeply flawed young Catholic engineer who achieves self-growth and eventual martyrdom after being rejected by the pleasure-seeking woman he loves.

19. Sylvester, *Dearly Beloved*, p. 13.

20. Sylvester, *Moon Gaffney*, p. 55.

21. Ibid., p. 56.

22. Arthur O. Lovejoy, *The Great Chain of Being: A Study of the History of an Idea* (Cambridge: Harvard University Press, 1936), p. 20.

23. Barth, *Flesh Is Not Life*, pp. 149, 188.

24. Ibid., pp. 201–202.

25. Dever, *Three Priests* (New York: Doubleday and Company, 1958).

26. Barth, *Flesh*, pp. 188, 307, 202.

27. Dever, *A Certain Widow* (Milwaukee: Bruce Publishing Company, 1951), pp. 159–60.

28. Leo Brady, *The Edge of Doom* (New York: E. P. Dutton and Company, 1949).

29. Ibid., p. 78.

30. Brady, *Signs and Wonders* (New York: E. P. Dutton and Company, 1953).

31. Dever, *No Lasting Home*, p. 244.

32. Hugh D. Rank, "The Image of the Priest in American Catholic Fiction, 1945–1965," (Ph.D. dissertation, University of Notre Dame, 1969). Rank's analysis of the self-critical theme in post–World War II American Catholic "priest-novels" was the starting point for this current overview of post–1935 Catholic fiction. While the self-critical motif is developed differently here, I am indebted to Rank's original insights.

33. *Catholic World* reviewer Thomas J. Beary wrote that while *Moon Gaffney* was well intentioned, its criticisms were too impetuous. "Had Mr. Sylvester been more selective in his charges," Beary argued, "his attack would have been more unified and successful." "Religion and the Modern Novel," review of *Moon Gaffney*, by Harry Sylvester, *Catholic World* 166 (December 1947): 210–11. Another reviewer for the *Catholic World* said this about *Dearly Beloved*: "It is not a story to be recommended. It leaves a bad taste in the mouth. It might, in fact, reasonably be classified as a nasty book." Review of *Dearly Beloved*, by Harry Sylvester, *Catholic World* 155 (April 1942): 117. For other negative reviews of Sylvester's books, see: H. C. Gardiner, "Course Confusion, Smooth Clarity," *America* 72 (31 March 1945): 513–14; and "Dearly Beloved and the 'Bourgeois Mind,' " *Books on Trial* (April 1942): 19.

34. Francis Downey, review of *Moon Gaffney*, by Harry Sylvester, *Commonweal* (20 June 1947): 240.

35. Hughes, "Three Americans," *Renascence* 1 (Spring 1949): 4–11.

36. Angeline Kraft, "Between Two Millstones," *St. Benedict Quarterly* 17 (March 1942): 14. "I knew him from A to Z," commented Sister Gable on Sylvester. Sr. Mariella Gable, O.S.B., interview with author, College of St. Benedict, St. Joseph, Minn., 15 November 1980.

37. Sylvester, "Problems of the Catholic Writer," *Atlantic Monthly* 181 (January 1948): 109–13.

38. *Flesh Is Not Life*, wrote Marquette University student John DeChant in 1939, is "an unprecedented oasis in a desert of namby-pamby modern Catholic fiction." Review of *Flesh Is Not Life*, by Hilary Barth, *Marquette Journal* 37 (March 1939): 26. Seasoned Catholic reviewers were less enthusiastic. Nevertheless, *Commonweal* reviewer Ed Skillin saw "a certain promise" in Barth's novel. Review of *Flesh Is Not Life*, by Hilary Barth, *Commonweal* 29 (6 January 1939): 306. Sister Gable likewise wrote that despite Barth's self-conscious style, he deserved "high praise" for his socially minded effort. "Catholic Fiction," p. 299.

39. "Joseph Gerard Dever," in Walter Romig, ed., *The Book of Catholic Authors*, Second series (Detroit, Mich.: Walter Romig and Sons, 1951), pp. 151–155.

40. See Hughes, "Three Americans," pp. 4–11.

41. Richard Sullivan, *Summer after Summer* (New York: Doubleday, Doran and Company, 1942).

42. See Sullivan, "Contemporary Fiction," *Catholic School Editor* 23 (March 1954): 19.

43. Gable, review of *The Edge of Doom*, by Leo Brady, *Today* (December 1949): 18. For another positive assessment of Brady, see Bernadine McKenna, "Leo Brady: Novelist by Indirection," *Today* (June 1954): 10–11.

44. The best full-length study of Powers is John V. Hagopian, *J. F. Powers* (New York: Twayne Publishers, 1968). Other major studies include Eleanor Buntag Wymar, "J. F. Powers: His Christian Comic Vision," (Ph.D. dissertation, University of Pittsburgh, 1968) and Michael Paul Murphy, "J. F. Powers: The Burden of an American Catholic Writer," (Ph.D. dissertation, University of Minnesota, 1980). Rank, "The Image of the Priest," is also useful.

45. Quoted in Hagopian, *J. F. Powers*, p. 21.

46. Powers's stories dealing with social injustice toward blacks include: "He Don't Plant Cotton" (1943), "Interlude in a Bookshop" (1944), "The Trouble" (1944), and "Blessing" (1945). "Renner" was published in 1944. Other early stories by Powers with strong social themes are "Night in the County Jail" (1943), "Day in the County Jail" (1943), and "Saint on the Air" (1943).

47. Powers, "Blessing," *Sign* 25 (August 1945): 18–20.

48. Powers, "Saint on the Air," *Catholic Worker* 10 (December 1943): 8; *Morte d'Urban* (New York: Doubleday and Company, 1962).

49. Naomi Lebowitz, "The Stories of J. F. Powers: The Sign of Contradiction," *Kenyon Review* 20 (Summer 1958): 494–99.

50. Sr. Kristin Malloy, O.S.B., "The Catholic and Creativity," *American Benedictine Review* 15 (March 1964): 69.

51. Powers, "Prince of Darkness," *Accent* 6 (Winter 1946): 79–107. The story was reprinted in Powers, *Prince of Darkness and Other Stories* (New York: Doubleday and Company, 1947), pp. 215–77.

52. Powers, *Prince of Darkness*, pp. 275–77.

53. Powers, "Lions, Harts, Leaping Does," *Accent* 4 (Autumn 1943): 12–29.

54. McCarthy, *Private Faces*, p. 105.

55. Sylvester, "Best American Short Stories," *Commonweal* 41 (10 November 1944): 101–102.

56. Hughes, "Three Americans," p. 4.

57. Gable, "Catholic Fiction Arrives in America," *Today* (April 1947): 12.

CHAPTER 10: "OUGHT THERE TO BE A CATHOLIC CRITICISM?" THE 1950s AND THE END OF THE REVIVAL

1. Philip Gleason, "A Browser's Guide to American Catholicism, 1950–1980," *Theology Today* 38 (October 1981): 378.

2. Ibid., p. 375.

3. John Cogley, "Some Things Are Not Caesar's," *Today* (November 1951): 12.

4. Editorial, "The Catholic and Modern Literature," *Commonweal* 56 (16 May 1952): 131.

5. Gleason, "Browser's Guide," p. 375.

6. John Tracy Ellis, *American Catholics and the Intellectual Life* (Chicago: Heritage Foundation, 1956).

7. Edward Watkin and Fr. Joseph F. Scheuer, *The DeRomanization of the American Catholic Church* (New York: The Macmillan Company, 1966), pp. 227–29. John Cogley in 1970 similarly characterized the "Catholic university" as a contradiction in terms while asking if it was "too much for Catholics to sponsor universities, period: without any overt apostolic or preservation-of-the-faith purposes, with no Revivals, Renascences, and Return-to-Tradition cultural imperalism in mind." Cogley shortly thereafter left the Church for the Episcopal congregation. "The Future of an Illusion," in Neil G. McClusky, S.J., ed., *The Catholic University, A Modern Appraisal* (Notre Dame, Ind.: University of Notre Dame Press, 1970), pp. 299–302.

8. John J. Cavanaugh, C.S.C., in Frank L. Christ and Gerard E. Sherry, eds., *American Catholicism and the Intellectual Ideal* (New York: Appleton-Century-Crofts, 1961), pp. 227–29.

9. See Gleason, "The Crisis of Americanization," in Gleason, ed., *Contemporary Catholicism in the United States* (Notre Dame, Ind.: University of Notre Dame Press, 1969), pp. 13–16. Gleason's discussion of the crisis generated by the 1950s intellectualism debate within the American Catholic scholarly community is particularly incisive. My analysis of the revival's dissolution is based in part upon Gleason's insights.

10. Henry Rago, "Catholics and Literature," in Commonweal ed., *Catholicism In America* (New York: Harcourt, Brace, 1954), pp. 181–90.

11. Dan Herr, "Reading and Writing," in Commonweal ed., *Catholicism in America*, pp. 191–99.

12. Rev. John W. Simons, "The Catholic and the Novel," *Four Quarters* 9 (November 1959): 16.

13. Justin J. Kelly, S.J., "Catholic Literary Criticism, Some Current Implications," *Critic* 21 (December 1962–January 1963): 49.

14. Ibid.

15. Mother Grace, O.S.B., "The Catholic Renascence Society: Its Past and Future," *Renascence* 1 (Spring 1949): 3.

16. Mother Grace, letter to the editor, *Thought* 24 (March 1949): 191.

17. Norman Weyand, S.J., *The Catholic Renaissance in a Disintegrating World* (Chicago: Loyola University Press, 1951).

18. Harold C. Gardiner, S.J., "Graham Greene: Catholic Shocker," *Renascence* 1 (Spring 1949): 12.

19. *Renascence* 6 (Spring 1954).

20. John Pick, "Hopkins' Imagery," *Renascence* 7 (Autumn 1954): 30; F. A. McGowan, "Symbolism in *Brighton Rock*," *Renascence* 8 (Autumn 1955): 25.

21. John Pick, "The New Criticism," *Renascence* 3 (Spring 1951): 106.

22. John Pick, interview with author, Milwaukee, Wis., 7 September 1980.

23. Andrew Greeley, *Come Blow Your Mind with Me* (New York: Doubleday, 1971), p. 112.

24. Will Herberg, *Protestant-Catholic-Jew; An Essay in American Religious Sociology* (New York: Doubleday, 1955).

25. Frank O'Malley, "Christ's College," Francis J. O'Malley Papers, Notre Dame University Archives, Notre Dame, Indiana.

Bibliography

MANUSCRIPT SOURCES

Chicago, Illinois. Loyola University of Chicago Archives. Joseph Reiner, S.J., Papers.
Milwaukee, Wisconsin. Marquette University Archives. Catholic Worker Papers.
Notre Dame, Indiana. University of Notre Dame Archives. Francis J. O'Malley Papers.
Washington, D.C. Georgetown University Archives. Francis X. Talbot, S.J., Papers.

DISSERTATIONS

Klein, John Leo, S.J. "The Role of Gerald Ellard (1894–1963) in the Development of the Contemporary American Liturgical Movement." Ph.D. dissertation, Fordham University, 1971.
Rank, Hugh D. "The Image of the Priest in American Catholic Fiction, 1945–1965." Ph.D. dissertation, University of Notre Dame, 1969.
Robb, Dennis M. "Specialized Catholic Action in the United States, 1936–1949: Ideology, Leadership, and Organization." Ph.D. dissertation, University of Minnesota, 1972.
Romito, Donald. "Catholics and Humanists: Aspects of the Debate in Twentieth-Century American Criticism." Ph.D. dissertation, Emory University, 1976.
Sicius, Frank. "The Chicago Catholic Worker Movement, 1936 to the Present." Ph.D. dissertation, Loyola University of Chicago, 1979.

COLLEGE NEWSPAPERS AND LITERARY QUARTERLIES

Ariston. College of St. Catherine, St. Paul, Minnesota.
Books Abounding. College of St. Catherine, St. Paul, Minnesota.

Clepsydra. Mundelein College, Chicago, Illinois.
Fleur de Lis. St. Louis University, St. Louis, Missouri.
Georgetown College Journal. Georgetown University, Washington, D.C.
The Juggler. University of Notre Dame, Notre Dame, Indiana.
Loyola Quarterly. Loyola University of Chicago, Chicago, Illinois.
Marquette Journal. Marquette University, Milwaukee, Wisconsin.
Notre Dame Magazine. University of Notre Dame, Notre Dame, Indiana.
Scrip. University of Notre Dame, Notre Dame, Indiana.
The Skyscraper. Mundelein College, Chicago, Illinois.
St. Benedict Quarterly. College of St. Benedict, St. Joseph, Minnesota.

INTERVIEWS

Sr. Mariella Gable, O.S.B. St. Joseph, Minnesota. 15 November 1980.
Donald A. Gallagher. Milwaukee, Wisconsin. 1 April 1985.
Arleen Hynes. St. Joseph, Minnesota. 16 November 1980.
Edward Marciniak. Chicago, Illinois. 14 February 1985.
John Pick. Milwaukee, Wisconsin. 7 September 1980.

SELECT BIBLIOGRAPHY OF SECONDARY SOURCES

I. Articles

Alexander, Calvert, S.J. "The Apostolate of Publicity." *America* 41 (18 May 1929): 128–29.
———. "A Cultural Revival in America Promises." *Queen's Work* 25 (June 1933): 3, 9–11.
———. "Scholasticism and the New Humanism." *Modern Schoolman* 6 (January 1930): 26–30.
Anthony, Catherine, M. "Frank Sheed Looks at Himself and His Church Today." *Our Sunday Visitor* 67 (28 May 1978): 3–5.
Barth, Hilary Leighton. "The Catholic Writer of Tomorrow." *Catholic School Editor* 9 (January 1940): 4–5, 14.
Bergonzi, Bernard. "A Conspicuous Absentee. The Decline and Fall of the Catholic Novel." *Encounter* 55 (August-September, 1980): 44–56.
Brien, Elsie Delores. "The Catholic Revival Revisited." *Commonweal* 106 (21 December 1979): 714–16.
Cameron, J. M. "Frank Sheed and Catholicism." *Review of Politics* 37 (July 1975): 275–85.
"Catholic Labor Theatre Underway." *Chicago Catholic Worker* 1 (March 1936): 3.
Dever, Joseph. "The Catholic Novel—Pitfalls." *Today* (1 October 1947): 15–16.
Ellard, Gerald, S. J. "The Denver Literary Congress." *American Ecclesiastical Review* 90 (April 1934): 407–18.
Ellis, John Tracy. "John Henry Newman, A Bridge for Men of Good Will." *Catholic Historical Review* 56 (April 1970): 1–24.
English, Jack. "Can a Catholic Write a Novel?" *American Mercury* 31 (January 1934): 90–95.

Faherty, William B., S. J. "A Half-Century With the Queen's Work." *Woodstock Letters* 92 (1963): 99–114.

Gable, Sr. Mariella, O.S.B. "Arrows at the Center." *Catholic Library World* 18 (April 1947): 219–24.

———. "Catholic Fiction." *Catholic World* 152 (December 1940): 296–302.

Gleason, Philip. "A Browser's Guide to American Catholicism, 1950–1980." *Theology Today* 38 (October 1981): 373–88.

———. "In Search of Unity: American Catholic Thought, 1920–1960." *Catholic Historical Review* 65 (April 1979): 185–205.

———. "Neoscholasticism as Preconciliar Ideology. *U.S. Catholic Historian* 7 (Fall 1988): 401–11.

Hitchcock, James. "Postmortum on a Rebirth, the Catholic Intellectual Renaissance." *American Scholar* 49 (Spring 1980): 211–25.

Lebowitz, Naomi. "The Stories of J. F. Powers: The Sign of Contradiction." *Kenyon Review* 20 (Summer 1958): 494–99.

LeFevre, Alice Louise. "Owen Francis Dudley and the Philosophical Novel." *Catholic Library World* 14 (April 1943): 195–200.

Lehman, Harvey C., and Paul Witty. "Scientific Eminence and Church Membership." *Scientific Monthly* 33 (December 1931): 544–49.

Lord, Daniel A. "The Great American Catholic Women Overlooked." *Queen's Work* 25 (February 1933): 2.

———. "Has Philosophy Failed?" *America* 36 (15 January 1927): 326–28.

———. "Schools of Catholic Action." *Studies* 22 (September 1933): 454–67.

———. "Sodalities in America and Catholic Action." *Studies* 22 (June 1933): 257–70.

McCole, Camile. "Humanism's Challenge to Catholicism." *America* 43 (24 May 1930): 163–65.

McCool, Gerald, A., S.J. "Twentieth Century Scholasticism." *Journal of Religion* (1978 Supplement): S198–221.

McDonald, John B. "Daniel A. Lord, S.J., Defender of Youth." *Catholic Library World* 13 (April 1942): 195–202.

Michel, Virgil. "Christian Culture: *Orate Fratres* 13 (14 May 1939): 296–304.

Neale, Catherine M. "The Gallery of Living Catholic Authors." *Catholic World* 165 (September 1947): 547–51.

O'Malley, Francis J. "The Culture of the Church." *Review of Politics* 16 (January 1954): 131–54.

———. "The Image of Man: Ten Years of *The Review of Politics*." *Review of Politics* 10 (October 1948): 395–96.

Rogge, Leonard J. "The Librarian's View of the Publisher in the Catholic Literary Emergence." *Catholic Library World* 8 (15 April 1937): 59–61.

Stritch, Thomas. "The Foreign Legion of Father O'Hara." *Notre Dame Magazine* 10 (October 1981): 23–27.

Sylvester, Harry. "Problems of the Catholic Writer." *Atlantic Monthly* 181 (January 1948): 109–13.

Talbot, Francis X., S.J. "The Best Ten Catholic Books." *America* 30 (19 January 1924): 332–33.

———. "Our Abject Book Poverty." *America* 41 (18 May 1929): 139–40.

————. "What are the Best Ten Catholic Books?" *America* 29 (6 October 1923): 590–91.

Weyand, Norman, S.J. "The Catholic Renascence, An Unexplored Horizon." *Catholic Library World* 23 (October 1951): 7–9.

Wills, Garry. "Catholic Faith and Fiction." *New York Times Book Review* (16 January 1972): 1–2, 16–18.

II. Books

Alexander, Calvert, S.J. *The Catholic Literary Revival. Three Phases in its Development from 1845 to the Present*. Milwaukee: Bruce Publishing Company, 1935.

Carey, Patrick. *American Catholic Relgious Thought*. New Jersey: Paulist Press, 1987.

Catholic Poetry Society of America. *A Congress of Poetry*. New York: Catholic Poetry Society of America, 1941.

Catholicism in America, A Series of Articles from the Commonweal. New York: Harcourt, Brace and Company, 1953.

Chesterton, Gilbert Keith. *Heretics*. London: John Lane, 1905.

————. *Orthodoxy*. New York: Dodd, Mead and Company, 1908.

Christ, Frank L., and Gerard E. Sherry, eds. *American Catholicism and the Intellectual Ideal*. New York: Appleton-Century-Crofts, 1961.

Dawson, Christopher. *The Modern Dilemma*. London: Sheed and Ward, 1932.

————. *Religion and Culture*. London: Sheed and Ward, 1948.

Dolan, Jay. *The American Catholic Experience from Colonial Times to the Present*. Garden City, N.Y.: Doubleday, 1985.

Desmond, John F. *Risen Sons. Flannery O'Connor's Vision of History*. Athens, Ga.: University of Georgia Press, 1987.

Ellis, John Tracy. *American Catholics and the Intellectual Life*. Chicago: Heritage Foundation, 1956.

————, ed. *The Catholic Priest in the United States: Historical Investigations*. Collegeville, Minn.: St. John's University Press, 1971.

Fiecke, Sr. M. J., O.S.F. *The Revival of Catholic Literature in Twentieth Century Germany*. Milwaukee: Bruce Publishing Company, 1944.

Fitzgerald, Paul A., S.J. *The Governance of Jesuit Colleges in the United States, 1920–1970*. Notre Dame, Ind.: University of Notre Dame Press, 1984.

Gable, Sr. Mariella, O.S.B. *Great Modern Catholic Short Stories*. New York: Sheed and Ward, 1942.

————. *Many Colored Fleece*. New York: Sheed and Ward, 1950.

————. *Our Father's House*. New York: Sheed and Ward, 1945.

————. *This Is Catholic Fiction*. New York: Sheed and Ward, 1948.

Gleason, Philip. *Keeping the Faith. American Catholicism Past and Present*. Notre Dame, Ind.: University of Notre Dame Press, 1987.

Griffiths, Richard M. *The Reactionary Revolution: The Catholic Revival in French Literature, 1870–1914*. London: Constable and Company, 1966.

Hagopian, John V. *J. F. Powers*. New York: Twayne Publishers, 1968.

Halsey, William M. *The Survival of American Innocence: American Catholicism in an Era of Disillusionment, 1920–1940*. Notre Dame, Ind.: University of Notre Dame Press, 1980.

Hoehn, Matthew, ed. *Catholic Authors, Contemporary Biographical Sketches, 1930–1947*. New Jersey: St. Mary's Abbey, 1947.

Hoeveler, J. David. *The New Humanism, A Critique of Modern America, 1900–1940*. Charlottesville: University Press of Virginia, 1977.

Kellogg, Gene. *The Vital Tradition: The Catholic Novel in a Period of Convergence*. Chicago: Loyola University Press, 1970.

Lord, Daniel A., S.J. *Armchair Philosophy*. New York: The American Press, 1918.

———. *Our Part in the Mystical Body*. St. Louis, Mo.: The Queen's Work Press, 1935.

———. *Played by Ear*. Chicago: Loyola University Press, 1956.

Lynch, William F., S.J. *Christ and Apollo, Dimensions of the Catholic Literary Imagination*. Notre Dame, Ind.: University of Notre Dame Press, 1960.

Marx, Paul, O.S.B. *Virgil Michel and the Liturgical Movement*. Collegeville, Minn.: Liturgical Press, 1957.

McGloin, Joseph, S.J. *Backstage Missionary, Father Dan Lord, S.J.* New York: Pageant Press, 1958.

McGucken, William, S.J. *The Jesuits and Education*. Milwaukee: Bruce Publishing Company, 1932.

Messbarger, Paul R. *Fiction with a Parochial Purpose: Social Uses of American Catholic Literature, 1884–1900*. Boston: Boston University Press, 1971.

Moore, R. Laurence. *Religious Outsiders and the Making of Americans*. New York: Oxford University Press, 1986.

Norris, Kathleen. *Noon, An Autobiographical Sketch*. New York: Doubleday, Page, and Company, 1925.

O'Brien, David J. *American Catholics and Social Reform: The New Deal Years*. New York: Oxford University Press, 1968.

O'Brien, John A. *Catholics and Scholarship. A Symposium on the Develoment of Scholars*. Huntington, Ind.: Our Sunday Visitor Press, 1938.

Piehl, Mel. *Breaking Bread: The Catholic Worker and the Origin of Catholic Radicalism in America*. Philadelphia: Temple University Press, 1982.

Rideout, Walter B. *The Radical Novel in the United States, 1900–1954*. New York: Hill and Wang, 1956.

Scott, Christina. *A Historian and His World: A Life of Christopher Dawson, 1889–1970*. London: Sheed and Ward, 1984.

Sheed, Francis J. *The Church and I*. New York: Doubleday, 1974.

———. *Sidelights of the Catholic Revival*. London: Sheed and Ward, 1938.

Talbot, Francis F., S.J., ed. *Fiction by Its Makers*. New York: The America Press, 1928.

TeSelle, Sallie McFague. *Literature and Christian Life*. New Haven, Ct.: Yale University Press, 1966.

Van Allen, Roger. *The Commonweal and American Catholicism*. Philadelphia: Fortress Press, 1974.

Weaver, Mary Jo, ed. *Newman and the Modernists*. Washington, D.C.: University Press of America, 1985.

Weyand, Norman, S.J., ed. *The Catholic Renascence in a Disintegrating World*. Chicago: Loyola University Press, 1951.

Index